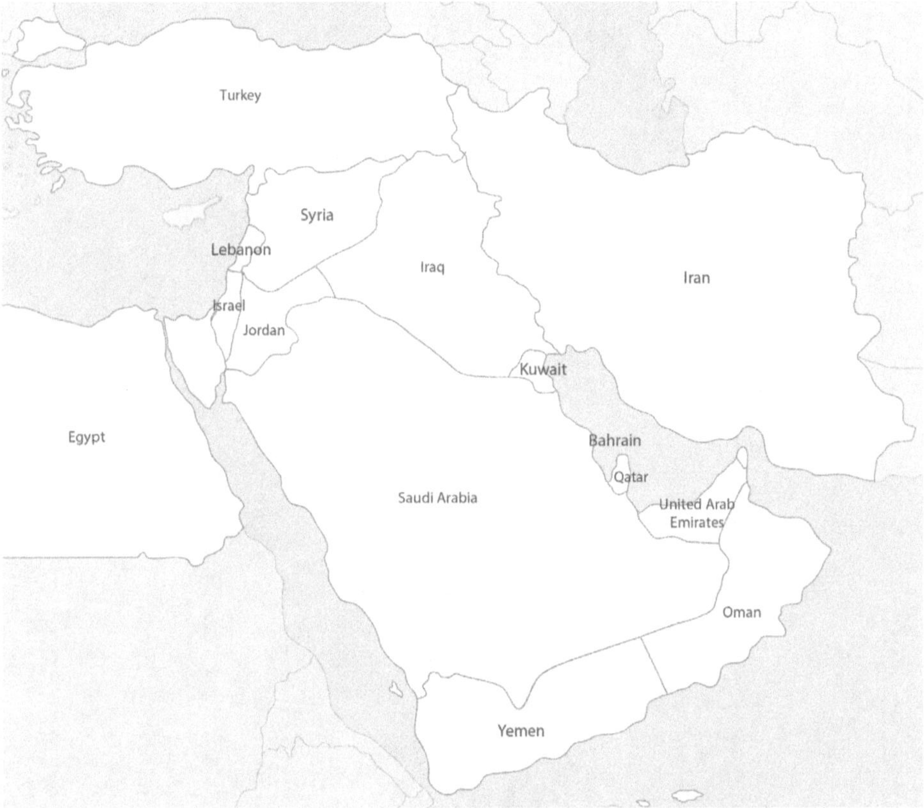
Turkey
Syria
Lebanon
Israel
Jordan
Iraq
Iran
Kuwait
Egypt
Bahrain
Qatar
Saudi Arabia
United Arab
Emirates
Oman
Yemen

VEILED
HORIZONS

Veiled Horizons
Copyright © 2025 by Mary Khouri

All rights reserved under the Pan-American and International Copyright Conventions. This book may not be reproduced in whole or in part, except for brief quotations embodied in critical articles or reviews, in any form or by any means, electronic or mechanical, including photocopying, recording, or by any information storage and retrieval system now known or hereinafter invented, without written permission of the publisher.

Disclaimer
The author and publisher have taken steps to maintain the integrity of the story while altering selected facts to protect the privacy of individuals affected by the events described herein.

ISBN (paperback): 978-1-963271-82-9
ISBN (ebook): 978-1-963271-83-6

Armin Lear Press, Inc.
215 W Riverside Drive, #4362
Estes Park, CO 80517

VEILED HORIZONS

AN AMERICAN WOMAN'S TREK INTO THE HEART OF ARABIA

MARY KHOURI

ARMINLEAR

CONTENTS

1	US-Saudi Business Council	1
2	Riyadh, Dammam, and Jeddah	23
3	The Months Before Saudi Arabia	37
4	First Hours in Saudi Arabia	59
5	First Weeks at Work	71
6	Desert Trips	89
7	Arab Hospitality	105
8	Work Life	127
9	9/11	143
10	Love and Marriage	155
11	Losing Nabil's Mom	175
12	Illness & Terror Attacks	197
13	Where to Relocate?	209
14	Move to Qatar	235
15	Caught Between Two Cultures	253
	Afterword	269
	About the Author	273

CHAPTER 1

US SAUDI BUSINESS COUNCIL

Heavily perfumed women enveloped in black, their charcoal cloaks fluttering behind them, stepped up to check in at the Saudia Airlines terminal gate at Washington Dulles Airport. My breath stuck in my throat; my anxiety heightened over what I was about to step into. These women, featureless, bereft of personality, stared straight ahead. Would I ever get used to this? Even my Arab-born husband was wary of this unlikely venture I insisted on pursuing.

We flew out of Washington Dulles on a frigid Thursday evening in February 2000. Having been provided an itinerary by the US-Saudi Business Council in advance, it seemed like any other conference-type event. There were meetings with Saudi companies, followed by receptions and luncheons with Business Council Board members, followed by more meetings and dinners and breakfasts with new companies. As a professional career woman, this was familiar. Despite my confidence, I had doubts. Not only about dress requirements but, after all, I was only an auxiliary member of the Council, soon to be in the Kingdom of Saudi Arabia, solely due to the relentless efforts of my Lebanese

American husband, Nabil. I was not even sure I would be allowed to attend the meetings because I was a woman. And if permitted to go to meetings, would I be taken seriously, or would I inadvertently offend someone and ruin my chances, as I was not yet accustomed to the cultural mores?

As we sat at the gate, I reflected on what might happen in the Kingdom. I was experiencing all the emotions – excitement and elation tinged with uncertainty but also a sense of surety that I was right where I needed to be. I faced hurdles before even getting to this place, and I certainly did not feel welcomed on this trip by either side. Despite these obstacles, I had an innate sense I would find a way to connect with Saudi business leaders.

We would have a layover at JFK and then fly into Riyadh, the capital of Saudi Arabia. Settling onto the plane in New York City with Nabil and other Council members on that wintry night, I put my carry-on in the overhead bin and squeezed into my seat. I watched the new passengers board the plane. They were a mix of men and women, primarily Saudis. The women working their way down the aisle were clothed in black *abayas* (loose robes) and headscarves with only a pair of inscrutable dark brown eyes peering through the head covering's two slits. I had seen photographs of Saudi women covered in ebony hues but seeing them in person was disconcerting. Each woman looked exactly like the next. The icy knot in the pit of my stomach tightened. Moments later, more women entered the cabin dressed in Western attire, some with form-fitting jeans and others with leather jackets. From their accents, Nabil determined they were Saudi. All women would be required to don the abaya before disembarking in the Kingdom. Several of the Saudi men wore white *thobes* (long robes) without the *ghutra* (headscarf); others were dressed in slacks, and all walked with their women following, managing the children who dangled precariously in their arms.

As the families pressed past me, the piercing scent of men's cologne burned my nostrils, augmented by the smoky and poignantly sweet scent of incense (*bakhoor*) attached to the soft fabric of the women's abayas. At times, young children broke free of their mother's hand. In a moment of abandon, they streaked down the aisle shrieking and squealing, inspiring other youngsters to join in the mayhem. Hapless stewardesses chased behind them, calling to passengers, "Take your seats, please! I beg you, take your seats!" The entire scene – the shapeless women, the stoic men, and the rioting kids – was perplexing for the way it felt completely alien. I looked over at Nabil to gauge his reaction. I knew this undertaking would be an emotional journey for him. After all, he was going back to a region he literally fled in the late 1970s. Nabil did not want to go back in the first place. He had grown up in the chaotic and conflict-ridden Arab world and held no sentimentality for the region other than missing his dear mother. I felt both pangs of guilt and a deep love for this man who was sacrificing so much for me.

The US-Saudi Business Council was completely against me accompanying their group on this trip to the Kingdom. However, Nabil insisted on taking me, as I was the one who wanted us to live and work in the Kingdom. I was not surprised Nabil wore them down; he did the same with me when we first met.

I was a graduate student in economics at the University of Florida in Gainesville when I first met Nabil. A big-hearted, serious-minded Danish woman, Inga, rented me a room in her ranch-style home near the campus. Other than going to class and attending the occasional graduate student party, I spent a lot of time in that room. That changed when, in March 1981, Inga introduced me to her niece, Belinda, who was visiting from Brazil for several weeks. She was several years older than me. Within a few days, Belinda gently admonished me for spending too much time in my small room consumed with studies and preparing for teaching my macroeconomics review class on campus.

"You are only going to be this age once, Mary," Belinda said with her thick accent. "When you get older you won't experience the same kind of happiness as you can right now. You need to get out more." I was surprised by Belinda's straightforwardness. I let her words settle a bit and reminded myself there was a life behind these walls. "Tomorrow is Sunday, and we can play tennis," she said. I love playing sports and was competitive. I relented and agreed to accompany her to a nearby tennis court on campus around noontime the next day.

We played for less than an hour. Belinda was a beginner and easily bored. I was fine with getting back to the house early to study. As Belinda and I crossed back over the grass stretch toward home, I noticed a group of young men playing soccer.

"Hey, ladies, would you like to come play soccer with us," I heard a voice with an accent call out. I turned and saw a group of around 10 olive-skinned young men. I thought it might be nice to hang outside for just a little while longer. Besides, how long could a soccer game be?

The young man who called out to us was the goalie, a tall, solidly built boy with an enormous afro and outfitted in a pair of garish neon-green shorts. I knew soccer was especially popular in Europe and other countries, and these guys were likely avid players. That is why I felt especially smug scoring goal after goal on the burly goalie. At some point in the game, I noticed that I was the only one able to get past the fashionably dressed goalie. The goalie with the ready smile, kept up non-stop chatter with the rest of his teammates, mentioning several times that he was studying hard for a physics test. I later found out he was an engineering student.

When the game ended, the goalie collected the ball and walked over to me and Belinda as we prepared to leave. I heard him say, "I'm Nabil! Would you two ladies like to play ping pong with me tonight at the student union?" I looked down at my sneakers and poked the grass. I knew it was rude, but I had zero interest in whatever this game was – the ping pong or anything else. I was very focused on my studies and was not dating or socializing with anyone. Trying to be polite but wanting to get out of this, I asked Belinda, "What do you think? Should we give him our number?" Everybody knows this is girlfriend code for "absolutely not." I expected Belinda to play the "bad cop" and refuse. Instead, I heard her cheerfully offer: "Oh, sure. It's 555-0000." I thought, "Great, now I have to deal with this; one more thing." Nabil smiled like a Cheshire cat and said, "I'll call you."

He did call me 17 times, Nabil claimed. Nabil wore me down. I couldn't win even though I came up with excuses each time.

I finally decided to stop putting him off, as I recognized I needed friends. I thought about what Belinda had said to not just hole myself up in my room. I did not want to be anti-social for the rest of my life. And I saw that this patient, joyful young man, at the heart of it, could be a good friend to me.

After meeting up several times, Nabil and I started having real conversations, and it became easier and more enjoyable. We had the chance to really talk. Nabil spoke more about his upbringing. I learned he was a Lebanese national, born and raised in a small desert town in Jordan. The youngest of six siblings, Nabil emigrated to the United States at the age of 19 to study engineering, fleeing a terrifying civil war and leaving the security of his family in Lebanon behind. He related his passion for structural engineering and bridges in particular. He talked about being thankful he was in the U.S. to complete his studies. After learning so much about him, especially from a life I could not even imagine, I appreciated his bravery and spunk in moving to a land so very different from his own. I had a difficult time imagining myself doing the same.

After a couple of months, Nabil and I began dating regularly.

He indulged me with his love of cooking, always making delicious Lebanese dishes, such as blended roasted eggplant with tahini, fresh garlic, and salt, and stew of potato with chicken, tomato paste, and onion over rice.

In the next two years, we studied together, drove in the middle of the night to watch the sunrise over the Atlantic Ocean at Crescent Beach, and frequented Flagler Beach and Lake Wauburg south of Gainesville. Along the way, Nabil taught me the art of spontaneity, like deciding, on the spur of the moment, to take an 8-day road trip on A1A to South Florida for our Christmas break on less than $100. Nabil brought a cooler with a bag filled with hummus and cold-cut sandwiches, along with tomatoes, sardines, and tuna fish cans that would tide us over during our travels. We navigated the byways along the coast and slept on pool lounge chairs at hotels, accepted $25 from a pastor to stay at a hotel, and dozed in the car. Not terribly concerned that I did not possess culinary skills, Nabil did all our cooking, Lebanese style, in his tiny efficiency apartment.

I finished my graduate degree in economics in 1982; Nabil was a sophomore at the university. Financial support from his family in Lebanon stopped that year due to the civil war. Electricity and phone line disruptions meant Nabil did not communicate with family back home for nearly a year. At that time, Nabil could only take half course loads each quarter. But I knew I wanted to work in Washington, DC, the seat of government, one of the most powerful and politically charged cities in the world. I wanted to make my mark there and was lucky enough to get a job as an economist at a governmental agency in the nation's capital in 1983. Nabil was still working on his engineering degree, and I was prepared to start a job. As much as I was grateful for and appreciated Nabil's unending support and love, I felt I needed to make sure I could depend on myself and was ready to move on with my plan.

Nabil helped me move to Washington, DC. Celebrating my birthday weekend in the mountain town of Front Royal, Virginia before Nabil went back to Florida, I told him I wanted to try the first year by myself. Nabil thought our relationship would continue as it had been, so he was distraught with this news. His eyes filled with tears. Upset, he argued that this is not what he expected from me. I had to hold back my own tears. I knew what Nabil meant, and my heart agonized, but I just knew I had to move forward. A couple of days later, I dropped Nabil off at National Airport. My hands shook as I held the steering wheel. Bottling my emotions, I reminded him I wanted to try making it on my own in the big city. Nabil said he loved me so much that he wanted me to be happy in any decision I made, even if it hurt like hell. The more he talked, the more I was ready to open up that bottle and ask him to stay. But I kept the bottle shut and my emotions in check; I wanted to test myself to see if I could make it solo. It was in October 1983 when Nabil and I shared a bittersweet embrace and said our goodbyes. I thought it likely I would never see Nabil again.

Even though we were broken up, we talked on the phone every day, which was confusing, but also comforting. Coming home to an empty apartment unsettled me. Within several weeks, I felt the full weight of being alone and losing the comfort of a loving confidante in a hard-hearted metropolis. One evening, feeling deflated after arriving home to my barren apartment from work, I phoned Nabil in Gainesville. As soon as Nabil answered the phone, I broke down, barely getting out what I wanted to say.

"Are you okay? Are you okay? What's wrong?"

I took a deep breath and answered, my voice thin and unsteady. "Please come."

"What did you say?" Nabil replied. The shock in his voice unmistakable.

"Come, I want and need you to be here."

"Are you sure that this is what you want?"

"Yes, Nabil, please come."

I didn't realize how hard it would be to make this call from the "heart," as I was so used to operating from my head, a place of logic and practical reasoning. These several weeks by myself made me realize how much I was connected to Nabil through my core. He was more than a friend or a companion; he was part of me, like an appendage.

Around midnight, a few hours after talking on the phone, Nabil loaded up the Pinto, which he bought from me a couple months earlier in Gainesville. He stuffed his clothes into plastic grocery and garbage bags and left the rest. One of his Spider plants dangling its legs over the side of the car the way dogs hang their paws out of the windows, Nabil drove up highway 95. He didn't stop, he just kept driving. We agreed where I would leave my apartment house key for him. Nabil dropped his items off at my apartment at around four in the afternoon, made a Lebanese vegetable stew, and sped off to my office. He alerted the security man at my building that he was looking for me. I was thrilled to get the call, and ran over to the elevator. When I reached the lobby level, I spotted Nabil. I ran into his arms, falling against his reassuring frame, tears poised in my eyes. Nabil's face became red, as tears collected on his face. It was a relief to be together.

It wasn't the first time we lived together. Nabil and I shared an apartment in Gainesville for almost a year before I moved to Washington, DC. When Nabil joined me, he landed a job at a discount department store with a plan to continue with his schooling in the DC area. Washington was an adjustment like it had been in Gainesville, but this time we were more serious and had to work through life's challenges with new jobs in an urban setting while trying to sustain a healthy relationship.

Ten years after moving to Washington, DC, in 1993, Nabil and I tied the knot. We had a church wedding with around 90 guests. Nabil's mother, Fatina, boldly made the arduous trip from Beirut, Lebanon by herself. Following Lebanese tradition, Fatina rose to meet me and my father as we walked down the church aisle toward Nabil as a gesture welcoming me, the bride, as her new daughter.

Particularly grateful that my entire family and Nabil's mother from Lebanon attended our wedding, I couldn't help but reflect on my parents' initial grave concerns over their daughter marrying an Arab man who they knew very little about. This tension between my family and Nabil was distressing at times.

A year following our marriage, we moved from a condominium in northern Virginia to our dream home, complete with white picket fence. For years, before and after marriage, although there were ups and downs, we savored weekends with friends in the DC area, Nabil drumming on his *durbakeh* (Arab drum), singing Lebanese folk tunes, and teaching belly dancing moves to our guests. It was a joy to come home to Nabil's cooking, the aroma of Middle Eastern spices filling our home. We delighted in drives to the bucolic Virginia countryside, overnight stays on the shore, and visits to the Aerospace and Natural History museums on the National Mall.

Within the span of a few years following our wedding, two miniature apricot poodles became like family to us. We were both living the life we had always dreamed of: I was managing multi-billion-dollar nationwide cost studies for a governmental organization in Washington, DC, as an economist, and Nabil was alternately working at private firms as well as with the Navy as a civil engineer.

One year fell away into the next. After seventeen years in the nation's capital, I turned forty and found my enthusiasm for the fast-paced and unyielding life in Washington beginning to wane. Did I really need the bigger house, the luxury car, another outfit? Would these things cure me of the budding feelings of disconnectedness? After years of riding on the Metro, Washington's subway, I increasingly found myself studying the bleak, implacable faces day after day. I silently dared them to break a smile or make eye contact, brokering some sign of human life and connection.

Even in our private lives, feelings of anonymity crept in. I rarely encountered even a neighborhood friend at a local grocery store or out running errands in the nearly two decades we lived in the DC area. Like the protagonist of Edgar Allen Poe's story, I was beginning to feel like just "a face in the crowd." The multitude of people in the city, like me, locked into their busy and self-important lives, often muted the possibilities for real bonding with other souls.

And we were finding that the accessories of the American Dream came with their prices. The cost of enjoying our weekends was becoming more exorbitant. A drive to the countryside meant neglecting our yard work and routine household errands being put off, making the workweek more harried.

I was afraid of becoming what I saw on the subway. There must be something like an emergency lever, a fire alarm, to get off of this tract. I knew I had to do something bold, outside my comfort zone, to feel alive again. At these critical junctures in life, I believe "going with your gut" is paramount. For me, it is more than trusting your instinct, but rather being a careful listener to the voice of a higher plane. My "gut feeling" was urging me to immerse myself in the unknown and intrigue of faraway lands and cultures. My spirit was thirsty for distinct change and a broadening of my worldview. I kept my feelings mostly to myself, not even sharing them with Nabil in the beginning. Listening to my insistent inner voice and responding in the only way I felt I could, I made initial attempts to seek employment with various international agencies like the World Bank, the IMF, and the UN, including several locations in the Middle East like Egypt and Jordan.

I eventually admitted to Nabil what was happening in my heart and what I'd been up to researching places to find work far across the globe. I gathered he didn't quite get it just yet but wanted to try and understand and support me. None of my attempts yielded success, or so it seemed. However, with each new search and each fishing expedition, I kept coming back to one country in particular: Saudi Arabia. Why Saudi Arabia? my friends and family would later ask. Why would a young, ambitious Western woman want to venture into a world of other women concealing their identities behind long black cloaks?

It was not enough to just say, "I have this gut feeling." As I turned my emotions over and over, I kept returning to the people and cultures that had informed me throughout my life. I recalled the sense of discovery and openness I felt, for instance, when I took part in my first powwow ceremony. My typical suburban life in the San Francisco Bay Area was altered most summers when as a young girl my family traveled to my mom's birthplace on the Piikani Indian Reservation sitting at the foot of the majestic Rocky Mountains. As a teen, I participated in powwow dances draped in a crimson shawl with red and black geometric designs and fringes. My cousins and others wore beautiful buckskins and eagle-feathered headdresses. At first, the blur of color and bizarre discordant drumming at powwows and the smell of raw earth was all foreign, otherworldly to me. However, over time, I came to appreciate these special rituals and my cousins with their warm hearts. I was proud, encouraged, and joyful as I participated in the tribal dances. It was as though I was connected to a higher spiritual realm, my Indian ancestry. I lost myself in the reverberating drumbeat, "heartbeat of our Earth Mother," and spirited chanting.

We regularly participated in a traditional Native American sweat lodge ceremony when with my mom's family. Inside a cramped, half-moon canvas tent, we crowded together while a cousin poured water on smooth stones ringing a small fire to create a sauna effect. In Piikani heritage, negative energy gets released during the sweat lodge ritual. Reaching your boiling point, which felt literal in some cases, the spirit is cleansed by racing and jumping into the frigid lake.

On the other side of my family, I had my German paternal grandmother, Oma. I was nine or ten when Oma moved from New Jersey to a town near us in the Bay Area. I was excited to be around someone from a foreign country who used words I couldn't understand, and spoke in an accent that sounded like some kind of unusual melody.

Lively and unconventional, Oma lived in an apartment complex with a pool only a few miles away from us. On our weekend visits, Oma would gather me into her arms in the shallow end of the pool, the gold fringe of her bathing cap brushing against my cheek. In her red-flowered bathing suit, Oma began to sway, listening to some music I couldn't hear. Singing a song in German, she danced me around the pool. And my sister and two brothers each had their turn.

Oma's European travel stories were mesmerizing. There was the time she got stranded in Europe and struck up a casual conversation with a couple near a train station. Oma ended up staying with the people in their family home for a month.

Oma could fill a room with her presence; she was so unusual. She had a way of bringing people to life; she brought me to life as a kid. When Oma was around, it wasn't weird to waltz and sing old-time German songs in the pool. I was elated when Oma followed us when we moved to the southeast in 1969. Without even realizing it, I was learning that bending the edges of the envelope and grabbing life was freeing. Amid it all, I did not know then that I would be continuously drawn to people who were different, people who were not afraid to be different.

I wanted to shake up my life as I did as a girl in powwows and in an ancestral sweat lodge on the Piikani reservation or at Oma's apartment, listening to captivating tales about historic and alluring Europe. Even Inga stirred me with her stories of being a refugee during WWII. And, now, Nabil's durbakeh drumming and Lebanese music and food made me more than a bit curious about other cultures.

There was something that told me I needed to put myself through new challenges. That was why I couldn't just go to the Czech Republic and paint or spend time working with the Peace Corps in Africa. I knew Saudi Arabia would crack me open, and I needed that. I relish challenges. I remember sitting behind the steering wheel of a single-engine, Cessna six-seater plane at sixteen as navigator along with my dad as the pilot, ferrying my sister, two brothers, and mother from our hometown on the southeast coast all the way out to California and Washington state. I wondered, "How would the Kingdom unlock me?"

I continued sharing more of my feelings with Nabil, trying to make him understand what I was going through. I told Nabil that I was intent on his part of the world, the Middle East, and Saudi Arabia, in particular. He said lovingly, I was crazy. He had escaped the Middle East to come to the land of opportunity. Nabil said the Arab world was unsafe; it was challenging for women to get jobs, and he was worried about how I would be treated as an American woman. Nabil was concerned about the perpetual and general unrest in the region. He wanted to pump the brakes and think about it, and I wanted to take the wheel and go.

We were sitting on our family room couch having mint tea when Nabil asked, "Why do you really want to go to this strange place, Mary?" I shrunk a little under Nabil's stark question, but I also trusted his earnestness. For one of the first times in my life, I had no facts, no logic, and no hard data to hide behind. I only had what was in my heart. "I feel like I'm spiritually dying," I replied, a truth that lay between us like a hot wire, but the whole truth nonetheless. Following this brief exchange, the two of us decided to go off into the unknown.

Truth be told, I also felt it important for Nabil and me to continue to grow as individuals and as a married couple away from familiar surroundings and distracting outside influences, such as my family's outspoken opinions surrounding Nabil's and my life together. I wanted us to become more fully faceted and authentic human beings.

As it turned out, Nabil was in between jobs at the time of our many conversations and was interviewing for engineering positions with several companies, including one that specialized in corrosion control – maintaining buildings that faced corrosion issues related to weather, humidity, and aging. This job was not his main interest, but the thought of joint venture activity with Saudi Arabia popped into Nabil's mind and sounded like a potential opportunity for the boss. I was heartened.

Nabil joined the company, and out of nothing, he made something happen. He contacted the Saudi Embassy in Washington, DC, and they provided the number for the US-Saudi Business Council, an organization that focused on strengthening business ties and job-sharing enterprises between the countries. Without skipping a beat, Nabil called and spoke to Jerry Roberts in Richmond, one of the leaders of the U.S. delegation. Jerry was surprised to hear from Nabil since he was heading up a group of small Virginia companies to travel to Saudi Arabia the next month, February. There would be a series of meetings in three major Saudi cities to discuss joint venture possibilities. Nabil called to let me know. I could not believe these pieces were falling into place. I was both nervous and excited but mostly looking forward to seeing what we would discover over there on this fact-finding trip. This was turning out to be easier than we thought. It was smoother than we could have dreamed, or so we thought.

When Nabil brought up the prospect of bringing me, though, there was immediate push-back. "Not possible, we can't have any women on this trip," Jerry said. Nabil remained quiet. But the next day, he called Jerry back and informed him that he could not go without his wife. Moving to Saudi Arabia was a critical and life-changing matter, and he needed to see if his wife could accept living there. He asked Jerry, "Would you do this to your wife? I'm serious about moving, and I'm serious about taking my wife with me." Jerry responded that they might not accept me and said he would be back in touch.

Jerry did get back in touch with Nabil, meeting with him and his boss. They both told Nabil it would not be their responsibility if they kicked his wife out of the meetings. Nabil said, "I speak their language and I know their culture, and they know mine, so I know they won't kick her out." Nabil's boss responded that he would not pay a penny for any travel related to his wife. And he would only pay Nabil's airline costs. While all the other members of our business group had airline seats upstairs in business class, Nabil and I would be downstairs in economy.

Even though the door was cracked open, it was up to me to kick it down.

Shortly before arriving at the Riyadh airport with the US-Saudi Business Council that mid-February evening in 2000, I watched Saudi women who boarded the plane in their western garments disappear into the restroom in the back of the plane. They returned to their seats wearing their abayas. I thought back several months ago to a co-worker Nabil introduced me to named Susan. Married to a Pakistani, Susan generously offered to provide me with "appropriate clothing" for the trip. She encouraged me to change into what would become my new wardrobe and see what I thought. I tried on my loaned garments, my new skin, in Susan's bathroom. My heart wilted at seeing my reflection for the first time; I looked menacing, a void. Nabil quipped that I looked perfect for a funeral, and my misgivings escalated. I hugged the dark robes tighter around me, willing myself to come to terms with the life shift I had committed us to.

Twenty minutes before landing in Riyadh, I reached around in my carry-on luggage for my abaya, pulling it unceremoniously over my head. I did not bother going to the restroom; I did not want to feel like a sheep, my identity branded like the others. I wanted to retain some small sense of control, even if it was only when I put on my new set of clothes. But I would have to conform. I knew this even as it made me feel like I was being untrue to some other part of myself.

At the moment of touchdown, metal clattered against metal as seatbelts were unbuckled, and Saudi men rose from their seats, straining to unearth carry-on luggage from the bulkhead compartments. Heedless of injuring themselves or others, the Saudi men scrambled down the aisle while the plane raced and skidded down the runway to its assigned gate. In the melee, flight attendants attempted vainly to cull passengers to their seats. The spectacle almost seemed "cartoonish" except I couldn't help but think how dicey this was and completely against airline policy. Still, the scene intrigued me, and I found I could not take my eyes off these rebels, oblivious to anyone's concerns or prying eyes. My inner control freak and rule-appreciating self recoiled from what I was witnessing. Where were they going in such a hurry? Was a broken ankle worth being the first one to step off the plane? As they stumbled around, grappled with their carry-ons, and slammed against seats and fellow passengers, it dawned on me that I was the foreigner, the westerner, the outlier here, who was not jumping up like the others to get off the plane.

The King Khalid International Airport in Riyadh was the largest in the Kingdom; everything about it was washed in opulence. Enormous gold-tiered chandeliers dangled from the rafters in the arrival terminal the way you might see an Alexander Calder sculpture or city banners in American airports. Moving through the terminal, I gawked at fountains spewing water from beds of white and beige stones, the droplets splashing against abundant green leafy plants. Entire pieces looked out of place in the desert kingdom. We weren't waiting too long before a Saudi official greeted us with handshakes and began escorting us to a designated VIP area where a member of the Council was expecting us.

As we walked past the immigration counters, I spotted a considerable congregation of young Asian women, primarily Malaysian and Indonesian. I could just barely hear them as we crossed the room. They spoke in placid tones and wore colorful ankle-length, formless dresses with headscarves. The women were gathered in a corner of the great hall, waiting to be processed through a specially designated area. I later learned they were housemaids who would work for Saudi families. Near the group of Asian women, I caught sight of several waiting lines organized as one for single men and another for families, which included single women. The Saudi culture was quite stringent about segregating women and men outside of the home. Mixing between unmarried men and women who were not relatives was *haram*, forbidden.

As I surveyed the room, a flurry of activity suddenly filled the space. I turned to find a large group entering the area -- women in abayas and men wearing long white thobes and ghutras, some red and white checkered, others white. I was startled as the Saudi men greeted each other with a kiss on each cheek. Some lightly touched the tips of their noses together. Many pairs walked away, hand in hand, gleefully swinging their arms in the air like schoolyard chums. The scene was so different from what you see in the U.S., where men are more prone to exchange quick pats on the back or half-hugs when greeting each other. The Saudi women seemed less emotional in their interactions, greeting each other reservedly with a quick peck on the cheeks. The room, however, vibrated with the women's constant chatter and the incessant motion of children, countless children like frenetic ants, always in motion. It made my head swim to see all the children racing around unfettered. Not what I expected to see in Saudi Arabia's strict culture.

The VIP room contained more of the elegance and style of the rest of the airport -- sumptuous furniture, overstuffed sofas, and chairs with intricate designs carved into golden legs. The head Saudi official of the US-Saudi Business Council met us. They offered us mint tea in miniature clear glasses along with local dates of every variety: plain, pitted, chocolate, or pistachio-covered. I gratefully nibbled on a handful of dates and took a moment to check myself. I could not believe we were actually in Riyadh. So far, our processing seemed easy and comfortable. Since this was not a "developed" country in the same sense as the U.S. or Western countries, I imagined there would be more chaos and confusion, even though we were hosted by the distinguished US-Saudi Business Council. Instead, our processing was orderly and even streamlined. We did not have to go through normal immigration or collect our bags. We simply gave our luggage tags to an official who located our bags and brought them to our waiting van. In the meantime, we sipped our mint tea and cardamom coffee. We took our time to sit back and relax as our Saudi counterpart talked to us about our itinerary and provided some further details about our time in Riyadh and the people we would meet.

As we settled in our plush red velvet chairs, exchanging pleasantries with our Saudi counterpart and translator, the thrum of my mind eased. I breathed in our luxurious surroundings and atypical scenes. Although feeling naturally unsettled and out of place, I was mesmerized, happy, and ready to suspend any apprehension and doubt I had to explore the rhythm of this unusual country.

As we exited the airport in a chauffeured car, we were jostled awake when the driver shot onto the highway like a rock unloosed from a slingshot. The speedometer quickly nosed to read 130, 140 KPH. Nabil and I fell against one another in the jolting of the catapulted car. Our breath caught in our chests. From in between the gathered curtains on the car window, I saw Mercedes, BMWs, and other luxury cars hurtle past us in smudges of white, blue, and black.

In contrast, duct-taped cars barely kept up with the others. Our driver remained undaunted. We did our best to settle in our seats, holding tightly onto our armrests for the rest of the trip.

I prepared myself to look upon crumbling, ancient buildings and cracked and worn streets as we drove toward Riyadh on that mild, sunny afternoon. What I saw instead was a modern six-lane highway with palm trees lining the medians. Entering Riyadh, I found an ultramodern city with high-end couture shops, quaint outdoor coffee shops, skyscrapers punctuating the skyline, five-star western hotels, and the seemingly ever-present McDonalds, KFC, Burger King, and Pizza Hut. The edges of the city held simple, unimposing, family-owned retail shops and cafes.

We arrived at our accommodations at the Radisson, tired and hungry. Nabil and I decided to have dinner alone in the hotel restaurant.

Sitting in a quiet corner of the room, I asked Nabil what he thought so far. He told me he was overwhelmed and did not like the driving. It concerned him that drivers haphazardly and aggressively passed us on the right shoulder of the highway as we traveled at speeds greater than 80 miles per hour from the airport. Nabil added that it would be hectic and confusing to live and work in the Kingdom, especially since he had become "Americanized." My face fell when I heard Nabil was not thrilled to be doing this. I agreed the driving was eccentric and frightening and harbored some of Nabil's other concerns, but I kept largely mum, as I did not want to feed into Nabil's initial adverse reaction. I knew this was neither a vacation nor a whim; it was something we had to do.

I gently told Nabil he needed to give the place a chance. He reluctantly agreed, indicating he would wait and see. To lighten the mood, we turned our talk toward the upcoming meetings to be held over the next 10 days in three major cities—Riyadh, Jeddah, and Dammam—beginning in Riyadh. I assumed I was not going to any meetings, so I prepared to call Saudi business executives from our hotel room the next day in an effort to get myself known and secure a job. I was excited we were in the Kingdom, but I knew I had work to do. I needed to gear myself up like I had done so many times before when preparing for a major presentation at work or a job interview.

We were thankful that Jerry quickly became an ally. He was sympathetic to our genuine interest in living and working in the Kingdom and provided me with a list of names and numbers. I was nervous each time I picked up the phone. How would I be received as an American woman looking for a job in the Kingdom? Would I be taken seriously? Would this ultimately all be for naught? After all, I was in a country where, simply because I was a woman, I was not accepted at meetings with the Business Council members.

I was both bewildered and reassured at the gracious and straightforward phone conversations I had with each Saudi gentleman. They wanted to know why I was choosing to work in the Kingdom, as this was unusual for an American woman. I responded, "I want to have a new work experience in Saudi Arabia and learn more about the culture and lifestyle. My husband is Lebanese, but I know Saudi is different, and I want to know more about the Arab world." I sensed that I piqued their interest. On one call, a Saudi businessman told me, point blank, that securing employment as a woman would be a major challenge, if not impossible. Apologizing as he spoke, he explained that he and his business colleagues received many resumes from accomplished Western women. Still, due to employment restrictions imposed upon women, occupations were limited to three sectors: academia, the medical field, and ladies' banks. In the Kingdom, great efforts are made to keep the genders separate, including in the work world. Women teach at schools and universities for girls only. In the medical arena, Saudi women doctors are completely veiled (including their faces), except for their eyes and hands. Women's banks hold money for women who work and for those who are independently wealthy, like women in the royal family. Female tellers tend to their women clients so that no temptations arise between the sexes.

After each call, the Saudi gentleman on the other end of the line assured me he would do his utmost to aid in my efforts despite the work restrictions for women. I was taken aback and relieved by the unexpected level of respect and interest in my job search and unusual preoccupation with living in Saudi Arabia. Even though Nabil had told me about Arab hospitality, I was still wary of the unfounded generosity. Not yet familiar with Saudi customs and business interactions, I thought that perhaps it was all too good to be true. I consistently encountered a listening ear; I was given contact names and encouraged to call back if I needed further assistance. I found these were not just empty words. It didn't hurt that the Saudis liked Americans, and the Western goal-oriented approach with a focus on deadlines and efficiency. Despite what seemed like insurmountable obstacles for me as a woman, I secured several promising interviews during our time in the Kingdom. I was hopeful, yet I didn't want to become too excited, knowing there was still a very long road from interview to employment.

CHAPTER 2

RIYADH DAMMAM AND JEDDAH

After the first full day in Riyadh, Jerry let me know that I would be allowed to attend a breakfast meeting the next day to include our Council members and the U.S. Commercial staff of the U.S. Embassy. I was overjoyed but kept my expectations in check. Along with mentally preparing for a meeting with high-level Saudis, I realized I needed to wear appropriate clothing. I would wear one of the extra outfits that Nabil's colleague, Susan, had generously offered me for this trip: a black tunic with a tan geometric design on the front over black oversized elastic pants. I would wear my abaya over this ensemble.

We drove from our hotel to the site of our breakfast meeting in a caravan of what the Saudis referred to as "limousines," but were more like chauffeured luxury cars, customary for these types of meetings. Our line of cars snaked through the heart of Riyadh, a sprawling city more than half the size of Rhode Island. I was dazzled by the sight of the Al Faisaliyah, an imposing three-dimensional triangular tower that rose to almost 900 feet. Horizontal sheets of steel running the length of the prodigious building would eventually house a five-star luxury hotel and principal shopping mall. The tower sported a precariously perched glass sphere near the tip with a three-story restaurant. The Al Faisaliyah was the tallest building in Riyadh. Years later, the Kingdom Center would overshadow it, rising to almost 1,000 feet. Overtaken by the grandeur of the city, it was not easy to imagine a life here.

When we arrived at the breakfast meeting, I was just thankful to be in the room. I knew I would have to figure out the business meetings as we went along, which did little to squelch my natural inclination to plan, prep, and have all my bases covered. It was not lost on me that I was going to have to be open to shifting in big and small ways while in the Kingdom.

I sat next to Chase Kennedy, an American of Jewish heritage and Senior Officer of the U.S. Embassy Commercial office, who knew everything about the Middle East; I understood only about half of what he said. Chase was in his late 40s with large brown eyes and tousled hair. He was in the Foreign Commercial Service and had completed tours across the Middle East, including Iraq, the United Arab Emirates, and Saudi Arabia. He had also been the Beirut Bureau Manager for NBC News in Lebanon. Chase was a connoisseur of the culture and politics in the Middle East, and he had a wife who was a professional belly dancer. Nabil had taught me a few belly dancing moves back home in DC, a wonderful mini-cultural adventure. Even though belly dancing outside the home was strictly forbidden in the Kingdom, I imagined Chase's wife plying her art behind closed doors – a jingle belt hugging her hips, arms whirling and undulating to some of the popular Arab music Nabil liked to play. In time, we became great friends with this couple and had some formidable belly dancing bashes. Jerry informed me I would attend the next meeting at the Riyadh Chamber of Commerce. A member of the Saudi Council told me I didn't need to wear the entire black ensemble. I could take off my abaya. I was glad to peel away my extra shell and feel more like myself.

We were cordially welcomed at the Riyadh Chamber of Commerce. As we entered the building, several commanding and majestic figures in crisp white thobes bowed slightly. In turn, each one reverently swept one hand to their chest and delicately shook the tips of my fingers with the other hand. I felt privileged to be the lone woman in the room.

The Chamber displayed vaulted ceilings with captivating colossal translucent chandeliers. Crown molding with complex circular designs marked the perimeter of the room, and at the far wall stood mammoth windows with drawn dark blue curtains and gold sashes. As papers shuffled and murmurs dulled, I fully expected to be seated in a corner or in the back of the room where I would remain fairly innocuous, content, and honored to simply have the opportunity to observe the proceedings.

I had just settled the papers on my lap, sitting well behind the U.S. team, when I felt a person standing next to me. It was one of the Saudi government envoys. For a split second, I wondered if he was going to gently apologize that they made an error and ask me to leave the room. He motioned for me to stand and follow him. I cast a worried look in Nabil's direction, feeling more than disappointed at how far I had come only to get kicked out of my first formal meeting with the Saudis. I steeled myself to remain calm and smile politely until I was out of the room. The man did not lead me in the direction of the doors but instead walked me over to a seat at the table next to Nabil and the American contingency. I sat down, feeling incredible, and saw a microphone sitting in front of me on the table. I sank further into the luxuriant black leather seat, delighted and appreciative.

Before the meeting began, each member of the American bloc,

including me, had the opportunity to address the Chamber and expound on their specific business interest. Following these introductions, the Secretary of the Chamber of Commerce told us he knew there were many misperceptions in the Western world regarding Saudi Arabia. The American group had been in the Kingdom for a couple of days, and he was curious to learn of their impressions. Nabil kicked me under the table, giving me a subtle glance, urging me to speak up. I knew it would be inappropriate for me to speak. What was he thinking? I felt a little irritated, but I knew Nabil wanted me to have this chance to show myself and begin to connect with these people. But I was not an official member of the delegation; it was not my place.

The Secretary turned his magisterial gaze in my direction, declaring he wished to hear from the lady first. I started to blush, sweat forming in my armpits. This could not be happening. The Saudi businessmen I had spoken to on the phone the day before had been most kind and supportive, but this was an official government setting. I was stunned at the level of interest and respect for this American woman by the high-ranking Saudi officials sitting across the table. I did not have time to think or prepare, so I decided to go with my heart and speak my truth.

I took a deep breath, leaned forward, and pulled the microphone toward me. I thanked the Chamber for meeting with us. I met the eyes of the Secretary and began. "Although I know that people who have visited and those who have not have certain feelings about the Kingdom, I wanted to come with a clean slate and form my own impressions. And, so far, they have been nothing but positive." I felt my hesitation and anxiety fade. "I have been calling Saudi business leaders from our hotel about getting a job, and each person I've spoken to has been nothing but gracious and respectful, wanting to help me." The room was deadly silent. Time seemed suspended, and my physical body numbed; only my mind whirred. I tried to ignore all the eyes on me. I talked about my interest in wanting to get to know the Saudi people and culture. I emphasized that I wanted to grow and develop personally while in the Kingdom and continue to form my own impressions. Before I realized I had finished speaking, spontaneous applause broke out on the Saudi side of the table. My face flushed with pride, and a renewed sense of energy, possibility, and power washed over me. I was beginning to think this might work out.

After that session, there was no question about me joining the other meetings; I could choose what was of most interest to me. At each destination we visited, we were welcomed with hospitality and warmth. Docile attendants, *tea boys,* typically of South Asian origin, endlessly scurried in and out of our meeting rooms. They served us Arabic coffee and mint tea on silver platters alongside plates of sweet pastries covered in crispy filo dough and filled with honey and pistachio nuts. The pungent and delectable aroma of cardamom radiated from the Arabic coffee and filled every molecule in the room.

The ritual serving of coffee, tea, and sweet pastries is a conspicuous element of all gatherings, whether formal or informal, in the Kingdom. I was baffled when cautioned repeatedly to move my cup from side to side with my right hand, signaling to the attendant that I was finished. Failing to do so meant receiving continuous refills, a "free refill" policy that, while appealing to many Americans, was not ideal in the Kingdom. One of the many lessons in Arab culture I would learn.

Nabil and I were really pleased with how successful my first day had gone. We had only two full days and three nights in Riyadh before moving on. I was ready to engage in the next parts of these meetings, and was feeling optimistic I would have good interactions in the coming days. I was feeling relieved—ready to let my abaya down.

After our daytime meetings and several hours after dusk, the city came alive with frenzied activity. The terraces of "male only" coffee shops opened their arms to young men with ghutras rakishly skewed to one side or in baseball caps turned backward. They sipped Turkish coffee and smoked *sheesha* (hookah), water-based tobacco, from a large pipe while speaking in hushed tones or whispering in each other's ears. Groups of women of all shapes and sizes, concealed in black, exited from the backs of cars driven by Sri Lankan or Bangladeshi chauffeurs. Their children burst out from behind them as their abayas danced to the melodies of the night air. Moving through the entranceways of upscale shopping malls and haute couture shops, the women immersed themselves in endless shopping, exiting in the late hours of the evening. Although we did not partake in mall shopping, Nabil and I did look forward to visiting a traditional Arabian *souk*—the marketplace—with its continuous stalls filled with every type of merchandise imaginable. My senses and spirit were aroused in Riyadh. It was not so much that I could see us living there just yet, but more of a feeling that my soul was coming alive.

Our next destination was one of the larger cities in the Kingdom. Dammam sits alongside the iridescent, calm waters of the Arabian Gulf (Persian Gulf), and is the center of the oil industry in the country. The city is home to prominent Saudi Aramco (Saudi Arabian Oil Company) and caters to foreign workers in the oil business who live in beautiful gated western compounds. We visited several leading Saudi companies and governmental organizations, including the Tamimi Group, the Chamber of Commerce, steel companies, and a high-tech hospital in Al Khobar. At each destination, I was, again, surprised when our hosts supported me in openly expressing my feelings and perspective, especially when I was the only woman present and had been discouraged from even stepping foot on the plane to come to the Kingdom. Now, here in the Kingdom, it was as though these Saudi officials were encouraging me to move forward on this unique journey I had started.

Much like Riyadh, the meeting rooms in Dammam were all incredibly lavish, with posh, colorful furniture and massive paintings, encased in gold frames, of Bedouin scenes. You could just feel the oil money dripping through the room. The display of obvious materialism was so over the top that you could not help but be awestruck.

We attracted scrutiny with our ongoing and spirited repartee surrounding our appreciation of the culture. I didn't expect to encounter so much progressive thinking in a room full of Saudi men, but on more than one occasion, our conversations turned to women not being able to drive. Several businessmen admitted they thought women should be allowed to drive. "You know, if women were allowed to drive, the growth of the Saudi economy would double," remarked one gentleman. Another went on to say, "If women drove, they could get to work and earn money, which would mean greater household spending and growth in the economy." "You are so right," I responded, a little bit thrown by this unexpected and forward-thinking comment. I found myself the center of attention. These business managers, who typically kept their distance from women, were taking a vested interest in my words, in me. It was a heady experience on a lot of levels, and it just reinforced that Nabil and I were doing the right thing for us and me.

We were finishing our first meeting of the day at the Eastern Province Chamber of Commerce when nature called. I glanced around for anything that would point me to the restroom or the universal sign for a "ladies' room." I could not find one. I alerted Nabil and asked what we should do. From out of nowhere, a Saudi participant from the meeting came over. He apologetically explained that there was no women's restroom. Was he joking? After letting his words settle, I realized that women were not in this building and probably never had been, but here I was.

"Okay, I'll take you," the man said. I frowned. "Take me where exactly?" I wondered. I assumed to a bathroom of some kind. But he wasn't giving me directions like, "It's over there. You need to take a left at the end of the hall." He seemed to want to take me himself.

I quickly recognized I would get the Beyonce treatment and full escort attention. Naturally, I was completely uncomfortable with an unfamiliar man guiding me to the restroom under such bizarre circumstances. Nabil, who is always very protective, showed no evidence of this being strange. I ultimately figured this must be customary, and I had to go with the flow (no pun intended) even as I was feeling very awkward.

We proceeded down a series of long corridors in what felt like a maze with a series of left and right-handed turns. All the while, the man told me to think of him as a brother. I started to sense this might be more of a familial duty—like a parent taking a child to the bathroom—and nothing untoward. We arrived at a large, shiny metal door. My companion pushed the door open and gestured for me to go ahead inside. That is when I realized he was not only escorting me to the men's bathroom but was going to stand outside the stall door. I was utterly self-conscious but felt I could not say anything and risk offending him. I thought about singing something like the "A. B. C." song as a distraction, but I thought that was too obvious. Ultimately, I put my mind over my "matter" and did what I had to do. Afterward, I followed my escort back to where we came from and asked Nabil if he thought that was weird. He shook his head and smiled.

"No, I knew he would treat you like a sister, and it would be one hundred percent okay." I appreciated Nabil's words but found the whole experience unsettling. I was uneasy about having my very own bathroom attendant, yet looking back, it was one of many minor happenings that would accumulate into an extraordinary experience.

Our third and final destination was Jeddah, located in the western provinces of the Kingdom, 150 miles west of Mecca. Adjacent to the radiant Red Sea, Jeddah was a beautiful and delightful city with an extraordinary mixture of traditional Arabic and contemporary Western architecture, including a scattering of mirrored skyscrapers. From the window of our chauffeured car, I strained my neck to get a better glimpse of an approaching roundabout. In the center were magnificent and modernistic sculptures of life-size cars jutting from concrete in incongruous directions. Another roundabout exhibited oversized Bedouin urns spewing water. Western expatriates told us they appreciated Jeddah, where there were opportunities to swim, boat, and dive in the Red Sea. I learned that the coral reefs of the Red Sea rivaled those of the Great Barrier Reef in Australia.

Jeddah also had fewer restrictions, particularly for women who frequented restaurants and sheesha cafes unaccompanied by men. Women were not afforded this privilege in Riyadh or many other cities in the Kingdom. In some ways, Jeddah felt more like being in a European town. I felt more relaxed, at ease, and at home in this seaside city. While Riyadh was a novelty, an assault to the senses, Jeddah was more liberal, familiar, and comfortable. This was a place I could see us living.

During a break in between meetings, Nabil and I ambled along the sparkling beach of the Red Sea, our toes caressed by the fine white sand. In the distance, Jeddah's picturesque skyline spread across the horizon. We found out there were sections of beach partitioned and earmarked for expatriates, allowing sun worshippers to strip down to as little as bikinis or Speedos. As Nabil pulled out our camera to take a picture of me against the backdrop of the dazzling sea, we were alarmed to see a uniformed gentleman rushing over, waving his hands and shouting in a blended language of English and Arabic. He forbade us to take photographs; there were Saudi women in the background. I was completely unnerved. Had we just broken the law? We had heard earlier from Council members that we needed to be careful about taking pictures in the Kingdom; the Saudis did not take kindly to this practice. Once the official turned away, I exhaled. We wouldn't be going to jail after all. My composure returning, I turned to the Saudi women who regularly swam in the sea clothed in their abayas, a sight that would always seem alien to me. I wondered how it must be to swim wearing full dress, and be both carried and weighed down by the ocean. I wondered if it was strange for them.

Most American beaches are overrun with umbrellas or hot dog and burger stands; there are a lot of things you expect to see in a beach setting, but a camel is not one of them. Further down the stretch of beach, I stopped in my tracks. Just up ahead was a camel decked out in a bright red and gold carpet with luxurious tassels over its back. It was being led by a thick-knotted rope through a vacant parking lot by a middle-aged man in an off-white tunic. I had hoped to see a camel on our trip to the Kingdom, although, in my daydreams, it would be ankle-deep in the sand with a tent and Bedouin in the background. Nabil saw to it to make another fantasy of mine a reality.

Arab bargaining is an art full of nuances. The vendor starts high; you go low. The vendor makes a slightly higher offer, the customer walks off in a huff, and the vendor eventually relents, calling you back to accept your offer. Mindful of the intricate movements of this marketplace dance, Nabil approached the man with a proposition. I watched as he expertly entered into negotiations with the man, and within several minutes, I was helped aboard the motley quadruped. Nabil eagerly snapped shots without a hint of opposition from the uniformed officer. I was on top of the world, so to speak. It was cliché, but when you're in Arabia you need a picture riding a camel.

As the last meetings wound down and we broke up for the evening, one of the American Council members suggested to Nabil that perhaps I would like to see the gold souk. Jewelry is not really my thing, but I was interested in seeing what I knew would be a traditional Arab marketplace. Nabil, however, wanted to buy me something. He hoped to purchase a "desert diamond" to serve as a reminder of our time in Saudi Arabia. Nabil made inquiries, and the Council connected us with a driver who, most graciously, on his own time and without accepting payment, escorted us to the Arabian souk.

The souk was an intricate maze of small shops made of concrete slabs offering a multitude of goods from spices, Indian silk, pots and pans, and children's toys to women's lingerie and 21-karat gold jewelry. The marketplace teemed with Saudis, other Arab nationals, and a sprinkling of expatriates. The souk tickled all of the senses. The scent of incense and spices infiltrated the winding cobble-stoned alleyways. We sauntered through the alluring hodgepodge. We often had to flatten ourselves against the side of walls to avoid the crush of wheelbarrows propelled by decrepit men in turbans laden with customer purchases or dodge the oncoming charge of women and children.

I spied an elderly Saudi man in the corner of the souk, a roadmap of wrinkles marking his face. He was tending to cardboard thin *saj* bread (flat bread) sizzling on a large, flat half-dome heated element over a wood block. Across from him sat a group of Saudi men on aluminum chairs smoking sheesha. One man rested his bare foot on the edge of the seat of the chair, and another stared off into nowhere in particular, plumes of smoke snaking from his nostrils and mouth, while the third companion spoke animatedly, his words peeling off his tongue like rocket fire. Down another maze-like alleyway, an array of women in black stood clustered in a tiny shop, fondling decadent, frilly lingerie. Children clutched the ends of their mother's abayas; South Asian men tended to their queries and purchases. Women were not allowed to work in the retail industry in Saudi Arabia, and Saudi men had little interest in menial jobs. The souk was pure enchantment and a staggering assault on my physical and emotional being. The abundance of community and culture in this chaotic tableau was in stark contrast to my more sterile life in Washington.

Our meetings behind us, Nabil and I regrouped as we packed our bags in the hotel room. We saw real opportunities that would go somewhere regarding employment. We looked at the business cards we received and talked about which companies might be well suited to Nabil and his company. And I talked about continuing to send my resume around to potential employers. I realized, though, that the things that made me excited might not make Nabil excited. I asked him how he felt about our time in Saudi Arabia.

"The time went so fast. I wanted to spend more time here. It took me back to when I was a child in the Middle East," he replied. Nabil went on to say he definitely felt like he was home, adding he never expected my reaction at all. He thought I would see it, change my mind, and want to stay in the U.S. Nabil was glad to see me happy and confident, and confided that he ended up feeling overpowered by the experience, wanting to come back as much as me, perhaps even more. I reached across our packed suitcases and squeezed his hand.

Knowing we would be in the Arab world, practically next door to Nabil's native Lebanon, we purchased round-trip tickets from Jeddah to Beirut before leaving on our Business Council trip. The plan was to travel to Lebanon as soon as our meetings in Saudi Arabia ended, spend a few days in Beirut, and then fly on to the U.S. The next morning, chauffeurs drove us and the other Council members to the Jeddah airport. We flew on to Beirut while the rest of the members flew back to the U.S. Nabil was excited about spending time with his mom and sister before heading back to the U.S.

Nabil's sister, Jehan, and a couple of neighbors were at the Beirut airport to meet us. We shared hearty embraces and conversation as we walked to Jehan's car. It felt good to be in Beirut, formerly known as "the Paris of the Middle East." The city had a wonderful and palpable spirit–the Lebanese people experienced years of civil war from 1975 to 1990 but refused to succumb, rebuilding their city and communities over the succeeding years. I gazed at the Mediterranean Sea through the right backseat window and the Lebanon mountains out the left window as we drove through the dazzling city.

As soon as we walked into Nabil's mother's apartment, we grabbed his mama in a bear hug, and everyone broke into tears. Her apartment sat on the second floor of a four-story building. It was a modest flat with two bedrooms and a tiny balcony off the kitchen. Located in the suburbs of Beirut, the area held a variety of concrete apartment buildings with balconies and awnings, stand-alone homes, and small retail shops. Relatives and neighbors freely flowed into the apartment to welcome Nabil and me. It took a while to get a hold of ourselves and move into the living room.

Our Lebanese family had many plans for us over the next three days. Party after party, belly dancing to durbakeh (known as *tabla* in the Arab Gulf) drumming, homemade food from Mama and his sister—tabouli, baba ghanoush, falafel, hummus, shish kabob, shawarma, fresh fish, and much more. Lebanese meals were typically vegetarian closely following the Mediterranean diet and included pita bread over customary western utensils. In the Arab world food is a connector of people.

This trip was comfortable for me; it was like coming home in a certain way. Many of the faces were familiar from an earlier trip we had taken to Lebanon in 1996. We felt the love not only of family but of the larger general Arab world as well. We were welcomed and encouraged with each new experience.

The last night in Beirut, as we settled into bed, I could tell by Nabil's plaintive eyes and quietness he was feeling emotional and sentimental. We agreed that a move to the Middle East would not only provide personal growth, but also a connection with his family that he had missed all those years in America.

On the plane trip back to the U.S., I had to get my head back in the space of going home to DC and the house, job, and life I had known while carrying around a scrap of the new life I might have. During our flight, while continuing to feel the glow of being with Nabil's family, we talked more about our opportunities for changing jobs and companies. Given the enthusiasm generated by our meetings with the Saudis, things were lining up and our prospects felt real. I could see myself moving to this world and away from what had been home.

CHAPTER 3

THE MONTHS BEFORE SAUDI ARABIA

The fax machine shrieked like a barn owl. I rocked on my heels as the paper inched out of the dispenser. Would this be the response from the Kingdom I had been waiting for since returning from our trip? I wrenched it out just before the final beep sounded and quickly scanned the text while my hopes plummeted. It was a polite, professional "thank you for your time and interest." Another dead end. We had thought there was every reason to expect a positive outcome from our trip to Saudi Arabia.

In the first few days after arriving home, still immersed in the luster of the trip, we pulled out every business card we received while in the Kingdom and sent out nearly 60 messages by fax, e-mail, and letter to Saudi governmental agencies like the Ministry of Higher Education, and private companies including the Tamimi Group, Aramco, Arthur Andersen, 3M Gulf Company, among many others. We thanked the businessmen and governmental representatives we met for "the invaluable information exchange." We inquired if they knew of employment opportunities in the Kingdom for a civil engineer and an economist.

Within the course of a few weeks, we heard various responses. Mr. Khalifa from Hidada, an industrial manufacturing firm, wrote that the Saudi Arabian government was pushing the private sector to employ at least 20% Saudi employees, and, therefore, most companies were looking to hire locals to fulfill the quota. "It would be somewhat difficult for your wife to have work outside hospitals or the universities." I knew, based on previous phone calls with Saudi officials, that it would be challenging for me to obtain employment in the Kingdom as a woman. These Saudization employment laws, a government mandate dictating that companies reduce their reliance on expatriate workers and hire more Saudis, would likely make the job search process for both of us even slower or, worse, irrelevant. Although we had heard rumblings of this when in the Kingdom, seeing it in writing made it more real and disheartening.

We did hear from Parsons, an engineering company, that "civil" engineering jobs were by far the most popular and plentiful of the engineering disciplines in the Middle East. We reached out to engineering firms repeatedly only to receive radio silence or more professional, polite rejections. It was discouraging to be faced with half-opened doors that now seemed to be shutting in our faces. I fell back into the funk of DC life, and that took me over again.

When we initially relocated to Washington, DC, we had a robust circle of friends and activities. However, a move from condo life to a suburban neighborhood meant families were often away with children at soccer, baseball, football practices, or other school events. Without children as a social channel, our community began a slow decline. At work, a restructuring was underway, which meant the organization would likely shrink with people being laid off. At his work, Nabil was getting bored with small projects that primarily involved renovation.

We felt isolated and uncertain, but I knew that with persistence and healthy dollops of blood, sweat, and tears, we would break through.

Determined to pull myself out of the impending doldrums, I decided to focus on all the positive interactions, all the words of support I had received from the Saudis, despite slim pickings in a decidedly restrictive workforce—particularly for an American woman. One of those positive points of connection was with a man named Alan Carter. Prior to our trip with the Business Council, we were encouraged to contact Mr. Carter, the head of a large private cell phone company in Riyadh. Alan was a tall, middle-aged man with a kind demeanor. He was a well-known entrepreneur in the Kingdom and could be helpful in providing all kinds of information on who to approach for suitable employment, and details on making a move to Saudi. We were grateful for this contact, and Alan was most generous with his time and reasoned and practical advice about life in Saudi.

Back in February, within hours of arriving in the Kingdom for meetings with the Council, we called Alan. He warmly welcomed us to the Kingdom, surprising us with an invitation to accompany him and his wife, Doris, to a traditional Saudi dinner. I was excited about indulging in a cultural activity during our time in the Kingdom. After a couple of days in Riyadh, we sat with Alan and Doris atop colorful oversized pillows in a tent. An enormous silver tray was piled high with mounds of rice and great slabs of lamb, a traditional Arab Gulf meal. It was my first time eating on the floor, so it took a few minutes to get my balance on the pillows as I reached out to ladle some of the fragrant coriander and shawarma flavoring mixed with the lamb. The communal sharing of food was very intimate, creating a special connection with our new friends. We had four waiters coming and going, serving us in the tent, which made us feel doted on and was a magnificent peek into the rich culture of the Arab Peninsula.

We had another glance at "real life" in the Kingdom for Westerners when Alan and his wife kindly invited us to a meal at their beautiful home in one of the high-end Western compounds in the city. A live-in housekeeper helped serve the meal. Live-in help, which was prevalent in the Arab Gulf, was a practice I would have to get used to.

On my first day in the Kingdom with the Council, Alan was kind enough to allow me to use the phone in one of his offices to call Saudi business executives about employment options, which led to an interview in Dammam, a city on the eastern coast, the second city on our itinerary with the Business Council. The International School Group in Dammam had an opening for an Assistant Superintendent for Business Operations. While I was not selected for the position, I couldn't help but think the interview was a good omen.

Alan continued his support after we arrived home in DC from our trip with the Council. He provided us with websites and connected us to people to aid in our job search. Alan's support and advocacy made me feel that we had a head start in creating a circle of expatriate friends in the Kingdom. We added the names and companies to our list and sent out more queries. We continued receiving muted responses. However, there were some vines we hoped might bear fruit.

Nabil continued working at the corrosion control company. Early one morning, several weeks after returning from the Kingdom, Nabil unexpectedly found a fax on the machine at his office. It was addressed to him by a Saudi Arabian Sheikh. The document revealed the Sheikh had been sending faxes to Nabil at work for the last two weeks, but he had not received a response. Nabil discovered from his company secretary that the boss had decided against pursuing a partnership with the Saudis and had instructed her to throw out all faxes from the Saudis addressed to him or Nabil. The fax read: "Our initial review indicates a high potential opportunity for your organization in the region. We have been looking forward to discussing the possibility of a co-venture arrangement to enable us to undertake job contracts expected to materialize soon."

Nabil phoned me immediately about the Sheikh's fax and picked me up from work.

"I can't believe it. It looks like this might happen," I said to Nabil on the ride home. Nabil grabbed my hand. "I feel like we're knocking down a wall, Mary." When we arrived home, we climbed the stairs to the bedroom and Nabil picked up the bedside table phone receiver. We both took a deep breath. I leaned toward the receiver, not wanting to miss a word, of the blended English and Arabic conversation.

"Hello, Sheikh Salem, this is Nabil Khouri. I know you have been trying to contact me by fax over the last few weeks."

"Ah, yes," came the response from the other end of the line. It sounded like he had been waiting for Nabil's call.

"I was happy to finally receive your fax. I am sorry to say that my boss has changed his mind about a joint venture with a Saudi company and has been, unfortunately, throwing away your faxes."

"I was wondering what happened to you. I sent you so many faxes and never heard back," the Sheikh replied calmly.

"I would love to work for you," Nabil said impulsively, "but before I make any commitment, I want to make sure my wife, Mary, has a job."

"What does your wife do?" Nabil took the opportunity to introduce me. I took the phone receiver. My spine stiffening, I bolstered myself.

"Hello, Sheikh Salem. As Nabil said, my name is Mary, and I'm an economist. I've worked for the government in Washington, DC for the last 17 years." I spoke at length about my remarkable visit to the Kingdom and my hopes to return in a more permanent capacity.

Nabil tugged at the receiver, leaning in to talk.

"We are both still very interested in getting jobs in the Kingdom." Nabil, my advocate, continued pushing, "With the employment restrictions that women face in Saudi Arabia, could you help Mary find a position, first, before me?" We held our breaths, wondering if this would be another dead end; however, surprisingly, without hesitation, the Sheikh was happy to agree. "Yes, yes, definitely, I will. Just give me a few weeks, and somebody will be calling you." We hung up.

"Oh, my God, that just happened," we said to each other. We hugged with tears in the corners of our eyes.

Nabil's initial elation later soured to disappointment toward his boss when he found out the faxes from the Sheikh had been thrown away. A couple of days after finding the fax, Nabil confronted the boss with what he felt was a betrayal, and this ultimately cost Nabil his job. He was given four weeks' notice to leave. We had already been pursuing jobs in the Kingdom on our own, as we knew the boss' heart was not into the prospect of partnering with the Saudis. Although the boss' behavior was discouraging, I told Nabil that everything happens for a reason. Now, we weren't entirely on our own; we had the newfound support of the Sheikh. Nabil ultimately secured a job with another engineering firm, and although satisfied with the new position, he stayed focused on a potential life for us in Saudi Arabia.

The next 24 hours were bliss. We knew we were in the game. We chatted excitedly about what those jobs might look like—perhaps project management for Nabil, and finance manager for me? By the next evening, as we watched the news on TV, we wondered what TV was like in the Kingdom. Would we have access to U.S. news? Was there cable TV, and were there sitcoms and movie channels? As the reality of the situation took hold over the next few days and we considered how we would get ourselves to the Kingdom and start a new life, our excitement turned to more specific questions. How did the internet work over there? Was it reliable? Were there internet restrictions? And the more mundane, how did you take out the trash? Were there private companies and bins; how did it work in the Kingdom? I began to feel the weight of the prospect of traveling halfway around the world to a new home and way of life.

A member of high-level management from King Faisal Specialist Hospital and Research Centre (KFSH&RC) in Riyadh called me in mid-April to request my CV. The Sheikh had been true to his word. KFSH&RC (also known as KFSH) officially opened in 1975 on land awarded by King Faisal Ibn Abdulaziz Al Saud and catered to the general population as well as to specialized medical cases and needs. I was not aware of this hospital or other medical establishments in the Kingdom, how they were run, or what their medicine was like. I would soon find out that KFSH&RC was a well-regarded medical institution in Riyadh initially run by Americans (Hospital Corporation of America) until 1985 when it was turned over to the Saudis. The hospital was massive; equipped with around 800 beds and 8,000 employees. In the Kingdom, healthcare was afforded to all—natives and expatriates—and was free of charge for those working in the government sector.

The call was from a man named Abbas Al-Ghal, Director of Operations at the hospital. He said they would review my CV and place me in an appropriate position. Mr. Abbas indicated I would be contacted by HCA (Hospital Corporation of America), International, to start the process. I was giddy with anticipation and knew our persistence was paying off. The light at the end of the proverbial tunnel was in sight. I just knew something would happen; I couldn't wait to find out what it would be. The HCA offices were in Nashville, Tennessee, and not long after that phone call, someone from their group contacted me about generating a work contract. By the end of the month, we received word I would likely receive a job offer from KFSH in Jeddah, a branch of KFSH&RC in Riyadh. Jeddah was the beautiful city on the Red Sea that left us awestruck last February when we visited with the Business Council. It was our favored choice of place to live; we already envisioned walks along sandy beaches framed by palm trees. My excitement was dashed when we ultimately found out the job would likely be in Riyadh, more conservative than Jeddah and nearly twice the size. We would have to think about this.

Job location would not be the only concern. I received intermittent mail from HCA about the process for creating an employment contract following the initial call. I tensed when I opened a mail piece from HCA and read the top of the official-looking document:

"Single Status Employment Contract." "You're kidding me," I told Nabil. Although it was a draft document that had not been signed off on by the requisite officials, I was anxious about the crossed communication lines. I wondered not only about how these issues would affect the timeframe for making the move to Saudi Arabia but if the move would happen at all. "It looks like I might be going without you, Nabil," I quipped. Nabil shook his head, knowing this would never happen.

Although some couples feel comfortable with long-distance commuter relationships, Nabil and I were "best friends" and enjoyed each other's company above all others. Besides, life would be interminably more difficult for me without Nabil's presence as my husband and official male escort. Having Nabil with me would definitely open up possibilities. Besides, no matter where Nabil was, he felt entirely comfortable with taking calculated risks; he was a free soul who did not always follow cultural mores. And it would be no different in Saudi Arabia. Some friends even cautioned Nabil to tone it down to avoid jail time in one of the most conservative countries in the world. They were only partly kidding. The thought of jail time half-crossed my mind, as well. But I knew Nabil would be able to finagle his way out of almost any tricky situation. He had encountered the horror of war in the Middle East as a young adolescent and survived many life-and-death episodes; I was completely confident he could handle any oddities of the Kingdom.

Then, another wrinkle: the HCA agent revealed the job was a staff position, not the senior position I had been promised in initial conversations with KFSH&RC. This was a major sticking point. Nabil and I agreed we would only relocate to Saudi Arabia if I were offered a salary that would make our move worthwhile, particularly since we would be giving up a myriad of job benefits, not to mention the closeness of family and friends. We wouldn't be willing to move to Saudi Arabia unless I could negotiate a higher salary.

I called Mr. Abbas immediately, unsure if he would be sympathetic or might decide that an expat was too much trouble. Mr. Abbas assured me he would speak with HCA and fix the issues. My mood lifted, and our outlook improved when HCA came back to us with all the snafus corrected. The job would be a senior position and entailed developing financial performance measures for hospital management, improved budget and financial reporting, and detailed income statements. While I had not yet heard about salary, the contract would be married status.

We were happy to hear that another major element of our move, housing, would be provided through the hospital or a housing allowance. I appreciated this perk and would find there were others associated with expatriate living, like free utilities, water, and electricity, all meant to entice job-worthy applicants to work away from the comforts of their home country. This helped to make up for the loss of job benefits we had become accustomed to.

We talked with the hospital administration about owning a car in the Kingdom. Of course, Nabil would be the only one driving, as women were forbidden to drive in the Kingdom at the time. Although we knew not everything would go according to plan in our life shift, the city location had been high on the priority lineup, as it could significantly affect our lifestyle. Riyadh and Jeddah were on the opposite ends of the spectrum. In the end, we decided since it seemed it would be Riyadh or nothing, we needed to accept this detour.

It became clear early on that this was not going to be a typical kind of international move. Unlike Americans who moved to France or Germany to start new lives and had to deal with the basics like shipping items or figuring out work visas, we were going to a place that was a bureaucratic and political morass. We would have to go through an additional set of hoops—a multitude of administrative forms, medical reports, family history forms, and the back and forth on contractual details. And on top of this, we would be moving to a region with a history of political instability.

Nabil knew this all too well. He was particularly concerned about my exposure to such an environment, one which he couldn't wait to escape as a young man. It was especially important, therefore, to negotiate a salary at the new senior level that supported a move forward. A salary negotiation never had so much at stake for me. It meant the difference between being stuck in the banality of Washington's endless bureaucracy with a deflated spirit and another new life with another kind of bureaucracy. But this new life was filled with the unexpected, the unusual, a whole new worldview. My mind swirled with concerning thoughts. Was I being too demanding? Was my inflexibility crossing the line of cultural norms? Would they rescind the job offer? Thankfully, we were able to settle on a number which, when supplemented with job benefits like free housing and medical care, made the venture justifiable in our minds. We would also receive reimbursement for moving expenses. Furniture and household items would be complimentary.

Two more months passed without any news about finalizing my contract with the hospital. E-mails and other correspondence dribbled in from the other companies and government agencies we had contacted earlier about jobs, but nothing panned out. As time moved on, what I thought was certain seemed to fade. What would happen if this all blew up? If all of it fell through, we couldn't "just show up" and figure it out as we went along like we might have been able to do in a European country. Saudi Arabia required sanctioned entry just to arrive. Nabil consoled me by saying that "Arab time" was different from "American time." Just hold tight, he said; we need to be patient.

Feeling a bit entitled, like we had done everything everyone had asked and were still dangling on the line, made me annoyed and anything but patient. While waiting for something to happen, I touched base with two Western women, Jane and Suzanne, who were referred to me by the US-Saudi Business Council before our trip to the Kingdom as sources of information about life as a Western woman in Saudi Arabia. Was it really as severe as I heard through the media, friends, and neighbors?

Jane and Suzanne had been candid in earlier e-mail messages when describing their perceptions of the Kingdom. Jane, a Brit, worked at the American Consulate in the Eastern Province of the Kingdom; she and her husband had lived in Saudi Arabia for a number of years. I asked Jane to tell me honestly how it was to live in Saudi Arabia as a Western woman. Jane wrote, *Although we do have a lot of fun, I must admit that sometimes I do want to scream about the place. I should add that life is very different, and the adjustment can be quite hard to make. Not being allowed to drive is the worst irritant so far as I am concerned, but there are others. Most of the 'long-timers' that I know of here have working wives. And most of the women who do not work get unhappy and want to leave.*

I was not particularly surprised by Jane's response; I knew the Kingdom was not a vacation destination. Although not fond of driving, the ban on women behind the wheel in the Kingdom was troublesome for me -- an example of prejudicial policies and practices against women. Jane's observations were like mental notes I needed to store away to remind me that life in Saudi Arabia would likely be peculiar at times, and indeed, many expatriates considered living and working in the Kingdom as a hardship.

Suzanne had a different perspective to offer. She was an American who had spent some time in Saudi Arabia as a "trailing spouse." Her husband, an American businessman, worked in the construction industry in the Kingdom. I didn't actually get to meet Suzanne; she had moved back to the U.S. before we arrived in the Kingdom. Her e-mails were spirited, and I could tell she appreciated the idiosyncratic nature of the place. In one of several e-mails, Suzanne wrote, *If you are a VERY flexible, adventurous sort of person, it's a great life. I miss it all very much. I took the train between Dammam and Riyadh by myself. I talked with anyone who would give me a second (including Saudi men). And generally had a sensational life. I had invitations to weddings, dinners, private operettas, and homes. I have been chased by the 'Mutawa' (religious police) and had my car run off the road. I would sit on the curb with the women during Isha's prayer and find someone I could speak with. Most of life in the Kingdom of Saudi Arabia is learned by doing and can be extremely frustrating by Western standards. Sometimes, western women in Saudi feel as though they are in a free fall into an abyss. It's Jumanji – you never know what's going to come through the wall. And it's not going to change any time soon. I hope this helps. 'Ma salama' (goodbye), Suzanne.* I was elated to hear Suzanne's account of her life in the Kingdom. This was a woman who rode the waves of quirkiness and was grateful for it.

One afternoon in late July as I was hurrying to shut down my computer and get home for the day, I saw a fresh e-mail slide into the top column of my inbox. I stopped and sat back down. It was from KFSH&RC, the subject heading: "IMPORTANT! King Faisal Specialist Hospital & Research Centre Employment." I clicked as I read the header, feeling like a high school kid getting an acceptance letter from her dream college. My job was part of a new group, "Financial & Management Reporting," which I would head up. The group would be responsible for creating and monitoring new financial reports for higher-level management decision-making. It was a worry that Nabil did not yet have a job; however, we were confident that this issue would eventually resolve itself.

With my employment essentially secured, we turned our attention to the challenging issue of finding a place to live. We weren't really sure what the housing options would look like. Our fortunate invitation to Alan and Doris Carter's home in a western compound during our Council meetings in February gave us some sense of typical living quarters. The compound was elegant, with lush and colorful landscaped grounds and large villas surrounded by a high cement wall meant to hinder peering eyes. Their villa was beautifully decorated with posh furniture and state-of-the-art appliances. We liked the compound and hoped we could consider it as a possibility. KFSH&RC's Housing Services provided contact information for housing compounds in the city, as did our newly formed Western acquaintances in Saudi Arabia.

One non-negotiable item in our move: our two miniature poodle pups would accompany us to the Kingdom. We acquired our beloved poodles, Maci and Coco, in 1994 and 1999, respectively. They were our complete loves. Much of our lives surrounded our precious pups; they accompanied us on errands when possible and often joined us on vacation.

We had a lot of questions regarding the transportation of our pups into the Kingdom. Chase Kennedy provided some early answers for us, and it wasn't great news. Chase had brought a dog to the Kingdom. He e-mailed a response after we wrote for his insight and advice:

I really do not know what to tell you – dogs are not the favorite animal here in Saudi! I have a dog and had a hard time bringing the dog through customs, so DO NOT SHIP the dogs separate from you – bring them on the same flight with you. Chase's forceful words were distressing. I worried about how we would get Maci and Coco on our flight and how Saudi immigration would handle the importation of two dogs. We were also concerned about how our pups would be treated once in the Kingdom. What would people think of us and our dogs, who were like furry family members? The issue surrounding bringing our pooches into the Kingdom was not just another major challenge, it was a deal breaker for us. We would simply not relocate to Saudi Arabia without our dogs.

We were dealing with a multitude of issues and didn't want to muddy the waters too early with the matter of our pooches. However, in early September, hospital administration instructed me to communicate with Paul, an administrative assistant for the Director of Finance at KFSH&RC, the group I would be assigned to, about any future questions or concerns. I wrote Paul an e-mail about bringing dogs to the Kingdom. I anticipated there would be complications, so I initially indicated we would bring one dog to soften the blow that would surely follow after learning about two dogs. After hearing about "dogs" (plural), in a later e-mail, Paul responded:

Dear Mary, yes, I did coordinate (verbally) about your problem of bringing the dogs here with our Housing Services and got a good response from them. (By the way, I thought you only have one – how many are they?) My pulse quickened. Paul went on to say that we could keep the pups in our assigned hospital housing unit for only a few days; he made it clear that this was a "special arrangement." The housing department would work toward getting us a housing allowance, which would permit us to rent a private accommodation. I made sure to copy all communication about the pooches and planned to carry these documents with us as we entered Saudi Arabia. We were pleased to hear that vets and dog groomers were available, and some provided home service.

In the coming weeks, the struggle to secure the paperwork for me and Nabil to enter Saudi Arabia was almost matched by the battle for the documentation required for our two pups. We endured numerous visits to the vet for vaccinations and health certificates, as well as trips to the Department of Agriculture Veterinary Service Office and the State Department's Authentications Office to have the veterinary health records validated. Finally, we had to make a trip to the Saudi Embassy to have all the documents certified. Since we felt strongly about having "the girls" travel in the cabin of the plane with us, we would have to buy specially designed airline doggie carriers. Off we went to that pet lover's haven, PetSmart, for soft-sided containers with ventilation strips along the sides and plush cottony mats inside.

Weeks after communicating with Paul about the pups, I received notice from HCA that the formal processing of my contract would begin. My employment contract would be for two years, with 50 days of leave per year, 13 of which would include Muslim holidays. Working hours would be Saturday through Tuesday, 8-6, and 8-5 on Wednesday. Thursday and Friday constituted the weekend, and Friday was a religious day, like our Sunday in the U.S. I was ecstatic we had finally arrived at this point and relieved to learn we would be provided a furnished apartment. Additionally, I would receive a generous severance package.

The details of our housing arrangement became clearer by September 2000. All hospital housing units (except for studios) had two bathrooms, linens, towels, and kitchen utensils and basic cookware would be provided. Paul suggested we might bring extra blankets, at least for the coming winter.

HCA warned me that the visa process was longer for married status contracts. I would also need a special exception on the Saudi side to bring my husband. I would be the sponsor and Nabil, my dependent. Due to my married status, I would need to provide a copy of my marriage certificate. It turned out I would need a copy of my marriage certificate on my person at all times while in the Kingdom since we needed proof we were married if authorities stopped Nabil and me. I found out later that jail or deportation could result if marital status were not proved. We also needed to note our religion on much of our official documentation, even though I do not confess to being very religious. These extra peculiarities brought early apprehension about the high levels of restriction and regulation in the Kingdom. How would we live our everyday lives in this highly controlled country?

Along with medical physicals, we needed to complete detailed medical forms for both the hospital and the Royal Embassy of Saudi Arabia. The medical testing went through mid-October. Our physical exams ultimately deemed us "Physically fit and suitable for employment and/or residence overseas with climate extremes and significant stress." I felt like we were being vetted for the space shuttle; however, at this point, we knew we were all in.

We also needed dental statements, family records, police clearance reports, and to sign a drug statement. The drug statement particularly struck me. HCA sent a document entitled "Drug Laws in the Kingdom of Saudi Arabia," which included excerpts of a letter from the U.S. Ambassador to the hospital's Executive Director. The letter outlined severe punishments, including jail time and hefty fines for smuggling drugs and possession of drugs. The Saudi side produced a document that drug use or possession could result in the death penalty in some cases. Although this would be a non-issue for us, these ominous documents gave me pause and made me reconsider our plans for a split second. How could I possibly build a life in a country where this sort of thing is a reality? After a couple of days, however, we both signed the documents.

With all that was happening, I kept my parents in-the-loop, so they wouldn't be taken by surprise when we relocated to the Kingdom. They were always glad to hear my joy but remained wary of this entire enterprise. I respected that. No matter how old I was or how my life unfolded, I was still their girl, Mary, and they would always want me to be safe and protected. Although they sounded calm on the phone, I knew they were deeply worried. They must have been incredulous at my new path but knew I was intent on moving forward, and they would have my back.

We then conveyed our plans to a wider circle—our friends and colleagues. It was difficult telling them about my interest in moving to Saudi Arabia. I worried they might think I was irrational or maybe deranged. I was heartened when some of our friends and my co-workers were supportive and admired our adventuresome spirits. But I never told friends, co-workers, or family about the severity of the rules in the Kingdom. And not all our friends were so supportive. Nabil, himself, was still very worried about me as an American woman who had never lived overseas. How would I fit there? I gently explained I was excited about moving there precisely because I wouldn't fit in; I would learn a new lifestyle and culture, rewire my brain, and refresh my spirit. This touched on Nabil's concern that if he hadn't fit in the Arab world as a little boy, how could he fit there as an adult? While I was sympathetic to Nabil's uneasiness, I hoped the physical closeness of his family would help him reconnect with his roots.

With more people aware of our move to this fraught and unusual place, there was one particularly alarmed neighbor. She had read a magazine news story about the Saudi religious police smacking a Western woman on the ankles for showing too much leg. The woman was later incarcerated. While I assumed the story was real, I was annoyed by my neighbor's forwardness, even though I felt a chill over the mental images of the religious police confronting the woman. I didn't want to engage with this neighbor on any level and wanted to push aside any of my fears. With Saudi Arabia controlling what media was released and no social media at the time, the limited news reports only served to add to the level of intrigue surrounding the Kingdom. Although we had a brief visit to Saudi Arabia the previous February, I was still fascinated by, yet somewhat wary of, the long black abayas, white thobes, and chaotic marketplaces in this distant region. I was determined, though, to fight for what felt like my soul; this is what was driving me.

One major challenge remained: Nabil's job or lack thereof. The Sheikh offered Nabil a job, but since it would mean extensive travel around the world without me, Nabil declined. Nabil was disturbed about not having employment yet confident in his own "go-getter" tenacity. He knew he would get a job in a few months. It didn't hurt that Arabic was his first language, and he had knowledge of the culture and traditions of the Middle East. I also knew that Nabil would apply himself tirelessly to secure employment once we were in the Kingdom. Looking back though, I am surprised we took the risk of going with only one of us having a firm job offer. There was no guarantee it would work. In any event, it seemed the girl who insisted on paying for her college tuition and copiloted a plane at 16 was all about risk, change, and uncertainty, and Nabil was ready to rise to this challenge alongside me.

As more documents were being finalized and hurdles seemed to lessen, there were still quirky details and rules regarding life in Saudi

Arabia that we would have to adapt to. Some of these extra rules seemed designed to limit the freedom of movement for expatriates within and to and from the Kingdom.

For instance, I had heard from Westerners in Saudi Arabia that expatriates were required to receive permission from their employer to travel anywhere in the Kingdom outside of Riyadh. I e-mailed Paul about this, and he confirmed this was true. The *Iqama* (residence permit) we would receive as expatriates once in the Kingdom was not sufficient for travel outside Riyadh. Employees needed the "In-Country Travel Certificate" from the hospital Personnel Department. And exit/re-entry visas would be required when taking leave outside the country. According to Paul, I would need to forfeit my passport to the Personnel Office for safekeeping. This made me more than a bit nervous. As if to lessen the impact, Paul indicated I would be able to retrieve my passport within a day after requesting leave time and could recover it more quickly in an emergency. These sorts of unstated rules made me highly uneasy. One evening, when sitting down for dinner, I asked Nabil what he thought about the latest developments. He said it was disappointing to hear about the extra restrictions, especially after feeling free like a bird in the U.S. Nabil emphasized that it sounded a bit like jail; it was hard to disagree.

In the midst of our administrative challenges and desire to know more about the unwritten rules of the Kingdom, Nabil and I endlessly discussed the possibility of starting a new life overseas. We spent many sleepless nights sharing our uncertainties about giving up our dream home, ending our stable employment with treasured health insurance and retirement plans, and leaving the nearness of our family and friends. We would particularly miss the freedoms of America; freedom of speech, movement, dress, and such. And we would greatly miss drives through the lush countryside of Virginia with the pups.

As it grew closer to our move date, I alternated between feeling giddy with excitement and weighted with dread and worry. In early fall, we determined it was time to put our house up for sale and begin selling, donating, or giving away our furniture. Neither Nabil nor I felt much of a sentimental connection with our furniture, most of which was second-hand. We had been much more interested in spending our money on travel. We had several discussions about moving our furniture out of the house. Storing it was never an option. Although there were residual emotional attachments to the furniture connected to memories of family visits, weekend parties, and cozy winter naps in front of the fireplace, we agreed that when we came back to the U.S. at some point, we wanted to start fresh.

Paul cautioned us to buy most of the things we needed once we were settled rather than trying to ship a ton of items. This advice didn't faze us, as we ended up bringing pots, pans, dishware, a knife block, and even hangars. I think we felt insecure and wanted to bring some of our old life with us.

Regarding our flight to the Kingdom, we preferred flying Saudia Airlines, as they hosted more direct flights out of New York City, and were the recommended airline of the hospital. However, Saudia told us in no uncertain terms that flying with our pooches in the cabin was impossible. We put the needs of our girls first and booked travel through Paris with Air France, a more doggie-friendly airlines than most.

By September 17, Paul wrote that the hospital Visa Section was doing all it could to accelerate the visa for me. By this time, our house had not yet been sold, so the delay was not all bad; however, it was stressful to always be house-ready amid everything else. We finally sold the house on October 31, 2000, a major relief and only weeks before our move to the Kingdom. Soon after, we had a going away party at our home with family members, neighbors, and friends. Another lovely but difficult time reminding us of all the family and friends we loved and would miss when halfway around the world.

On October 10, 2000 I sent a letter to my boss and Human Resources that I would be leaving my government job. I had agreed with my boss that I would take 90 days of leave without pay beginning 11/13/00, and if I did not return to my current position within this period, I planned to resign from my job.

Only two days later, on October 12, 2000, we learned of the suicide bombing of the USS Cole off the coast of Yemen by Al Qaeda. My heart felt like it would pound out of my chest. Yemen was the poor neighboring country to the south of Saudi Arabia. The incident sparked new questions about the wisdom of living a life in a region that was like a tinderbox. We both questioned an imminent move to the Arabian Peninsula. We immediately wrote our Saudi Arabian contacts and checked online at "Travel.State.gov."

Later, on October 12, American citizens were cautioned about heightened tensions in the world. We sent e-mails back and forth to folks we had met in Saudi Arabia to assess safety levels. Chase Kennedy indicated: *No restrictions. State Dept. is advising all Americans traveling abroad, especially to the Middle East, to exercise caution and to consider carefully the issues around travel, but there is no absolute ban. 'Ahlan wa Sahlan' (welcome), we hope to still be here when you arrive!*

Alan Carter echoed a similar sentiment after attending a meeting at the American Embassy. There had not been any incidents or threats on Americans in Saudi Arabia. However, the two Consulates in Jeddah and Dammam would be closed to outside services effective immediately for precautionary purposes.

Paul was the most encouraging. He wrote: *The situation in other parts of the Middle East is not affecting us here at all. The danger for Westerners in Saudi Arabia? I never heard of such a thing. It's always been very calm here – I mean, very minimal disturbances. You don't have to worry about it. Will see you in about two weeks.* And Paul had good news about our visas: they were finally approved by the Ministry and HCA. Nashville would have them before long.

On October 22, we began notifying friends about our specific plans to leave for Saudi Arabia. My family and work colleagues already knew of our arrangements. I had a beautiful send-off luncheon before leaving my government job. There were lovely speeches. I hugged everyone in the room before leaving the restaurant. It all made departing the U.S. bittersweet; however, it was good to leave on a high note.

Our original departure date had been December; however, we were able to move it up to November 1. HCA International sent me envelopes from Employee Relations and Family Health, an original contract plus two copies, a name badge, an arrival information page, and reimbursement checks for our physical exams. Getting these materials in my hands made me feel like the first wall had been knocked down. While excited, I tried to keep the thought, "Be careful what you wish for," at bay, although the sentiment was at the edges of my mind.

In the days and weeks leading up to our flight, I had been nothing short of a minor train wreck – excited, nervous, and distracted by the mundane yet daunting task of packing up our house. Our departure day finally arrived. After numerous farewell gatherings and the last of our belongings readied to take or donate to the Salvation Army, our intrepid family headed to Dulles Airport outside DC. It took three oversized airport carts and three porters to convey our 42 pieces of luggage, along with our two pups in their containers, up to the ticketing counter. As I stepped away from my old life, I was filled with anticipation and curiosity about what lay ahead.

CHAPTER 4

FIRST HOURS IN SAUDI ARABIA

The man at the Air France counter surveyed the piles of luggage with an expression that can only be interpreted as one of growing dread. "You can't take all that luggage on the plane!" he groaned. Coco began yapping.

"What is that?" He snapped. "You have two dogs?" he asked, catching sight of the second doggie carrier. I jumped in, "We already called the airlines to say that we would have extra luggage and two dogs, and they said it would be okay."

Nabil leaned in and reminded me softly, "Mary, we told the airlines we'd only have 15 pieces of luggage."

"Well," I continued, feeling anxious yet determined, "We're here with confirmed tickets. What are we supposed to do now?" The man at the ticket counter regained his authority.

"You're going to have to send most of this by cargo on a separate flight. There is no way you're going to be able to board this flight with all of that luggage."

Taking in our nervous looks for a moment, the representative relented slightly. "If we checked in all of this luggage it could create a weight imbalance in the plane, which could be dangerous." Dejected, with all our respective tails between our legs, we lugged our 42 pieces down the corridor to the cargo office. We spent the next several hours sorting through our suitcases and collecting our toiletries and other essentials to include in our checked luggage. The remaining 34 pieces would travel separately by cargo. Besides our suitcases, we had trunks and boxes filled with an assortment of household items and clothes for every season we naively felt compelled to lug halfway around the world. "Crazy" was the consensus from our friends in the U.S., and from the compatriots we met later in the Kingdom.

In contrast, a Canadian family of four, who became fast friends within a month of our arrival, had brought only eight pieces of luggage for an indefinite stay. I felt discouraged and weary after the airport incident. I didn't even call family or friends on our way to a nearby hotel. I knew it would be just one foot in front of the other in the coming hours and wondered if this was an omen of what was to come.

Our flights the next day from Washington, DC, to Riyadh, which entailed nearly 20 hours of travel time, were mostly uneventful. Having flown several times domestically with our pooches joining us in the cabin, we knew that it was like the spin of a roulette wheel as to whether or not the airline crew would be good-natured about bending the rules and letting us take our pups out of their bags while in the cabin or if they would sternly adhere to protocol.

After take-off from Washington Dulles to Paris, I tested the waters by opening Maci's carrier. Out popped her furry little head. In a flash, she was in my lap, but not before I threw one of those blue airline blankets over her. She shrugged off the blanket with a jerk of her head and started planting sloppy kisses all over my face. A heavily made-up stewardess wearing a grimace as severe as her rouge rushed over. "Put that dog back into its container!"

Red-faced from this brush with the airline police, I quickly put Maci into her carrier and pushed the bundle under the seat in front of me. There would be no more puppy kisses for the rest of the trip.

Another challenge awaited us when we arrived at Charles de Gaulle, France's biggest, busiest, and most confusing airport. Released from their containers and on leashes, Maci and Coco jogged alongside us to keep up as we rushed to catch our connecting flight. Suddenly, Maci let out a shriek of pain; her right front paw had become stuck in the tread at the end of the moving walkway. I pulled on Maci's leash with all my might, but needed Nabil's extra strength to wrench her free. Terribly upset, we thought Maci could be permanently injured or worse. How could we continue on our final flight with Maci in this condition? A maternal instinct taking over, I rushed Maci into a women's restroom and hoped against hope that I could stop the bleeding. Despite the deep cut, I managed to rinse her injured appendage and made a bandage of sorts out of paper towels that I wrapped around her battered paw. Undeterred by her ordeal, Maci was quite the trooper and barely even whimpered during the remainder of the trip. I did start to wonder, though, if I was receiving an assortment of signs that we made the wrong decision about both our Middle East adventure and bringing the dogs.

An hour before landing at Riyadh airport, I pondered all that could go wrong once we landed and began moving through immigration, my sense of apprehension growing. After all, we had not one dog but two, and we knew that the Kingdom was not a particularly dog-friendly place. As we learned from our prior inquiries, and as Nabil knew only too well, Arabs rarely kept dogs as pets. Their primary exposure to "man's best friend" tended to be from films or American sitcoms. Nabil had warned me that Arabs' unfamiliarity and discomfort with dogs could extend to an aversion to touching them; there were cultural and religious customs that required strict cleanliness around prayer time. In addition to gathering all the immigration paperwork for me and Nabil, I took out the pups' documents and looked them over to make sure all was in order.

Coco was slung over Nabil's shoulder in a doggie carrier. As we moved through immigration, she let out a small yelp. The tall and officious-looking immigration officer turned toward us, "For God's sake, what was that?!" he hollered.

"That's just our dog," replied Nabil quietly.

"How many dogs?" the official asked, eyeing the dog carrier hanging off my shoulder with a menacing look.

Nabil answered even more quietly, "Two."

"*Haram, haram* (forbidden, forbidden), we cannot touch them. Let them go through." With a fling of the official's arm we were through immigration without so much as a peek at the carefully prepared paperwork for our cherished pups.

We greeted our Saudi contact with eight pieces of luggage and Maci and Coco in their carriers and piled into a van with other newly arrived expatriates. It was hard to imagine there were others like us, but, of course, none of them had two dogs. Hurtling along the modern causeway with its pristine medians cradling palm trees and colorful flowers, I was reminded of the unusual driving habits of our Saudi hosts, which I experienced during our trip to the Kingdom nine months earlier. Many cars rode two abreast in a single lane. Others cruised along the white line of the lane divider itself, which we came to find was a frequent occurrence. Even more alarming was the practice of cars switching lanes from far right to far left to make a left-hand turn or vice versa in one swift maneuver, a compulsion we found happened far too regularly. The car horn surpassed all other signals as the driving sound of choice. It was not unusual to be stopped at a red light and hear car horns start to chorus from all sides. Saudi drivers made New York motorists seem sleepy in comparison.

After a heart-stopping ride, we finally arrived at our new place of residence, Olaya 8, an eight-story apartment building in the heart of the city and right across the street from the soon-to-be-completed Kingdom Center that would hold nearly limitless haute couture shops.

I turned to Nabil and said, "We should be alright with the doggies at this point. I have all the copies of the e-mails from Paul indicating the dogs are approved to live with us in the apartment." As we approached a security guard near the entrance of our apartment building, both pooches began whooping and hollering as if they knew we were nearing the end of our journey. The guard, a stocky man with a formidable look on his face, practically fell off his feet with surprise.

"What is that?" he asked in limited English.

"These are our dogs," Nabil said, trying to remain calm and keep his voice friendly. "We are KFSH employees, and we have been approved to have the dogs live with us."

"What are you saying?" the guard shot back.

Nabil repeated, "These are our dogs, and they have been approved to live with us." The guard looked skeptical. His face continued to cloud.

"Oh, no, no, no!!" he shouted, his voice rising with each syllable. "No dogs, no dogs!" My adrenaline flowing, "You've got to be kidding me!" I screamed inside my head.

"Look, here's a document showing we have been approved," Nabil said. Scowling, the guard grabbed the document out of Nabil's hands. He stared so hard at the paper that I expected a burnt hole to appear at any second. It was obvious he still did not understand. "No dogs!" was the insistent reply. It was time for Nabil to use his powers of persuasion. With calm conviction, Nabil began speaking in Arabic.

"We have just flown halfway around the world from America, and right now, we are exhausted." Nabil continued, "I do think this is something we can settle tomorrow." After falling silent for a minute, probably thinking things through about this odd foursome and surprised that Nabil spoke Arabic, his rancor turned to sympathy. The guard's shoulders relaxing, he pointed us to the double glass doors of the building's entrance.

It was becoming increasingly clear that there were definite shades of gray in the Kingdom. Even with the rules and regulations in place, there were many cases where the edges could be bent with sufficient determination. Such was the case with our fixation on bringing our pooches with us to Riyadh. We were willing to hold our breath for longer than the other side.

The white marble floors of the apartment building sparkled, specks of brown and gray reflecting off the long fluorescent lamps running along the ceilings. We squeezed into one of those smallish, cramped European-type elevators to carry us to the seventh floor. The KFSH representative led the way into our apartment. Piling our luggage in a corner and setting our pooches free, we began surveying our new home away from home.

The apartment was a cavernous place, nearly the size of our 3,000 square foot home outside of Washington, DC, and fully furnished. Colorful reds and greens threaded through the material on a supple couch, a love seat, and two chairs in a very long and narrow living room. A large dining room contained a hardwood table with chairs to seat eight and a matching armoire stocked with plates and glasses. The ample yet somewhat dated kitchen contained all the necessary utensils, pots and pans, and cooking sundries such as a microwave, blender, and knife block, and dry goods like bread, peanut butter, granola bars, and cereal. A washer and dryer occupied a side room off the kitchen. A long hallway led to three expansive bedrooms with more than sufficient closet and cupboard space. Two and a half bathrooms were strategically located in the apartment with the half bath in the foyer looking like something out of *Homes and Gardens* with its finely curved golden fixtures.

Earlier, as we approached our apartment building in the KFSH van, we were happy to see large balconies running the length of the imposing edifice. Nabil and I had lived in an apartment building when we first married and, unlike many of our neighbors, made very good use of our spacious balcony. We loved to barbecue on the terrace and relished weekend breakfasts in the early morning sun.

I tugged at the balcony door and was unable to budge it open. Even Nabil's brute force was ineffective. Peering behind the curtains of the pane-glass window, I found a thick chain lock threaded through the door handle and another protruding piece of metal clamped to the outside wall. I asked the KFSH official, who was about to depart for Riyadh airport, to assist another group of incoming KFSH employees, about the lock. "All of the balcony doors of the building are locked," he said matter-of-factly.

Nabil whispered in my ear, "That's weird." I felt disappointed, already realizing my personal space would be restricted, and a bit sad that we wouldn't be able to enjoy a morning sip of coffee on the balcony as we watched the world go by.

Despite the effects of jet lag, by early evening hunger pangs dictated that we brave the streets of downtown Riyadh on foot to pick up some dinner. Given the problematic driving conditions, we were certain this would be a challenging task. Our doubts were well founded. We learned the hard way that there was good reason to be wary of both the streets and the cars in the Kingdom. Flagging down a policeman standing near the intersection outside our building, we told him our concerns about crossing the street.

"If God wills, you will make it across." The policeman deadpanned. "Good luck to you." Incredulous, I leaned over toward Nabil and whispered, "He's not going to help us across the street?" Nabil seemed not to hear. He told me later he didn't want to distress me. It was unfathomable to me that the policeman wouldn't help and that crossing the street would even be an issue.

On top of it all, I was still unaccustomed to my abaya, which I was regularly tripping over. Nabil and I decided that we would hail a cab to cross the street. We were ultimately successful in crossing the street in a taxi; however, the situation was more than a little freaky and worrisome. If we didn't feel a police officer could ensure our safety, then who would?

After searching for a grocery store, we finally settled on a shop around the corner, where we encountered freshly cut lamb and crisp vegetables. We found it a bit easier to communicate with the Pakistani and Nepali shopkeepers. After getting separated in the honeycombed aisles of the shop, Nabil reappeared with a broad smile.

"They've got Budweiser. I can't believe it, they've got Budweiser!"

"It's non-alcoholic," came a voice just over Nabil's shoulder. The curves of Nabil's mouth straightened, and a baffled look replaced the sparkle on his face. The shop vendor continued, "There is no alcohol in Saudi. Only non-alcoholic drinks." We had read about this in our information packets regarding Saudi culture and general "do's and don'ts." The promise of a tasty beer, snatched from Nabil's palate, left him perplexed but he wasn't a real beer drinker anyway.

As we left the store, the bag boy, slightly built with mussed, thick hair, followed us out with our full cart. We stepped out onto the sidewalk, and Nabil turned to take hold of the shopping cart for the trip home. The young man pulled the cart away and continued forward with an expression of steadfast purpose.

"It's okay, we'll take it from here," Nabil told him politely. Expressionless, the bag boy continued marching forward along the sidewalk.

"Thank you, you can give me the cart now," Nabil repeated. The bag boy appeared not to have heard or was ignoring us completely. We gave up. We neared the corner, and Nabil pointed toward home. Down the street to our apartment building, up the elevator, and into our apartment—the bag boy remained with us the entire way. As we stepped through the doorway, our girls, Maci and Coco, immediately began their ritual of zealously welcoming a visitor. The girls leaped up against his legs, playfully nibbled his hands, and cried pitifully—all of which garnered the first emotion from this goodhearted young man: sheer terror. Cornering our pups, coaxing them out of the room and into a bedroom, we shut the door. Returning to the front door, we told the panic-stricken young man that all was safe and under control. His composure slowly returned, and our compassionate attendant pulled the shopping cart into the kitchen and proceeded to empty the bags, placing the items on the counters. Nabil slipped our friend a hefty tip, and he silently made his exit.

We finished putting the groceries away and could tell the pups were agitated and likely needed to go out to "do their business." Some hours earlier, we had let our pooches relieve themselves in enormous potted plants in the corner of Charles De Gaulle Airport in Paris and then in the parking lot just outside the Riyadh airport terminal after landing in the Kingdom. It was apparent that nature was calling once again after a long night and day traveling in the confined space of a doggie carrier. This was a new problem. We were in an apartment building in the middle of the capital city, and our query about grassy spots around town had been met with bewilderment and shoulder shrugs. The only grass to be found in Riyadh was a park that was miles away, and the Diplomatic Quarter, an approximately three-square-mile quadrant of the city that housed many of the country's embassies, was even further away.

We needed to explore our neighborhood and determine what makeshift arrangements we could organize for "our girls." It was time to pull out my abaya once again. Near the end of our previous stint in Saudi Arabia earlier in the year, I had begun to accept the abaya as a second skin. For my friends back home, though, the abaya always seemed to be a point of contention and encapsulated much of what was incomprehensible and wrong with Saudi Arabia. Their perspective always bothered me, and I hoped to enlighten myself and my friends with a broader viewpoint about this place.

The abaya is the traditional dress for Saudi women. I respected their culture and understood the need to conform to their traditions. One great feature of the abaya I discovered once in the Kingdom was that you could wear anything under it; it was a bit like a security blanket. And if you're having a bad hair day, you could wrap a scarf around your head and fit in perfectly. Pajamas typically became my attire of choice under my abaya when Nabil and I walked the dogs before going to bed and first thing in the morning before breakfast.

On the first sojourn through our neighborhood, we wandered down neighborhood streets with stone wall perimeters enclosing stand-alone concrete homes, looking for a suitable place for the girls. We spotted an empty lot with beige coarse sand, chunks of concrete with jagged edges, and assorted odd bits. It wasn't the green grass of home, but it seemed like our only alternative. Maci and Coco weren't entirely receptive to squatting amongst twigs, scattered brush, and the odd empty soda can. But they soon realized that this was as good as it was going to get.

A middle-aged Saudi gentleman with bright white thobe and ghutra, who lived across the street from the empty lot, spied us on this first night and asked if the dogs would like to come into his courtyard to eat grass. Evidently, he thought our fluffy, curly-haired companions were sheep and not doggies looking for a spot to "do their business." Our girls were "people pooches" and only too happy to pounce all over and lick the tip of the nose of this unsuspecting benefactor, very unsheep-like behavior. It put this kind man in a bit of a tizzy. "Uh, oh," Nabil exclaimed as our pups began eyeing the lush green grass just inside the courtyard, and not as an appetizer; with a yank on their leashes, we were out of there, the gracious gentleman waving us off with a crooked smiled plastered on his face muttering something unintelligible as we scampered off.

On that first night in Riyadh, Nabil and the pooches ensconced comfortably in bed, I wandered in the darkness to the bathroom, switched on the light, and stared at my weary face. "What have I done? How could we have left two good jobs, our family, and friends for this strange place?"

CHAPTER 5

FIRST WEEKS AT WORK

On one of the first Sundays in the Kingdom, I walked into the living room after doing dinner dishes and did a double take. There was Nabil settled in an oversized living room chair, watching the Redskins playing football on TV. It was hard to believe that just days before, we had traveled to the other side of the world, and here it was just like a regular Sunday back home. A representative from Housing Services had assisted us several days earlier to connect our cable TV. We were pleasantly surprised to have access to the regular American network channels, ABC, NBC, and CBS, as well as CNN, ESPN, and movie channels. Although I knew the internet had found its way to the Kingdom, allowing us real-time correspondence through e-mail with family and friends, we didn't think we would be watching American programming.

Within our first week, we met Hanaa and Samer, a wonderful Lebanese couple who both worked at KFSH. Hanaa was secretary to the Director of Finance, and Samer was a radiology technician. Hanaa and Samer graciously helped us run mundane errands. Each weekend, they drove us to a new mall in the city. While we welcomed the time and effort to help us acclimate to shopping in the Kingdom, we were much more interested in the chaotic and traditional Arabic souks planted throughout the city. Over our years in the Middle East, we would continue seeking out the old over the new. Venerable long-standing markets and wrinkled men bartering over centuries-old daggers were more to our taste.

My first official day at work was on November 9, 2000, but I visited the hospital several times before then for pre-employment medical appointments and to sign my final contract. I learned the massive KFSH property catered to Westerners, primarily single, expatriate nurses, by providing a large array of amenities. From housing, swimming pools, grocery stores, and flower shops to a bowling alley, post office, Dunkin' Donuts, hair and nail salon, and several dining facilities, the grounds included everything an average Western woman needed to feel at home, minimizing her exposure to the Kingdom's unfamiliar customs. Western expatriates were coveted at the hospital due to their perceived superior organizational skills and conscientious work habits. I was astounded at all the conveniences and pleased to be the recipient of the unexpected niceties.

I would work in the Finance Department located in a four-story administrative building near the hospital's primary medical facility. The building was outlined with tan bricks in a rippled architectural style, and gray slate covered the upper floors.

I swallowed nervously in the elevator as it rose silently up to the second floor where the finance offices were housed. As I made my way down the hall to the offices, a young Saudi woman approached and announced, "We're so happy to have you here to train us." Feeling a boost, I replied, "Well, I'm happy to be here." I could feel the young woman's eyes focused on me as I passed her and walked further down the corridor. A middle-aged Indian man rushed over, declaring, "We've been waiting for you for a long time. We thought you'd be here months ago." "The visa took longer than we expected," I lamented. The man nodded. I felt a bit less nervous. Out of the corner of my eye, I spied Abdullah, my new manager. I had met him briefly a couple of days earlier in the office when finalizing my employment contract. I walked over and extended my hand. "Good morning, I'm Mary. I met you earlier this week. Today's my first day." Abdullah looked at me with blank eyes and spoke in a soft monotone. "I never wanted you here. When they asked me, I told them you were all wrong for the job."

My blood went cold; I felt limp. This couldn't be happening. I looked at Abdullah but couldn't discern his face. Time seemed suspended; those seconds seemed like minutes and even longer. This wasn't supposed to be happening. I had to shake off this shock. In my haze, I knew I had to persist.

I stared dumbstruck at the bits of frayed, brown mesh office carpet, the afternoon sunlight filtering in through the building windows. "Abdullah," I began, finally finding my voice. "I came here to be a team player, to work hard and assist your department to be the best it can be." Abdullah's face changed. I hoped it might be remorse. Maybe it was too soon to tell. "Well," he retorted, "I really don't think you have the appropriate background to be part of our group."

The spirit of that 16-year-old girl who navigated the single engine Cessna across the U.S. so many years ago persevered. I willed myself to stay steady, although I could have cried out, "What are you talking about?!?!" I was not about to let one man's biases stop me here. "Abdullah, I am interested in learning, and I'm a quick study; I'm sure that any weaknesses I have can be overcome."

Abdullah fixed me with a stern, quizzical look before turning his back and striding down the corridor. I remained rooted to the spot, unsure as to what just happened. Several minutes passed, and neither Abdullah nor another superior appeared to politely "escort" me out of the building. I began to realize my job remained intact and let out a thin sigh of relief. The truth was Abdullah's statement had knocked the wind out of my lungs. I knew before arriving in Saudi Arabia I would need to adjust to a new work life, with a new set of rules and expectations flavored by a distinct culture and lifestyle. However, I could not fathom how I was going to work alongside a boss who didn't want me there. And even more disturbing—what if Abdullah was right? What if I wasn't right for the job?

I switched to automatic pilot as I was shown to my office, and left to my own devices without any work for a couple of weeks. As I sat at my desk, day in and day out, the quiet buzz of office life—the click-clack of typing on PCs and the drone of voices conferring on some financial report or another— filled my workdays. I was treated politely, but also kind of like a child being told even minor things because people were also adjusting to me. I felt isolated, stifled, and deeply bored. I let Nabil in on some of my worries. However, I didn't want to overly burden him, as he was still looking for a job and acclimating to a more conservative Arabian Gulf culture, very different from his upbringing in Jordan and Lebanon. My stomach churned.

One day dissolved slowly into the next. The hum of the office was occasionally interrupted by the soft voices of Saudi women in nearby offices conversing over cardamom coffee, a fundamental part of Saudi life. I could tell the banter centered on subjects like children, family, and preparations for upcoming family meals, as I could make out Arabic words like *atfal* (children) and *kabsa*, a traditional Saudi meal of lamb and rice. These junior staff members, usually wives and mothers or young single women recently out of college, were hardworking and dedicated to their jobs. Many of the younger women were also the caretakers in the family and knew the importance of balancing work and home life. The hospital, and society in general, also placed great importance on preserving the family (a tribal-type concept) and a proper work-life balance. New and young mothers were often given the option of adjustable hours and gladly allowed office respites. In my experiences working in the government and corporate America in the 80s and 90s, companies didn't give much flexibility to mothers. The Kingdom was ahead of the game in that respect. While a proponent of accommodating mothers in the workplace, I was not entirely satisfied with the periodic chitchat, the same way I chafed at the "around the water cooler" babble I experienced in U.S. office settings.

I had to decline an early offer of coffee with two young Saudi women on my first day of work. I just couldn't justify it; I had to at least appear busy for my emotional comfort, and I knew Abdullah had his eye on me. In the days and weeks to follow, I considered changing my mind because I was lonely. I needed to connect with my female colleagues; I would have to let my guard down and be vulnerable.

I eventually gave in to the Saudi women's invitations to join them for coffee. While I was somewhat concerned about what to say and not say, the young women immediately riffed easily from topic to topic, focusing primarily on their evening plans. Faten talked about making *hamour* (grouper) with her maid who would scale and clean the fish. Alia, who was single and living with her family, said her cousins would be visiting, and she wasn't entirely sure what they would have that evening for dinner. In the Arab Gulf, single women and men live with their families until marriage. Expertly pouring from a large thermos into small delicate demitasse cups, the warmth of the spicy brew and easy conversation helped lighten my mood. The art of pouring and sharing coffee surprised me. A grab-and-go kind of coffee and soda drinker, like many Americans, I never would have imagined that pouring and serving coffee could have its ritual and beauty.

In late November, as the end of the year neared, the pace of work and the need for year-end financial reports and additional resources heightened. I was available and anxious to support and show my worth. Thus began my intense training on all financial systems and how they interacted with one another. My colleague, Laila, spent the time she didn't necessarily have going over the ins and outs of using SmartStream, Oracle, and other financial programs. Even Abdullah began showing up at my office, inviting me to group meetings. I was encouraged; it felt good to finally be viewed as a valued member of the team.

In addition to being challenged by the work, I was extremely conscious of everything I wore in those first few weeks. In the States, I might have decided on my outfit for the day in the precious minutes between drying my hair and heading downstairs for a bite of breakfast. Although my clothing options were more limited in the Kingdom, my early days at KFSH found me devoting significant time to picking out clothes that were both respectful of the strict cultural customs and professional. Certainly not a "clothes horse," in time, I adapted fairly easily and ultimately found it a nice change NOT to have to fuss so much about what I was wearing.

During my induction at KFSH, I half expected to be greeted with a neatly divided fleet of robes and pantsuits. Instead, Western women like me were permitted to forgo the black abaya on the hospital grounds; we were strongly counseled, though, to have our arms and knees covered. Low-cut blouses were strictly prohibited.

When off hospital grounds, Western women typically wore the abaya; in some shopping malls, they were required to wear a headscarf or otherwise risk an encounter with the *Mutawa*, the religious officers.

In extreme circumstances, a woman or her husband, who in the Mutawa's eyes allowed her to dress indecently, might face jailing.

Like most other female expatriates, I normally wore a mid-calf (or longer) dark-colored skirt or pants and a long white lab coat to work. My colleagues' fashion, however, reflected both the cultural and stylistic diversity in the workplace. The Saudi woman working at the passport desk was completely covered in black, her eyes, two charcoal pools, stared back at me. Her Sudanese workmate at an adjacent station wore a colorful yellow and blue sarong and head covering that exposed her entire unmade face, leaving wisps of hair peeking out from under her scarf.

At the hospital, Lebanese women stood out in stark contrast to all others, not only in attire but also in their confident demeanor. These women sported tight pants, immaculately coiffured hair, and painstakingly applied makeup, demonstrating their knowledge of the latest fashion trends. Lebanese women followed the same kind of cultural protocol as other Gulf Arab women, such as covering their arms and legs while on the hospital grounds and wearing the abaya and headscarf in public (with their faces exposed) when off the hospital premises. Yet it appeared as if there was an unspoken understanding in the Arab world that granted Lebanese women more fashion freedom; they often wore form-fitting clothes on the hospital grounds—definitely pushing the limits. I knew that this nonconformity was due in part to the regular influx of Western European tourists into Lebanon during its golden age in the 1960s and early 1970s, before the civil war, when it was known as "the Paris of the Middle East."

It became increasingly apparent to me that women from Gulf countries such as Saudi Arabia, Kuwait, and Bahrain were more reserved and demure in dress than those women from non-Gulf countries, such as Lebanon, Syria, Egypt, and Jordan. I soon found that, despite the divergence in clothing styles and presentation, women were not typically the objects of unwanted stares that tend to find their way into Western workplaces dominated by male colleagues. In fact, great lengths were taken to shield women from this unwelcome attention; Arab women's offices were never positioned along a main corridor, and some women even hung curtain material over the entrances of their partitioned offices. Not so for me; my office was along a main corridor, something I was used to, and it did not disturb me in the least.

Meanwhile, on the home front, around a week and a half after landing in the Kingdom, we were informed by the Hospital Transportation Department manager that our prized cargo had arrived at Riyadh airport.

We had met regularly with the manager about the estimated arrival time of our luggage as well as how to transport our items from the airport to our home. We stopped by one day to check for any updates, and the manager waved us inside. He was on two calls when we entered: one a business call on the office phone, and the other a personal call with a friend he proudly told us was from the U.S. As we waited, a third call came in on a second cell phone sitting on the desk. Nabil and I had to restrain chuckles as the manager tucked the first cell phone under his chin, kept the office phone in his right hand, and answered the third call with his left hand. The manager was able to maintain the three separate conversations, although inelegantly, for several minutes. While the manager promised to investigate using one of the department's larger trucks to handle our sizable cargo of 34 suitcases, boxes, and trunks, it became apparent that they would not have the proper resources to help us. It would have taken several pick-up trucks and additional labor, which the manager did not have. Nabil hired a private truck and Sudanese driver to transport our luggage. I accompanied Nabil and the driver to the cargo section of the airport.

Given the strict rules on gender separation in the Kingdom, it was unusual, and probably unheard of, for a woman to enter the cargo area of the Riyadh airport. But Nabil and I decided once in Saudi Arabia, I would accompany him on as many outings and errands as possible. We always did things together and wanted to continue. While I did not want to offend cultural dictates, I didn't want my gender to hinder me either.

My persona non grata status helped me enter the cavernous restricted cargo area without incident. I crept into the space with its intertwining conveyor belts and clusters of burlap hampers practically undetected. Nabil said they probably allowed me in because they wanted this woman in and out of the area as quickly as possible and didn't want to deal with me. Nevertheless, knowing I was more dexterous and physically adventuresome than Nabil, I climbed up onto the sides of the conveyor belts, carefully moving from one to another. When I unearthed the first piece of luggage, I yelled out to Nabil. "This is number '14 of 42,'" reading from the top of the suitcase. Nabil flagged down a cargo workman to retrieve the piece of luggage. This continued for nearly two hours; I felt secretly pleased with my prowess in maneuvering the intricate configuration of the conveyor belts. The workers looked at us like we were from another planet. No one ever questioned if the luggage belonged to us.

I took a hospital shuttle bus between the hospital and our apartment building for work, but we couldn't really get anywhere else in the Kingdom without our own car. We certainly wouldn't be able to take day trips or other excursions with friends to many of the places we had dreamed about visiting. We were barred, though, from buying a vehicle until Nabil obtained his Iqama, a permit required for expatriates to establish residency in Saudi Arabia. Expatriates were compelled to have their Iqama on their person when outside the home. When we first arrived in Riyadh, the hospital said that until we received our Iqamas, we should stay close to home and work, as we would not be official residents of the country until we received these permits.

Everything took time in the Kingdom; there were multiple sign-offs required by both the government and hospital when applying for the Iqama, as well as basic inefficiencies common to a developing country. By late November, Nabil had his Iqama, and I received mine around the same time. We were close to buying a used Jeep Cherokee from a Canadian, Bob, who worked in the Microbiology Lab at KFSH. Nabil would need to have the car checked out by a mechanic for any irregularities before the transaction was finalized. Nabil and Samer went to the car mechanic section of Riyadh. Women weren't known to frequent this area. I would be a distraction and, therefore, was left out of this particular adventure. Most mechanic shops were conveniently located in one sector of the city. Blocks of shops side by side, practically clones. Thankfully, the mechanic determined the car was in excellent shape.

Although Nabil established residency and bought the car, we still had one more hurdle to clear. Nabil would have to secure a driver's license. We hoped Nabil's U.S. driver's license would be accepted. It turned out the hospital had its equivalent of a DMV on their premises. I was forever surprised at the range of services provided by the hospital. I did go with Nabil on this venture, although we knew due to the prohibition on women driving, I would likely be the only female in the building.

When we arrived, the reception area was filled with men, mostly Saudis but some expatriates, milling around. We thought it would be a relatively easy process particularly since, in the hierarchy of expatriate nationalities, Americans were highly valued. We were relieved to find out that Nabil didn't have to take a driving test, only a vision test.

We went up to the counter, Nabil checked in, and his name was added to the queue. A Mutawa with a long gray beard, wearing a ghutra without the *agal* (black coil over the head keeping the ghutra in place) and a shorter thobe (long-sleeved robe), was standing near the counter, glowering at me. He growled something in Arabic, and Nabil leaned over and whispered, "He's asking what you're doing here, Mary." In the next moment, the Mutawa had a fellow worker grab a chair for me. The worker motioned for me to sit down, although no one else was seated. I was startled by the gesture but pleased I wasn't shown the door.

When Nabil's name was called, the same Mutawa ushered Nabil and me into the examination room. He directed Nabil to move toward a counter with a metallic box: the vision test devise. Nabil was told to place his eyes up to the two lenses and read numbers and letters on a black background. He succeeded in reading the characters correctly. However, when it came to a vision depth exam, Nabil failed four times to correctly identify which one of three lights appeared closer.

I was alarmed. I saw the color drain from Nabil's face. Nabil rallied, however, and said, "We don't have this type of test in the U.S. Why is this so important?" The man countered in bits of English, "Without this exam, you cannot have a driver's license." "Can my wife take the test? She's always with me when I drive," Nabil quickly responded. While surprised by Nabil's boldness, I was used to his unusual negotiating style. "What do you mean by this?" came the reply. "Whenever I drive, my wife is always with me, and she can help by telling me the distance of the approaching cars. And I only have a problem with determining depth at night."

The man stroked his beard and, with a firm voice, said, "Women cannot drive in Saudi Arabia." Nabil replied that he wasn't telling the man his wife was going to drive. She was only going to be his driving assistant since he couldn't see depth. The man said, "Nobody ever asked me this before. What if your wife isn't with you?" Nabil replied, "Then I would take a taxi." The man scratched at his beard again and told Nabil, "Okay, let her take it, but I'm not responsible if you have an accident." Bowled over, I couldn't believe it when Nabil pulled me over and asked me to take the test. I passed the test, and Nabil received his driver's license after having his picture taken.

A couple of days later, Samer went downtown with Nabil to transfer the car from Bob's name to Nabil's, which completed the registration process. I was agitated over Nabil driving our new car for the first time through the perilous city streets to our apartment building, particularly since he would be driving through the "death roundabout"—a circle aptly named due to the disproportionate number of deadly car accidents that occurred there. My worries were only slightly alleviated when Samer kindly agreed to have Nabil follow him to our apartment building. I relaxed only when Nabil strode through our apartment door with a wide grin across his face. "I made it, Mary."

Otherwise, we settled into a familiar routine. We grocery shopped at Al-Azizia, a huge store near the hospital, popular with KFSH expatriates and locals. There was plenty of fresh seafood and a wide variety of essentials like meats (however, no pork), vegetables and fruits, canned goods, and such. Pharmaceutical items were only available at established pharmacies. Nabil did all the cooking, just like back in the States. We had vegetable omelets for breakfast and delicious chicken and vegetable stews for dinner. And we enjoyed exploring the city with our new car.

Our apartment building, Olaya 8, was filled with KFSH expatriate families. At least one, and sometimes both, parents worked for the hospital. We were surprised to see children roaming the building by themselves or in bands relatively carefree, oftentimes playing chase in the large hallways. We were always happy to hear a knock on the door and find a cherubic little face on the other side. "Can we come in to see your puppies?" Evidently, these children had spied us on walks or in the lobby of the building with Maci and Coco and found out where we lived. The pups greeted the children with playful yaps, licks, and paw strokes along tiny legs.

These visits didn't always end well, though. One weekend afternoon we had two lovely boys playing on our living room floor with the pups when we heard a brusque knock at the door. It was the mother of one of the boys. Stony-faced, the woman told Nabil, "I don't want your dogs to play with my child." Nabil timidly replied, "Sorry, Madam, but your child came to our house asking to play with the dogs." "Next time he comes to you, don't open the door for him," the mother declared. "I can't do that; he's too cute not to let him in." This drew a subtle smile; the woman took her child's hand and the two left. The boy did return to play with our pups; we couldn't turn him away.

That mother was not the only one unhappy with us. Other troubled parents had circulated a petition for our removal and submitted it to the KFSH Housing Department. We were astonished to learn our neighbors went through formal channels to make certain our pups left the building. Although we were both disappointed and embarrassed, Nabil reminded me that dogs were viewed differently here. We needed to accept this and move on. We had received correspondence from Housing Services prior to the incidents between our pups and the children indicating that only fish and birds were allowed in hospital housing. The hospital was doing us a favor by allowing us to keep two dogs at Olaya 8. We should use our hospital housing allowance to find suitable accommodations in a private community as soon as possible after arriving in the Kingdom.

On November 26, 2000, we were notified by the Head of Housing Services that we would be moving out of Olaya 8 to the Diplomatic Quarter on December 25, 2000, Christmas Day. We were to move our "Personal Belongings, All Personal Set-Up items, and Issued Linens." I felt defeated; we had only just packed and unpacked our 42 suitcases and trunks several weeks ago.

We had visited the Diplomatic Quarter several times before we knew about the move, as it was one of the few areas in Riyadh with grass—a prime location for our pups. Among our highest priorities upon arriving in Riyadh, up there with receiving our cargo shipment and finalizing my work contract, was to find a location where our girls could "do their thing."

We had not heard of the Diplomatic Quarter before arriving in the Kingdom; our accommodations at Olaya 8 had been pre-arranged for us by the Housing Department. Had we known and been given the choice, an apartment in the Diplomatic Quarter would have been our preferred accommodation. The Diplomatic Quarter, a Western haven, housed many of the foreign embassies. The area held a multitude of lush gardens and fountains, a walking trail along its periphery, and laxer rules. Expatriate women weren't required to wear an abaya in the Diplomatic Quarter, and residents rode bikes and jogged. Al-Kindi Square, a favored outdoor shopping plaza located in the center of the Quarter, was filled with cream-colored marble tiles, along with retail shops and alfresco cafes along its perimeter.

What was, at first, a bit of bad fortune turned out to work in our favor. I was surprised that our initial upset was a kind of blessing in disguise, and I wanted to secretly thank everyone who signed that petition. We were pleased to meet and befriend a lovely Polish-Canadian couple whose apartment we would move into. Minka, a KFSH microbiologist, and Jacub, a photographer, were from Canada. They were leaving the Diplomatic Quarter for a housing compound next to the hospital that had larger apartments and a pool.

It was funny how we met Minka and Jacub. Soon after learning of our move to the Diplomatic Quarter, Nabil, on the spur of the moment one evening, told me he was going to call the residents of our soon-to-be new apartment. We had not met Minka and Jacub, nor did we know their names. Nabil was determined to make them our friends, though. I chuckled. "Nabil, how do you know we're going to get along?" The next moment, Nabil was on the phone, introducing himself to Minka, and asking if we could come over to look at the apartment. Before Minka could respond, Nabil explained that we had two miniature poodles. He asked if we could bring them along. I could hear Minka's excited voice through the receiver, "Oh, we miss our dog, a Bijon, that we had to leave in Canada. Please come over this evening with your wife and dogs." I let out a bigger chuckle, "Wow, you're unbelievable, Nabil," even though I knew this was standard Nabil.

That evening, we had a delightful visit with Minka and Jacub. Minka offered us coffee and sweets and the pups some cuddles, which they returned with sloppy kisses across the faces of our new friends. It turned out our new accommodations would be much smaller than the apartment at Olaya 8. Only two bedrooms and one and a half baths in the Quarter as compared to three bedrooms and two and a half baths in Olaya 8. What we'll do for our pups! In those early days, Jacub and Minka spent many a weekend with us pointing out the best hardware store in town, introducing us to their Polish-Canadian friends and Minka's work colleagues, and sharing in our first *iftar* meal.

The iftar meal takes place at sundown during the Muslim month of Ramadan. One of the holiest times for Muslims, Ramadan occurs during the ninth month of the *Hijri* (Islamic calendar) and begins when the crescent moon is first sighted. Since the Hijri calendar is lunar-based, the month of Ramadan shifts by 10 or 11 days each year. During Ramadan, Muslims fast from sunrise to sunset, and expatriates are asked to respect this holy time by not eating or drinking in public during the fasting hours. However, KFSH opened its cafeteria for non-Muslim expatriates, who comprised a significant portion of the hospital staff. Ramadan is not only a time to refrain from eating during daylight hours but also an opportunity to exercise self-restraint and sacrifice and to purify body and soul.

Several weeks after arriving in the Kingdom, I experienced my first Ramadan, which began on November 27, 2000. I received information from the hospital on Muslim practices during Ramadan and rules for non-Muslims. Since Muslims would be fasting from sunrise to sunset, their work hours were limited to six hours a day. Non-Muslims would work normal hours and were asked to forgo eating (even gum chewing) and drinking in public during fasting hours.

During Ramadan, stores are generally open from 10:00 AM to 3:00 PM and reopen from around 9:00 PM to 1:00 or 3:00 in the morning. Minka and Jacub were excited about us experiencing a mall visit during the nighttime hours of Ramadan, so we joined them one Wednesday evening (beginning of the Saudi weekend). It was close to 1:30 AM, and apparent that things were just starting to roll. During Ramadan, day turns to night and night to day. The mall corridors were plastered with wall-to-wall people, and a loud hum of dissonant chatter rang through the shops. The spectacle spellbound me; I felt too overwhelmed to shop.

In comparison, our iftar meal at the Sahara Hotel with our new friends was rather sedate, except for the ubiquitous bands of children running between restaurant tables. Minka and Jacub picked us up, and we drove to the hotel, which was near the airport and surrounded by miles of desert.

The iftar feast is traditionally enjoyed at home by gatherings of family members and friends. It usually begins with cardamom coffee and dates and moves on to sumptuous Arabic dishes on massive silver trays dominated by lamb and rice. We were fortunate to attend our iftar meal atop the Sahara Airport Hotel with Saudis and a smattering of Westerners. The restaurant hosted a splendid panoramic view of the surrounding desert. Food was served buffet-style and seemed to stretch on for yards. Many of the starter selections were of Lebanese origin (at least according to Nabil). We chose from hummus, baba ghanoush, tabouli, *fattoush* (Lebanese salad with pita chips), *ful medames* (fava beans), and much more. If not for the men dressed in white robes and the women in black, I could have been in Lebanon; it felt sentimental and comfortable.

The coup de grâce was a massive platter of lamb, *Mandi*, originating from Yemen and now popular in the Arab Gulf and the broader region. There are several steps in preparing Mandi. The first is to dig a hole in the ground, build a mud cone, and burn wood within the enclosure. When the fire turns to embers, the meat is hung over the hot ashes, and the hole is sealed. The oxygen is consumed within 30 minutes, but the residual heat continues to cook the meat for around 90 minutes. Nabil smiled ear to ear; we had never tasted such tender lamb! After dinner, we entered a large tent, a *majlis* (sitting area), with vibrant red rugs next to the restaurant, where diners enjoyed sheesha, fruit-flavored tobacco smoked from a Middle Eastern water pipe. Although Nabil had a hookah pipe when we lived in the U.S., and we did partake on occasion, it always seemed like a distinct cultural experience. In this particular private setting, sitting on conventional *sedu* pillows on the floor in a Saudi tent made the experience seem more natural and gratifying.

Our move on Christmas Day 2000 fell just before the end of Ramadan. I worked for much of the day, and when I mentioned to Abdullah it was Christmas, he was oblivious to the fact—I guess like we are in the U.S. to Muslim holidays. When I arrived at Olaya 8 after work, Nabil had hauled all our suitcases and boxes to the foyer area and was directing the staff from the KFSH Transportation Department to load our luggage onto the hospital pick-up truck. After tying down the contents of our life in the Kingdom, Nabil, the pups, and I followed the truck to our new apartment in the Diplomatic Quarter. I was concerned at the prospect of changing to new accommodations and the work that entailed. Although my aim in moving to the Kingdom was to have an Arab cultural experience, I was comforted to know I would live in an oasis of greenery, grass, and Westerners. And the dogs were accepted. It felt good to have familiar elements around me; it cut some of the edge.

Nabil and I would have forgotten that it was Christmas except that friends of Minka and Jacub kindly invited us to a Christmas dinner at their home. Christmas dinner, something we had done countless times in the States, was now being celebrated in this far-off land that didn't even acknowledge the holiday. Even so, we sat down at a beautifully decorated table lit by the bulbs of the family Christmas tree and relished our turkey, dressing, and the rest of it. And that was okay; all of it was okay.

CHAPTER 6

DESERT TRIPS

We were looking at a 15-foot arched wall of rocky sand that we were expected to drive over with our "smallish" SUV. My jaw clenched. "How the heck are we going to get over that dune?" I asked Nabil. We were on a highly anticipated desert trip with a group of friends. We had just watched the three cars ahead of us ascend the formidable-looking ridge, jerking, sputtering, and lurching until they cleared the top. And now it was our turn. Scanning Nabil's face, I caught an aura of seriousness and sensed he didn't want to worry me. Nabil later admitted being fearful of our Cherokee Jeep flipping on the ridge. After all, this was our first attempt at scaling a large desert dune. We were the only "newbies" on this trip.

Nabil said it was best if the dogs and I got out of the car before he maneuvered over the ridge. I definitely did not want to leave Nabil alone. I breathed easier when our friends, Damien and Jacub, jumped out of their massive SUVs to guide us over the steep embankment. "Go slowly, Nabil, keep your tires straight, and make sure you keep moving," Damien yelled out. Nabil leaned forward, firmly grabbed the steering wheel, and, fixing his eyes ahead, said, "Here we go!" I held tightly onto the armrests, anticipating a rough ride. Stepping halfway on the accelerator, it was as much Nabil willing the car up the arduous dune as the car's engine propelling us forward. Bracing myself against the seat as we made our way up and over the stony hill, I only relaxed after we crested the top of the dune. Jacub and the others clapped as we came into view on the other side. Nabil couldn't help but break a smile.

Only a few weeks after arriving in the Kingdom, and before we even had a car, we began hearing about weekend trips to the Red Sands, Hidden Valley, and the desert destination all the expatriates talked about, the Edge of the World. These desert locales were part of a Saharan-type tableau located outside Riyadh, each with its unique topography—from large swaths of fine-grained sand to rugged buttes and distinct canyons. The Edge of the World was approximately two hours outside Riyadh. The origin of the place's name remains a mystery. It could have earned its name from expatriates taken by surprise by spectacular views and the precipitous drop at the end of a rugged desert plain. There was no way to know for sure, as guidebooks did not exist for the Edge of the World, nor websites promoting this uncommon site or the other distinctive desert locations. And Google was not widely known in Saudi Arabia in the early 2000s. We learned about the Edge of the World primarily through conversations with expatriate friends at social gatherings. Word of mouth was standard advertising for expat events like desert trips, locally produced plays, choral concerts, and such. Expats kept many of these ventures "under wraps" to not infringe on strict Saudi practices surrounding traditional lifestyle and religious practices in the Kingdom. The Saudis tended to "turn a blind eye" to many of the more innocuous events, as they wished to retain their expatriate working base.

It never entered our minds that the Saudi desert would be anything other than a sea of flat white sand peppered with undulating dunes. We were intrigued by chatter about the unconventional landscape of the Edge of the World and the sheer excitement about the place from our expat friends. My initial thoughts of life in Saudi did not include forays into the desert. I had seen beautiful desert photos, but never really saw people in the pictures and knew there wasn't a formal tourist industry with expeditions into the desert. You could not even secure a tourist visa to enter the Kingdom; only work-related or business visas were accepted. I just didn't think the desert was accessible.

Misguided by Western books, TV, and movies that exoticized the Arabian desert, I somehow envisioned scorpions and venomous snakes hiding in uninhabited tracts of sand across much of the country. I was much more curious about the lifestyle and worldview of the Saudis. I wanted to meet and get to know the locals, and there weren't many of those in the desert. Little did I know, at the time, about the rich lives and history of the desert Bedouins.

Our trip with the US-Saudi Business Council to Saudi Arabia a year earlier changed my outlook. Jerry Roberts, a principal member of the Council and newfound friend, recounted stories of camping trips to spots outside Riyadh on his previous trips to the Kingdom. There was an intense peace, Jerry told us. He talked animatedly about looking at the spray of stars across the sky that filled him with awe. Jerry had never seen anything like it, and he strongly encouraged us to visit the desert.

Damien, a Greek-Canadian expat and Minka's colleague, brought up the Edge of the World at a Friday fish dinner at Minka's home. He described bulging dunes at impressive heights and trails that felt like you were walking along the seam where the earth and sky meet. Damien was part of an expat group called the "four-wheel drive club" that regularly took trips to the desert. Would we be interested in accompanying the group to the Edge of the World the weekend following next? We were both intrigued and happy to be included and even happier to find out it would be okay to have Maci and Coco along for the adventure.

The trip would be caravan-style with around seven cars and would require extra supplies, like chains and ropes, in case a car became stuck in the sand. Unlike other day trips where the packing might include only snacks and drinks, this one required jumper cables, first-aid kits, and cans of air-forced tire inflators. Damien made it a point to have us flatten our tires slightly before the trip so as not to sink into the soft sand. The thought of ropes and chains hauling us out of the desert miles away from civilization made me wary. But the anticipation of what we would experience chased away any anxiety about the travel.

I had adolescent memories of family trips to the southwest, The Painted Desert, Zion Park, and Bryce Canyon, which weren't particularly memorable. As a young child, all I saw were a lot of rocks, odd-looking stone formations, and vast areas of desolation. Years later, as a young adult, the harshness and isolation of America's southwest deserts acquired more of a mythical quality as I gained more interest in the area. I developed an appreciation for the exceptional formations spawned over millions and billions of years.

On Wednesday evening in early January 2001, the night before the start of our weekend desert trip, Nabil made sandwiches of pita bread with *za'atar* (spice mix with thyme) and homemade hummus, and brought out our cooler. Filled with impatience, it was hard for us to sleep that night. Even the pups seemed restless.

Strong coffee and excitement fueled us in the pre-dawn hours of Thursday as we loaded up the Jeep with sandwiches, dog food, several gallons of water, blankets, folding chairs, plastic utensils and cups, and toilet paper. The pups settled on my lap, Nabil climbed into the driver's seat, and we headed over to Damien's housing compound. Nabil fretted about having enough food for the group, which included several families with young children. I interrupted Nabil by reminding him that everyone would be bringing food and drink to share. Nabil always cooked for an army when we had people over or shared in a potluck, as it was shameful in Arab culture to have a shortage of food.

The city scenery that had become familiar to me by now slipped by the window. We settled into the quiet of the drive over to the compound. I felt small waves of worry pulse through me. What if we got stranded in the desert? I kept my concerns to myself. I didn't want to spoil the trip for either of us. The group had already told us about high winds and loose rocks on the cliffs. There was a story out there about a Western nurse visiting the Edge of the World several years earlier who had lost her balance in the wind on a bluff and tragically fell to her death. This horrifying anecdote stayed with me before and during our trip. Nabil and I agreed to stay extremely sensitive to the dangers and take special care of Maci and Coco. I decided to keep the angst to the back of my mind and focus on the thought of meeting up with friends and our new adventure. It didn't hurt that Damien had visited the Edge of the World multiple times and was highly attentive to safety. Besides, Nabil always had a way of making me feel safe and comfortable.

By the time we made it to Damien's compound, I was more excited than nervous. We found our friends already gathered in their cars near the entranceway of the compound. Within short order, Damien yelled out that we needed to get going. The SUV's lined up, military-style, one behind the other. Damien took the lead, and Nabil was instructed to position our Jeep midline. Damien had GPS, as did most of our friends. We did not. There was no cell phone reception in the desert—both additional concerns for us. Before heading out, Damien told each driver to maintain the same position behind the car in front of them and to flash headlights and emergency lights if a car fell out of line.

We cracked our windows and were on our way. It was a beautiful cloudless morning, like most mornings, and temperatures were already in the low-70s. We all moved, single file, to the main road and then the highway. A bit tense about making this longer drive out of the city, we made sure to always keep the cars ahead and behind us in view. We certainly didn't want to lose sight of our friends and become adrift in the sprawling city or its outskirts. The drive would be one hour on paved roads and the second hour through unmarked desert. Nabil and I listened to the Riyadh "American Oldies" radio station featuring popular U.S. tunes from the 1960s and 1970s. Once out of town, it felt good to be out of my abaya and in casual western wear—long-sleeved t-shirt and khakis—though I felt a start every time we passed a car with a Saudi family, men in ghutras and women in abayas. Did the women see me? Were they offended? I felt I was betraying the culture. Even when home in the U.S. for our summer break, I felt underdressed when wearing a tank top and looked around for nonexistent Mutawa.

As we drove away from Riyadh, the tall sparkling glass-paned high-rises gave way to mini-plazas filled with one-story beige family retail shops and simple walled-in residences. Finally, large spaces of sand came into view. They lasted for miles and miles, with the occasional camel off in the distance. After driving for around 45 minutes, Nabil exclaimed, "So far, so good, Mary. We haven't lost anybody."

At close to an hour into our drive, the convoy slowed. I wondered if a car went missing. "What's going on, Nabil?" "I don't know," he said, shaking his head. We slowed further and glimpsed Damien several cars ahead, waving out the driver's window and pointing to the right. Evidently, Damien found the huge boulder placed by another intrepid expatriate, signaling the turn into the desert. As we stopped alongside the other cars just off the road, I looked at the nondescript slab of rock and wondered how Damien distinguished it as the signpost for our turn. We would be looking for makeshift signage throughout the desert portion of our trip. Damien stepped out of his truck. He took a count of each car in our group to make sure everyone was present. Soon, we were lined up once again and started our travel over the washboard desert. I was exhilarated.

Jostling and stumbling over the rocky plain, I held onto the grab handle of the car ceiling with one hand and gripped the pups with the other. Nabil and I had never been off-road driving, so it was both enthralling and intimidating to be rough riding through the desert, rocks spewing out from under our tires. Could one of those rocks land through our windshield or a car window? I tried to block out that thought. The dust from car tires ahead of us created cloudy mists. The bumps were constant and unforgiving. I had to steel myself, expecting to be caught off guard by a particularly large jolt. It wasn't easy to know how to position myself and the pups to soften the blows. Yet, I was captivated, riveted by our ride through the stark Saudi desert. I felt alive, and my adrenaline flowed. And it didn't escape me that we were among the few Westerners who had followed these desert trails.

We encountered several onerous dunes along the way, which became progressively easier to scale; Damien and Jacub eventually kept watch over us from inside their cars. The dried river beds led to stretches of uneven plateaus with collections of Acacia trees and Saltbush, the scrubby plant with spiny leaves that grows everywhere in the desert.

Goats and sheep and a pair of camels were close enough to look them in the eyes. We drove along tread markings for a portion of the trip. At other times, we motored along jumbled rocks and hard earth. Damien stopped and backtracked from time to time, forcing us all to stop and watch him inspect the area to ensure he didn't miss a signpost, normally made of a pile of smooth, flat stones. It was incredible that anyone could find their way. There were no maps. Damien stood beside his SUV, hands on hips, scratching his head. He assessed the situation, relying on memory and the sometimes elusive signage placed by fellow expats. The uncertainty in Damien's eyes made my stomach roil a little. Nabil looked at me with a half-hearted smile, "Don't worry, *habeebtie* (sweetheart), remember I speak the language." The only problem was there was not a single soul outside our caravan to ask for directions.

Completely mesmerized by the car ride and fixated on the surrounding landscape, I caught my breath when Nabil slammed on the brakes. He barely missed crashing into the SUV ahead of us. Nabil and I, startled, looked at each other. What just happened? Up ahead, Damien, with a wide grin, shouted out, "We're here." We had reached the Edge of the World, just yards away.

I climbed out of the car, pulse rising, and hooked the pups to their leashes. Gingerly making our way over the pebbly ground to "the Edge," my heart thumped as I came upon the 1,000-foot sheer drop just steps away from our car. Below were impressive cliffs, part of the Jibal Tuwaiq escarpment, that loomed high over the plateau and our vantage point. The red-brown cliffs were lined with clear sedimentary layers, and the lower tiers dated back 150 million years to the Jurassic Age when the plain was sea-covered. I was rooted to the spot, captivated by the majestic cliffs, buttes, and massive desert below, all set off in various shades of red. Nabil and I lingered, astounded.

Maci and Coco must have sensed our excitement and were anxious to explore themselves. As we started a trek along a narrow trail on a nearby bluff, the dogs suddenly pulled on their leashes. My knees buckled. I almost lost my footing on the loose rocks with the persistent tugging of the pups and the whipping wind. Frightening visions of tumbling off the cliff flashed in my brain. Nabil, alarmed, rushed over to grab the leashes. He led the pups down to flatter ground where several friends had gathered. I was right behind them. Our friends had watched our misadventure and were relieved when we were all safely off the bluff. And they were only too happy to look after our furry daughters, especially the children of our friends, as Nabil and I continued our careful expedition over the rocks.

As we reached ever higher buttes, we stood in awe of the magnificent geological panoramic view. I couldn't believe I was in Saudi Arabia. Although the Edge of the World is not one of the Seven Wonders of the World, thoughts of a lesser Grand Canyon popped into my mind. One could almost imagine the caravans crossing the expanse, stopping to exchange myrrh, frankincense, and precious stones with fellow traders in an ancient period.

Tired and sweaty after climbing along the sometimes precarious cliffs, we made our way to our cars, which had all turned a dusty brown. With a wave of Damien's arm from his car window, our convoy followed to a nearby, quiet area with a beautiful sweeping acacia tree. Three hearty trunks from one large base held a canopy of small feathered prickly green leaves, providing considerable shade for our group. Out came folding tables and camping chairs, quilted blankets, and a portable barbecue grill. The grill was soon filled with sizzling shish kabobs. tabouli, hummus, and brownies were laid out on the folding tables. We were delightfully exhausted and welcomed rehashing the day's events as we savored our feast. Minka and Jacub talked about hunting around in the rocks for evidence of fossils. Jacub enthusiastically pulled out several stones from his pocket -- shell imprints on thin pieces of limestone. I asked Jacub if I could look at one of the rocks, and he happily obliged. Fascinated by this small stone, I turned it over in my hands, feeling the outline of the shell design. It was hard to fathom that this imprint sketched a sea creature that lived in this place millions of years ago. Damien upped the ante by telling us about other desert trips when companions found ancient sharks' teeth. As evening approached, the light muted, and the horizon tinged orange and red against the ashy buttes; an exquisite sunset.

The natural landscape, culture, and spirit of this place took me back to my native lands in the Rocky Mountains of Montana. Although the topographies were distinctly different, the imposing mountains and clear aqua-colored lakes of Glacier National Park and the austere beauty of the Saudi Sahara conjured up similar feelings of wonder and flashes of ancient lands. Two vistas, worlds apart, both arising from large-scale movements in the earth's crust eons ago; the sheer artistry and serenity of each made me catch my breath. In both, I was caught up with ancestral spirits and the sacredness of the land.

Satiated, the drive home was filled with babble about our intriguing trip. We were grateful for a trip that bonded us to this place.

Other desert odysseys similarly filled my spirit. The Red Sands was a massive span of fine sand and dunes, likely named due to its iron-enriched components. And it was only around an hour outside the urban sprawl of Riyadh. Dunes rose like several-story buildings, providing ample sand-surfing for children, pups, and adults alike. We all became 12-year-olds. One after the other, children and adults planted their behinds on top of a dune and, with a forward motion, careened down the slopes. Our pups took their turns, somersaulting behind. Maci and Coco found newfound freedom off their leashes, trekking and digging through the sparkling coral-colored sand as young children chased after them. Nabil and I aimlessly climbed dunes together, finding solitude and grace scanning the boundless, rippled rose desert.

That same trip brought us to nearby Hidden Valley. Smooth red sand transformed into hard rocky passages, craggy buttes, and alluring mesas. Hidden Valley bore an uncanny resemblance to Monument

Valley, which straddles Utah and Arizona and is the site of several U.S. Western movies. Finding a secluded area bordered by sheer ledges and a wide-fanned acacia tree, we laid out our blankets, chairs, and food. Several of us hiked into a circuit of caves, marveling at the intricate formations carved out by tectonic shifts ages ago. As we moved through the area, we became attuned to spotting fossils – the golden ratio of spiraled shells.

Belly dancing led by Nabil's *tabla* (Arab drum) playing rounded out the afternoon. Memories of belly dancing parties in the States with good-natured friends filled my mind; it was somehow nostalgic and fitting that we were now in the Saudi desert with new expatriate friends dancing to spirited Arabic music. Married to a Lebanese native and having visited Lebanon several times, where I learned new dance moves from Nabil's family and neighbors, I coached our expat friends in their natural hip movements. A novel experience for most, adding a special Middle Eastern flavor.

I had heard of Bedouins, and now that we lived in the Arab Gulf, I was appreciative to see hints of this uncommon and historic community on our desert drives. Oftentimes, when least expected, Bedouin goat and camel herders could be seen from the roadside, tending to livestock in bare oceans of sand, children playing nearby. On occasion, we spotted several of their white and brown tents. Bedouins, nomadic desert-dwellers, lived a simple life and were known for their generosity.

On a later trip to Hidden Valley, while we indulged in a picnic lunch of Kentucky Fried Chicken with expat friends, a haggard figure in a worn tunic and ghutra appeared, his arms waving and incoherent words spilling. The man, with a gray straggly beard and sunken eyes, shakily stuttered, "*Alsalam alaikum*" (Peace be upon you). Nabil said he recognized the Bedouin dialect. The man continued in Bedouin slang, "Do you speak Arabic?" Nabil nodded at the man, and told our group the man might need some help. Approaching the man, Nabil spoke to him for around 30 seconds and then walked back to us. He said the man needed assistance with "jumping" his pickup truck, which had stalled out some distance away in the desert, and Nabil was going to help. One of our Canadian friends wanted to accompany Nabil, probably as much to be supportive as to have a new experience. The threesome got into Nabil's Jeep and drove away.

As the Jeep disappeared in the dust of the desert, I realized that Nabil's offer of help and the Bedouin's quick acceptance happened in a split second, and didn't give me the chance to discuss the matter with Nabil. Who was this man, after all, and what was his true motivation? And why had Nabil instantly agreed to go off with him? It calmed me to know he was an older man who truly looked in distress. However, around 45 minutes later, my worry increased even though I knew, deep down, that Nabil had good survival instincts if needed.

Not too soon after, I recognized the rumble of our Jeep and was relieved to see Nabil and our friend coming toward us. We huddled around Nabil to hear what happened. Nabil described driving the man to his weather-worn truck adjacent to one of three large black tents lined with red. Several women dressed in black from top to bottom were surrounded by children chasing after each other. Camels roamed in the distance. Nabil questioned "jumping" the man's truck, as it was larger than his Jeep. Saudi natives are known for their love of oversized American SUVs and trucks, like Toyotas or Chevrolets. After a few attempts, Nabil was successful in getting the truck engine to start, which brought a toothless smile.

The women were shyly curious about Nabil and his friend and likely had not seen men in shorts before. A few children came over yelling, "Hello, hello, hello," obviously proud of their English. I asked Nabil why he so readily left with the man; wasn't he suspicious? Nabil replied, "Not at all. I lived among the Bedouins in Jordan. They are my culture and are completely harmless, transparent, and genuine people." Returning to his story, Nabil said that as he and our friend were leaving, the man asked Nabil to bring his tribe (*rabaa'k*), those of us left behind, to have dinner with him and his family. As a gesture of his gratitude, the Bedouin wanted to slaughter one of his camels, which meant sacrificing prized and valuable livestock. We were all shocked at this level of generosity. Nabil explained that it was not unusual for Bedouins to be exceedingly hospitable when it came to paying back favors. I would come to find that generosity existed across all socio-economic groups. Though excited about the possibility of sharing in a special feast with a Bedouin community, we ultimately had to forgo this magnanimous offering, as Nabil said it could be an all-night event and most of us had to work the following morning. The man's graciousness left its trace, though, creating great admiration for these unassuming people.

While our daytime desert sojourns were awesome, some of our more notable times in the Kingdom were overnight camping trips with our friends from all over the world. Arabs and Bedouins, particularly those from the Arab Gulf where nomadic tribes originated, are people of the night. It seems generations of Arab Gulf desert dwellers, the Bedouins, found it necessary to do core activities, such as cooking, grooming, or traveling in the evening or early morning hours because it was simply too hot to do them during the day. This established a skewed 24-hour cycle favoring the night, which carries on today. While most Arab Gulf natives and others in the region are concentrated in urban centers with fully functioning air conditioning, they continue to reserve the nighttime for important rituals and traditions, celebratory occasions, and special gatherings of family and friends.

The night is a singularly auspicious time in the Middle East for other reasons, as well. The Muslim calendar is based on the lunar cycle.

The night gets top billing in song, poetry, and assorted stories. Nighttime has been immortalized in the revered folk tale, *One Thousand and One Nights*, based in the Arab region and Persia, which includes stories told by Scheherazade to King Shahryar for 1,001 nights in a bold attempt to save her life. The Arab fascination with the night extends to name choices, as well, with Laila (which translates to "a night") being one of the most popular Arab female names.

Our first camping trip was 10 months after arriving in the Kingdom. We were at a dinner of expatriate square dancing friends when we struck up a conversation with a couple who were members of a formal camping group. Caroline hailed from Canada, and Victor from Belgium. The pair told us of their many and varied camping trips, including to the Empty Quarter, an enormous, remote stretch of desert in the southeast quadrant of Saudi Arabia. In awe of their spirit and audacity, we delighted in sharing stories of trips to the desert and our interest in an overnight stay.

This led to introductions to another couple, Sandy from Canada and Craig, a New Zealander, who would be leading a trip to the desert the next weekend. They worked for the Eye Hospital in Riyadh. I was thrilled when they invited us to join their weekend camping trip. We were thankful it would be an "easy drive"—some highway driving and no challenging desert dunes. The couple kindly offered to let us use their camping tent. They would sleep on cots alongside their 4-wheel drive vehicle, assuring us they would not use their tent anyway, as this time of year, late September, they always used cots in the open air.

Our escapade began mid-afternoon on the first day of the weekend. Two other SUVs and our "little ones" would join us. Our destination was an area near the Edge of the World. We dutifully followed our new friends on the paved road and eventually along car tracks in the desert. The area surrounding the Edge of the World was stunning, with strands of buttes and cliffs. As we arrived at our destination, the sun was descending, setting the whole scene aglow in burgundy. Sandy and Craig quickly scouted out a good area to set up our borrowed tent, as they had been to this site several times before.

We were adjacent to a canyon wall that cut deep into the earth, with towering rock formations in the distance. Sandy nimbly helped us set up the tent, a high-end version used in the Arctic. The expat gentleman in the third vehicle would also be sleeping outside on a cot. I felt spoiled with our plush accommodations that had siding, privacy, and a moonroof.

We were helping Sandy organize the tent when I heard a clamor in the distance. It sounded like birds shrieking in agitation. Curious, I looked in the direction of the commotion. I made out the silhouette of a person against the ruby-colored sky. I looked at Nabil, his eyes trained on the distant movement. As I looked back at the figure, I was incredulous to make out Craig marching along the horizon playing the bagpipes, bounded by the desert, adjacent canyons, and imminent sunset. Nabil and I were floored. I turned to Sandy, "That's Craig playing the bagpipes!" She simply grinned.

Following our sublime serenade, we set up for dinner. There were portable tables, canvas camping chairs, and our contributions to the impending meal. Always the cook, Nabil had prepared tabouli, hummus, and *kafta* (hamburger meat mixed with tomatoes, parsley, and onion) at home, and Sandy and Craig packed steak, baked potatoes and salad. Craig started a fire with charcoal and lighter fluid over a natural pit and placed a grill under the steak and kafta. We had a most delicious meal and good conversation, a powerful fusion of tranquility and camaraderie. A time to simply breathe. We retired to our tent with the pups after 11:00 PM. The mesh netting of the tent afforded refreshing desert breezes and a deluge of twinkling stars as we cuddled in our sleeping bags with Maci and Coco—a glorious night. I could see what Jerry Roberts was talking about.

I took particular notice of the full moon and flash of stars, trying to make out the design of constellations through our moon roof. The night seemed to close itself around us like the walls of a cave or an immense shell—it cradled us. I had the slight sensation of being suspended in space with only the polished steel of the stars to orient me. My breathing slowed. My heartbeat settled. I struggled to remember ever feeling more at peace. As a young child, I remember the night invoking images of ghosts, goblins, and the bogeyman under the bunk bed I shared with my sister. The night was a time of eerie silence punctuated by strange creaks and a fuzzy, dreamy awareness. Now, however, I was experiencing the magic of the night in the middle of the expansive and solitary Saudi desert.

CHAPTER 7

ARAB HOSPITALITY

We met Reem Al-Omari, a 16-year-old Saudi from a prominent tribe, only weeks after arriving in the Kingdom. Taking a stroll with the pups one Thursday afternoon, we found ourselves at Al-Kindi Plaza, the massive square near our residence in the Diplomatic Quarter. Because it was Ramadan, all the shops were closed. The square was empty except for a single figure in black. Our youngest pup, Coco, spotted the lone teenaged Saudi as soon as we arrived at the square. Without warning, Coco broke loose from her leash and bounded over to the girl as she roller-bladed on the light beige tiles, black headscarf flowing behind her. Within seconds our Coco reached the girl and leapt up to grab the scarf in her mouth. Coco was pleased; the girl was horrified. She spun around, shrieked *haram* (that's forbidden), and glared at us.

I went to grab Coco. Nabil instinctively ran over and hugged the teenager, trying to comfort her and apologize. *La telmesny* (don't touch me) she shouted. Nabil froze. While Nabil's actions were very "Nabil," they were strictly against Saudi mores. It was forbidden for men to touch women in public. Flustered, I went over and spoke to the girl, hoping there were no serious repercussions. "We are so sorry. Our doggie loves people, and sometimes it's hard for her to control herself." The girl's eyes lightened, and she looked at me with an inkling of recognition.

"Are you American?" she asked.

I nodded, not sure what was coming next.

"I really want to learn English, and I love American people."

Feeling relieved, "Oh, that's great. But your English is very good."

"I want to improve, though, and maybe visit the U.S. someday," she asserted.

I explained we were from Washington, DC, and new to the Kingdom. We lived in the Diplomatic Quarter. Not surprisingly, the girl said she was part of a large family, the youngest. Her older sister and two nieces were in another part of the square. By this time, the girl had introduced herself: Reem. She cradled and cooed over Coco and Maci. As the sun lowered in the sky, we told Reem we needed to leave, as we were expected at an iftar meal with expat friends at the Sahara Hotel.

"I'll call my mother and see if I can go with you," Reem said cheerfully, already taking out her phone as she walked over behind a nearby building. I had mixed feelings about Reem's reaction. I was pleased she was comfortable with us but surprised at her presumptive behavior. I told Nabil I wasn't sure how Minka and Jacub would react to us bringing a teenage Saudi girl to our dinner. Nabil didn't have a chance to respond. Reem reemerged, shoulders sagging as she walked toward us. Her cousins were coming to her house that night so she couldn't join us. I suspected that Reem's mother was wary of us.

Following our meeting at the square, Reem came up in our conversations now and then. We appreciated her spirit and hoped to see her again. We had exchanged phone numbers but misplaced a scrap of paper with her number, and unless Reem called us, it seemed unlikely we would see her again. At the end of January 2001, we were heartened to have another chance meeting with Reem at the square.

This time she was with her mother, an uncle from the mother's side, and two sisters, one with children. They seemed as happy to see us as we were to see them. The mother and uncle kindly offered to buy us lunch. We declined politely, having just eaten. But we did accept their offers to treat us to tea.

The uncle asked if we ever had Moroccan tea.

"No, never," Nabil said.

"That itself is an experience," replied the uncle.

The waiter came with an Arab teapot. It was gold with a domed cover, rounded handle, and long spout. He began the ritual, pouring the tea close to Nabil's tiny clear glass. Slowly and gracefully, the waiter lifted the teapot while continuing to pour from as far as his arm could reach above him. Gently bringing his arm down he kept pouring the crimson blend until the glass was filled. This was one custom I had never seen nor heard about, and felt lucky to experience. Captured by the occasion, I couldn't look away from this exquisite scene; the waiter's movements were as fluid as a dancer's and just as beautiful. Solemnly, the waiter ceremoniously poured each of us a glass of tea in the same manner. Despite the chaos in the square—kids screaming, a housemaid yelling at a toddler not to jump in the fountain, and children laughing as they fell off their scooters—the waiter never spilled a drop.

The family was pleased that Nabil was Lebanese and spoke Arabic fluently; these characteristics helped us in meeting locals and Arab expatriates. Many Saudis liked the Lebanese for their industriousness, warmth, and spirit. The mother talked about her family. She had seven daughters and two sons, ranging in age from 16 to 32. Everyone lived under one roof except for one who was married with five children. I could just imagine the line for the bathroom. Even with help, I couldn't get past having all those people to care for.

One of Reem's nephews playing chase with his siblings caught sight of the dogs and yelled out, "Look at the doggies!" The other children ran over, and they all gathered at a safe distance from Maci and Coco, some with mouths agape, others with huge grins. I was charmed by their innocent intrigue. They were accustomed to long, lanky desert dogs native to the Arab Gulf called salukis, similar to greyhounds. They had likely seen larger breeds like German Shepherds or Golden Retrievers on TV or in the movies. One boy began to put his hand out, but Coco's exuberance to lick and play startled him, and he shrank back, looking a little overcome. A couple of youngsters managed to pet Maci, the quiet one. The mother, Reem's sister, asked if we would be willing to sell one of our pups and how much it cost. Nabil tensed and said they were like our children. "Would you be willing to sell one of your children?" The young mother caught off guard, replied, "Of course not."

"Nabil, you can have my children for free!" quipped Reem's sister. We all burst out laughing.

Just before leaving the café, Reem's mother and uncle insisted we come for a barbecue at the mother's home the following Friday. Nabil and I exchanged confused looks; we barely knew this family. And we were astonished when Reem said to bring Maci and Coco and nobody objected. Perhaps Reem wanted to make up for the fuss over the pups a few weeks earlier or the sister for wanting to buy them.

This would be our first visit to a Saudi home. I had always wondered what was behind the tall, whitewashed concrete walls concealing locals' houses. Although excited, we were apprehensive. How would Reem and her family receive us? Would we need to watch what we said? Were there certain codes of behavior we should follow as guests?

And I kept reminding myself we were in a country we knew very little about. Just three months ago, there had been the Al-Qaeda attack on the U.S.S. Cole. In the weeks before we departed from the States, we received several alerts from the U.S. Department of State about other potential terrorist attacks in the Middle East. What if we were kidnapped or worse? We even asked Canadian friends to call mid-evening to check on us the night of the barbecue. Later, we felt embarrassed for thinking in terms of stereotypes.

We were to arrive at the Al-Omari home at 8:00 PM. In preparing for a typical Saturday night out in DC, I might spend 15 minutes in front of my closet pulling out this or that outfit. Any concerns about what to put on for our visit with the Al-Omaris were pointless. I would wear the abaya and a scarf around my head in deference to the family. And rather than the customary shorts Nabil wore at Western gatherings, he slipped on dockers and a collared shirt.

My eyes widened as we stepped through the courtyard door and approached an Arabian mansion with bleached marbled steps leading to an alabaster mortar exterior: Reem's home. I grabbed Nabil's hand as we climbed the steps under an imposing arched portico. Two housekeepers greeted us deferentially at the stately inlaid wooden door. The women, southeast Asian, spoke a fusion of broken English and Arabic. They wore light blue uniforms—long pants with buttoned-up shirts and white aprons and collars. We were guided to a spacious living area and instructed to sit on an elegantly appointed cream-colored sofa. Another similar sofa and several stately straight-back chairs with the same posh cushion texture sat close by. White marble covered the floors, much like a five-star hotel lobby, and the ceilings stood high and majestic. There were at least three sumptuous chandeliers with round crystals in rows of ever-larger concentric circles dripping from golden chains. The scent of *bakhoor* (a form of incense) in incense burners floated through the home. Squeezing Nabil's knee, I whispered, "This is a lot grander than I expected." Nabil took a gulp and softly said, "I feel like I'm in a Hollywood movie." I steeled myself and thought about how this evening would broaden my view of Saudi tradition. I hoped, though, that neither of us said or did anything off-putting to our hosts.

We were served *gahwa*, cardamom coffee, and khudri dates on silver platters by the housemaids, who seemed to be the only people around. I wondered if we came too early; however, Nabil reminded me that Arab time often lagged behind Western time. We tried to appear nonchalant when Reem came down the semi-circular staircase nearly half an hour later. Approaching with a muted smile and reserved body language, Reem shook my hand and leaned forward to kiss me once on each cheek. She bowed her head slightly in Nabil's direction, probably concerned he might grab her in a bear hug, and turned to wave at the dogs. Vanishing into the kitchen, Reem reappeared after a few minutes, holding a tray edged in gold handles carrying a mixture of Swiss and German chocolates. Reem sat with us, inquiring about our day and how we liked her country. Was it what we expected?

We didn't have a chance to answer. The mother entered the room, throwing up her arms and hollering, *Hala wa ghala!* (warm greetings). She rushed toward me, grabbed my cheeks, and brusquely pecked each one. She acknowledged Nabil and the doggies with a nod. Then she cracked a smile and asked Nabil, "How are your children today?" Nabil, surprisingly quiet, smiled back.

Six more sisters and one husband trickled in, each similar to Reem in their welcome; all the females wore the required black. One of two brothers and many children—nieces and nephews of Reem—followed. The brother was hesitant, and the children were mostly interested in Maci and Coco. The uncle and his wife arrived around 10:00. I was bewildered when he turned on the TV and flipped through mostly

European programming, bragging that they had over 300 channels. It struck me how this would be considered terribly rude in the U.S. But here, the family appeared to be fine with the disruption, and it was soon integrated into the rhythm of the evening. While a melodramatic series or world news droned on in the background, we talked about regional politics, our time in the Middle East, and Nabil's life in Lebanon and Jordan. Children dashed from room to room. The talk halted, though, when a particularly compelling scene in a show or news report focused eyes on the TV screen. Then it would pass, and conversation resumed. I felt reassured the family felt relaxed enough with us to continue with what must have been their nighttime ritual of TV watching; I sensed a degree of acceptance. Our Canadian friend did call to check on us, although I barely noticed. While housekeepers circled through with more treats—chocolates, fresh fruit juices and nuts, ever-flowing mint tea and coffee—there was that question, "Are you happy? What can I get for you? Would you like more chocolates, more dates?"

Although appreciative of the generosity and attention, I was somewhat overwhelmed by the frenzy. I tried willing myself to settle in, and appreciate the first hints of Saudi homelife and fellowship while wondering if "the dinner" might be confined to dates, chocolates, and nuts. Just as my stomach began begging for protein and carbohydrates, the commotion level seemed to swell. It was nearly 1:00 AM when housemaids and female family members collected trays of chocolates and dates. At the same time, other house staff carried out slabs of lamb and beef in aluminum pans and heaps of fresh fattoush laden with greens, mint, cucumber, tomato, onion, olive oil, and bits of fried pita bread. As they headed outside, we were corralled and swept up in the forward motion to the outdoor courtyard. A cadre of servants and a couple of daughters had already started a barbecue on a shiny gas grill poolside.

We sat at six-foot-long tables covered with light plastic tablecloths – white with green swirl trim. Although there was no assigned seating, Nabil and I sat together with the pups between us under the table. The nice china was set on the tables, and shish kabob, lamb steaks, and kafta sizzled on the barbecue grill. The chatter, although subdued, was constant, as was the movement around us – to the kitchen, to chase a child, to answer phones. Dinner was served as mild pandemonium ensued, similar to a happy, hectic big family event like Thanksgiving or an anniversary party in the States, but on steroids. The pups were overjoyed to receive substantial portions on the same fine china, under the table.

We spent some time chatting with the mother about Nabil's family in Lebanon.

"I like to go shopping with my daughters in Beirut," the mother revealed. "We love going through the racks of designer clothes."

Nabil and I nodded, acknowledging that Beirut was known as a clothes designer's haven.

Chuckling, she added, "When we come back to Saudi Arabia, though, we have to cover up the new clothes under an abaya."

I laughed along but felt wistful for the mother and her daughters.

I found it odd that Saudi women tended to wear the latest fashions under their abayas, which would only be seen at women-only gatherings or in the family home. In the States, it's so often about being noticed and "seen." Good first impressions are often achieved, at least in part, through attire. I learned that Arab Gulf women get around this by wearing extravagant footwear and handbags, accessories that can be seen despite the abaya.

Similarly, the relationship between Saudi women and their hair was curious, at least by Western standards. Many familiar with the Arab world know that Saudi women exercise careful attention to keep their hair covered, with few exceptions. What I was not aware of, though, were the pains Arab Gulf women took to style their hair based on the current rage. They generally sported fashionable cuts and trendy highlights, often using henna. Outside the family home, I only ever saw a Saudi woman's hair free from a headscarf when at work, either in the women's restroom or at end-of-the-week women-only breakfasts of *mezze* (Arab finger food, dips, and pita bread) behind closed doors—both a refuge for female co-workers. I often felt voyeuristic in these settings as Saudi colleagues uncovered their finely styled hair, as though I were intruding on private scenes. Inevitably, I found it hard to look away. Reem's sisters and mother wore headscarves during our early visits to each other's homes. Once the women became comfortable with Nabil, he was seen as a brother or an uncle, and it was, therefore, no longer necessary to wear a headscarf. This was highly unusual. The women conceded that they, as was the custom with Gulf women, had never revealed their hair to a man except for their fathers, brothers, uncles, and nephews, men they could never marry.

Most of Reem's sisters were outgoing except for the eldest, who was divorced, and the middle daughter, who was serene and aloof. We found out later that this second sister was betrothed to a high-level prince who she only saw one weekend a month. He was married to several other women (but no more than four at a time based on Islamic beliefs), which was commonplace for royalty. It was also not unusual for Saudi royalty to marry women from large Saudi family tribes, as this helped support their standing. We told the princess we were glad we didn't find this out earlier, as we would have been intimidated, and might not have become so close to the family. With a restrained smile and composure befitting a princess, she said, *Aadi, aadi* (it's okay, it's okay).

Music began playing from a boom box, mostly Lebanese and

Egyptian, with a belly dancing beat. The women opted not to play Arab Gulf music, *Khaleeji* tunes, popular in the Kingdom; they likely did not want us to feel uneasy. Nabil held out his hand to me. I shook my head. No way. Deflecting the persistent prodding, I mentioned hearing that the mother had a sensational singing voice. I would only dance if the mother sang first. One of the daughters turned on Toni Hana, a popular Lebanese singer. The mother crooned in aching silky tones about lost love, her face drawn and eyes downcast. Nabil asked a sister if they had a tabla. "No, but I'll get something close." She scampered away and returned with a huge, deep kitchen pan. Nabil said, "That will do the job." He turned the pot sideways, positioning it just the right way on his lap. With a couple of claps to the aluminum bottom, Nabil caught the rhythm with fingers and palms, creating a pulsating echo from the hollow of the pot. Drawn into the sublime reverberation and less embarrassed with attention averted from me, I fell into a slow belly dance. The girls soon followed.

Flush with excitement, I sat down after our intrepid belly dance. I noticed a spectacular azure handbag with off-white circular and geometric designs at the princess' side. I told her it was unique and beautiful. Nabil pushed his elbow into my side, startling me. Had I said something wrong? Anyway, it was too late. With no qualms, the princess emptied the belongings and insisted the purse was mine. "No, I was only admiring it," I said. The sister seemed offended, and I knew I shouldn't continue with my protest. Nabil whispered to never tell an Arab you like something, as they would give it to you. It was an insult to refuse. I was taken aback at the young woman's extreme reaction in wanting to please me with the purse, and Nabil's explanation. This was generosity at another level. It was clear a guest was to be treated with the utmost hospitality in a Saudi home. I would come to find that this Saudi trait, typical in the larger Arab world, draws from both religion and culture. In the Middle East, it is an honor to have a guest enter your home, whether announced or unannounced, friend or foe.

Around 2:30 AM, I was full, drowsy, and relaxing in one of the chairs upholstered in some luxurious fabric, smiling at what a beautiful evening it was when I realized I hadn't seen Coco in almost an hour. I sat upright; my heart stopped. I rushed from sister to sister, putting a hand on their arms and asking," Have you seen the doggie? The little doggie, Coco?" They smiled, shrugging. How could they be so casual? My skin went clammy as I pretended to enjoy myself.

After nearly two hours of enduring anxiety, a young child of Reem's sister whom I had missed said, "I know where Coco is. She went off with Uncle Ahmad." Alarm gripped me. "What! Where are they?" Just then, Ahmad walked through the gates of the courtyard. Coco lay comfortably in his arms, her tongue dangling, her tail wagging. She looked smug and simply blissful. Nabil leaned over to tell me, "Mary, this is the Arab way. What's mine is yours, and what's yours is mine. You don't have to ask permission for this kind of thing." Trying to remain calm, I asked, "Where did you all go?" "Oh, I took Coco through the MacDonald's drive-thru to get a Big Mac," Ahmed replied. "We shared it, and then I took her to all of my friends' houses. They've never seen a dog like this!" I chuckled, my limbs finally loosening, my mind unwinding. While we would often meet with our Saudi friends, we knew to keep our pups away during prayer time, occasions steeped in purity and cleanliness. Our Saudi friends understood our deep devotion to Maci and Coco; it was an "American thing."

We danced and sang in the early morning hours. All the while being asked if we were happy. Did we want to change the music to Western style? No, we could always listen to American music. We had CDs, and there was an American military base in Riyadh with a radio station that played 60s and 70s music. As traces of crimson shone onto the courtyard, the girls coaxed Nabil into reading Turkish coffee grounds. Nabil explained he learned how to read coffee grounds from his paternal grandmother in southern Lebanon when he was a young boy. His grandmother was adept at reading fortunes that often rang true and pinpointed specific times of the month and year, past and future. Nabil revealed he was not as accurate as his grandmother but did readings for fun. A housemaid brewed the coffee, and the girls lined up on dining room chairs around Nabil to have their demitasse cups read. Several requested a private reading. The eldest daughter slipped away, telling Nabil it was against her beliefs.

Surprisingly, this sister worked at King Faisal Specialist Hospital in Social Services. She was divorced with two children who she rarely saw and who were under the care of her former husband. Her younger sister, the princess, had her own small business manufacturing the luxury purse style that she had graciously given me. None of the other sisters worked. However, Reem went to high school. It was normal for single women in the Arab Gulf to sit at home waiting for a potential suitor's family to approach her family for a marriage proposal. This traditional process often began at women-only functions, especially weddings where women—mothers, aunts, and grandmothers—had their eyes out for potential marriage material for their sons, nephews, and grandsons. We left as the sun rose, thanking our hosts for an incredible night as we stepped through the courtyard gate. The women whispered, "*Ma salama*" (goodbye) as they huddled behind the metal gate, steadfast over being invisible to the public.

We had many more festive gatherings within and outside the family home, including at our apartment. When at our home, Reem's family brought at least one housekeeper who, unsolicited, did our dishes, vacuumed, or ironed. It seemed the hospitality went both ways: showered on guests and hosts. Like most, we heard of a darker side: domestic abuse cases in the Kingdom involving family and housemaids. In these situations, sadly, the housemaid has little or no recourse. Fortunately, we did not witness anything like this personally with this family. However, over our years in the Middle East, we found that emotions could run high in the Arab Gulf. From the extreme generosity and kindness we encountered from Saudi and other Arab Gulf friends to several second-hand stories we heard about disputes that abruptly escalated to a precarious physical level. Whether we were just lucky not to see this behavior first-hand, we don't know, however, the wonderful intimate moments with Saudi nationals who became cherished friends were among the welcome respites from a rigorous work schedule at the Hospital.

Even though we were relatively content in the Diplomatic Quarter, we became more and more worried about increasing acts of violence in Riyadh. In 2004, after a horrific spate of bombings at Western expatriate compounds by Al-Qaeda in 2003, Nabil and I moved to the neighboring Gulf country of Qatar. Qatar, shaped like a lightbulb, is nearly the size of Connecticut and measures around 100 miles by 50 miles. In contrast, Saudi Arabia is nearly one-quarter the size of the United States. Qatar had a booming economy with good career opportunities for an economist and civil engineer in its capital city of Doha. Although Saudi Arabia is the most traditional and conservative country in the Gulf region, we found the same consummate hospitality through our new Qatari friendships.

I had the opportunity to do some writing for a local magazine about Qatari culture, women's roles in the Arab Gulf, and the effects of westernization on Qatar. That's how I met 19-year-old Suad[1]. She

---

1   Sadly, Suad died in a tragic car accident on November 22, 2013, at the age of 23, a few months after her college graduation and a special desert trip. Nabil and I were heartbroken. She taught me more than most about the culture and lifestyle of Qatar. I hope that Suad's voice and sentiments live on in the dreams of other young Qatari women.

was Qatari with penetrating eyes and a quick laugh and attended the Academic Bridge Program at Qatar Foundation's Education City. Planning for a law degree, she wanted to become the first female judge in Qatar—an ambitious goal for a young woman in the Arab Gulf. Suad graciously agreed to be interviewed and encouraged other young Qatari women to do the same. Through Suad's efforts, I was grateful to interview five young women for my magazine articles focusing on perspectives, cultural and otherwise, amongst the newer Arab Gulf generation.

Early on, I was captivated by my new young friend. Although short in stature, Suad's candid charm, infectious spirit, and commanding manner always filled a room. She loved her cell phone, texting, and shopping at Doha's malls for designer jeans, handbags, and shoes. She regularly stood up for those less fortunate than herself. When only 18 years old and just starting at the Academic Bridge Program, Suad worked closely with a human rights conference in which domestic abuse and inadequate migrant workers' conditions in Qatar were discussed. As part of the conference, Suad and her group developed potential solutions for pressing issues that weren't normally addressed in the country.

Suad was aware of the challenges and rewards of "Western creep" within her country and was one of the very few young Qatari women who chose to attend university abroad in Swansea, Wales. Although her parents were acutely concerned over Suad's choice, they were encouraged when she ultimately decided to live with her female cousin who resided in Swansea. As was the tradition in the Arab Peninsula, Suad would not have been allowed to go abroad for university studies otherwise.

Suad was nothing if not open and transparent, more so than most other young women I met in the Arab Gulf. Although sensitive to subject matter, I felt comfortable asking Suad a wide range of questions during our interviews regarding her life as a young woman in the Arab Gulf. I remember her telling me about arranged marriage, an important and sacred tradition in the Arabian Peninsula. With a glint in her eye, Suad divulged she was "not comfortable" when asked if she was being encouraged to get married and settle down. "My family wants me to get married as soon as possible. I don't know, I like my freedom. I'm not even trying to meet anyone." I was taken with Suad's straightforwardness.

Sipping cardamom coffee together one afternoon, she told me, "I'm not going to say I agree one hundred percent with arranged marriage. I know it is my culture, but I want to actually meet the person I'm going to marry before getting married." Suad's family's concerns were understandable in the more conservative Gulf region, where an unmarried woman in her late 20s is considered an "old maid." Suad, however, was adamant about not getting married prematurely. "My focus is on my education. My education comes first." She wanted to learn how to be independent and take care of herself while at Swansea University.

Suad and several other young Qatari women attending university in Doha's Education City conveyed their thoughts on the abaya during an informal group interview on campus. I asked how the young women felt about the obligatory abaya. Suad spoke first. "You start wearing the abaya when you reach puberty." Her eyes intent on mine, she continued, "I didn't see any problem with wearing the abaya. I was cool with it because I believed in it. Not only because it's our social custom, it's our religion, first."

Reserved and soft-spoken, Sameeha divulged, "When I was ten or eleven years old, I wanted to wear the abaya, but my mom didn't want me to. I cried to my mom, 'Please, I want an abaya.' I wanted to look older." Taking a sip of water, Sameeha resumed, "When I first wore an abaya, I was happy. It was amazing." Sameeha added, "If you have skinny jeans or something tight, you just wear the abaya to cover over it and become decent."

Bold and resolute, Mona, a Journalism student, declared she was around thirteen when she started wearing the abaya. "At first, I didn't like it. Because back then I couldn't run around; I had to be careful not to step on it, but, in time, I learned to love it." Mona highlighted the importance of accessorizing the abaya, asserting, "I think some women look extremely beautiful in the abaya, especially when they know how to present themselves with the handbag and the shoes, even the way they wear their headscarf."

I was curious if the young women ever felt compelled to wear the *niqab*, full black face covering. I had seen older, more conservative, Qatari women wearing the niqab, covering not only with an abaya and headscarf but their entire face except for the eyes. Sameeha, her dark opals studying me, replied, "When I go to a wedding party or something and have a lot of makeup on, I like to cover my face. Our custom is to not show our face with lots of makeup, so I do cover my face at those times, but a lot of young women don't."

I asked the girls about the traditions surrounding the abaya. I knew young women were required to wear the abaya in public settings where men were present, but what was the tradition for wearing the abaya around male relatives? Mona explained the abaya must be worn around those men you could marry, which included cousins but not uncles. In the Arab Gulf region it is not only common for cousins to marry, but it is encouraged and considered honorable, as it tightens the family circle.

I noticed there were differing opinions concerning the abaya. It was intriguing to hear another perspective from a male KFSH manager at an iftar meal we attended soon after arriving in the Kingdom. While claiming it was important to dress modestly in the Arab Gulf, wearing the abaya, in particular, was not part of a religious framework. The KFSH manager felt that, in fact, compelling women to wear the black robe (abaya) served men's egos. I heard this same sentiment from some others when living in the Arabian Peninsula.

At another sit-down, Suad emphasized that she was spoiled in Qatar; everything was done for her by the household staff—maids, cooks, and drivers. When it came to family, Suad wanted to have a maximum of two to three children once married. Her perspective was practically unheard of in a region where five or more children in a family were often the staple. Always the realist, she wanted to provide not only the appropriate financial support but emotional support, as well, for her future children. While serious-minded, Suad had a wonderful sense of humor. I asked her once if she would prefer to be a man rather than a woman. She flashed me her trademark toothy grin and said, "Of course, a man! I could marry four women."

Soon after knowing Suad, she insisted I meet her family, the Al Hamdans, to experience "Qatari hospitality." Nabil was soon drawn into our circle. We spent much time at the family's home enjoying mezze, sharing news stories of the region, and meeting extended family members. After an evening with Suad's family, her mother lit incense in a *mabkhara* (incense burner). She waved the smoke with her hand into our clothes and hair as she moved the mabkhara up and down our silhouettes. This was meant as a form of hospitality and, we believed, to ward off evil spirits. Oily perfume followed, which she daubed on our wrists and necks.

Suad's mother was Saudi. It happened her tribe had close relatives in the Al-Omari tribe of Riyadh, which created a bond between us. In the car after one of our early visits with Suad and her whole family, Nabil remarked that he was impressed at being included in these special rituals with the females of the family. He felt Suad's parents must consider him as a brother to be so accepting and open with him. If the extended family was visiting, however, it was not appropriate for men and women to mix; at those times, Nabil and the men sat separately in an outdoor majlis (sitting area).

After a few years of precious time spent at each other's homes or neighborhood restaurants, we were excited to receive a special invitation from Suad's father and mother. They had graciously arranged for a day with us in the desert at their family farm. We met at their home, a typical Arab Gulf residence with two majlises, plush furniture threaded with red and gold, and light-colored tiled floors covered in maroon Arabian throw carpets.

Greeted warmly by Suad's parents, I was surprised when Suad's mother handed me two gifts. "What is this?" I asked, stirred by this unexpected kindness. I felt badly not having brought a gift ourselves in thanks. "Open them. They'll remind you of us." Intrigued, I carefully untied the blue ribbon and opened the first box. I had to muffle a chuckle when I pulled out a ceramic bobblehead of an Arab woman dressed in a stereotypic black robe and headscarf, her face covered. "I just love it!" I exclaimed. I opened the second box with another bobblehead of a man wearing a goatee and dressed in thobe and ghutra. I grabbed Suad's mother in a bear hug. She was taken aback but flashed me a huge smile. I had thought about buying these funny caricature mementos but never anticipated receiving them from an Arab Gulf woman, the object of the parody. I appreciated Suad's mother's humility and our connection.

A convoy of four cars—ours and three family cars with two drivers and four housemaids—ferried us the nearly two hours outside of Doha. I tried to imagine what a Qatari farm would be like as I looked out the window at the changing landscape. Colorful irrigated vegetation in the city turned to a monochrome canvas, miles and miles of sand along a remote highway passed by with the occasional residence and strips of shops—beige on beige. Within an hour, we turned into the desert. We followed the cars ahead on a worn, makeshift, sandy, gravelly road. Suad's father in the first car slowed when we fell behind trying to avoid the spraying of rocks from car tires. We eventually arrived at an isolated span of desert. I eagerly scanned the horizon. The scene was more rustic than I imagined. One side of the farm held several rows of large cages filled with goats, sheep, and hay scattered throughout the pens. On the other side, a simple open tent with red cushions was designated for the men with a grill prominently displayed out front. Nearby stood a closed four-flapped tent for the women.

We were delighted when additional family members arrived during a farm tour by Suad, who was now twenty-two. She was joined by several brothers of the patriarch, their wives, two sisters, their husbands, and children. Suad's mother and two of her mother's sisters, who had come from Saudi Arabia, covered their faces with scarves as the men approached. The male relatives hugged and rubbed noses with Suad's father. They politely shook hands with Nabil and nodded their heads in my direction. It was becoming clear that this trip, in some part, was planned for us. Suad revealed she had not been to the farm since she was a young child. And as they were preparing to eat dinner in the men's tent, Nabil overheard someone remark in Arabic, "Let our guest of honor serve himself before anybody." Nabil later said that the men shredded bits of lamb with their hands and offered them to Nabil as a sign of respect as the group sat together on the ground. I was astounded and deeply honored that we were at the center of this. Other than our wedding, I could hardly recall another celebration with this level of energy and love directed at us.

Following introductions, Suad's mother guided me by the arm to the women's tent where the housemaids had placed swaths of plastic sheets along the floor over colorful carpets. They laid down platters and trays of rice and lamb, hummus, baba ghanoush, stuffed grape leaves, macaroni, and salad with tomato and onion. We all sat on the floor around the platters. As a guest in the women's tent, I was encouraged to eat first and well. Using my right hand, I dipped into the communal dish of rice and lamb. This was customary for these sorts of occasions. As the feasting got underway, I was astonished to see the women's restraint give way to deafening discussions and lively gestures, from hand waving to back-slapping. They made my Italian relatives look tame.

Where were the reserved, soft-spoken aunts I first met a couple of months earlier? I would never have imagined their tough exteriors cracking. Now, sitting shoulder to shoulder with the women in the tent, the laughter and jokes were free-flowing and sometimes awkward. The Gulf dialect was always difficult for me -- harsher than the Lebanese dialect with a lot of hard *"ghahs"* for words beginning with a vowel, and some words completely different than those in the Levant region. It was apparent, though, that the women enjoyed making innocuous fun of each other. Although puzzled at the extreme shift in demeanor and behavior of the women, I felt privileged to be brought into this personal family time. I let myself be taken into the joy.

One of the aunts played the slow, steady beat of Khaleeji music on her cell phone.

"Mary, do you know how to dance Khaleeji? Suad's sister asked.

Although uncomfortable, I knew I needed to try. "Not really. Can you teach me?"

Up jumped several of the women. "The movement is mainly in the shoulders," said one.

"Like this," said another as she swung her shoulders from side to side.

The women cupped their hands to their mouths, ululating as I attempted the dance. I felt encouraged. Several joined me, pivoting their shoulders, moving in circles, and cocking their heads forward and back. Some swung their hair around their heads.

Sputtering through the technique, I watched my hosts spin gracefully through the tent and began feeling the transformative energy of dance and the spirit of the women.

Nighttime fell as we danced, lounged, nibbled, and chatted about everything and nothing. I felt happily weary as I lazed against a colorful cushion. One of the women called out that she needed to use the *hammam* (toilet), and the others agreed. I had been so engaged I didn't realize that I, too, had a full bladder. But where was the toilet? I hadn't even thought of restroom facilities and hadn't noticed porta potties in the area. During our desert trips in Saudi Arabia, we did "our "business" in the open desert, with instructions to cover our waste with sand so as not to attract desert animals, wolves and wild dogs.

There was a clamor to put on face masks and get through the tent flap to what I understood to be a bathroom. I followed the trail of ladies as they headed for a huge Chevvy SUV. As I settled into a back passenger seat, I was startled to see some women climbing up onto the running boards with gleeful smiles. I heard one woman say, "Be careful. We don't want the men to see us." After passing behind the men's tent, one of the women streamed Arab Gulf tunes on a phone. Some sang while dangling out car windows, and those on the running boards balanced precariously.

I was seriously worried about the women's safety, yet I admired their unfettered spirits. The toilet turned out to be a little more than a hole in the ground, enclosed like an American outhouse with some weathered wooden planks. It seems like a five-star hotel, though, when you're in the middle of the desert having to consider baring it all in the open. Again, the women were generous in letting me be among the first to use the hammam. After all the women had their turn, it was another wild trip back to the women's tent, where we wound down the evening munching on chestnuts and corn roasting on a portable grill.

We left the desert farm after midnight, following Suad's father's car, the other vehicles sandwiched between his and ours. At the junction between the desert and the highway, Suad's father made his way to our car, asking if we knew the way home from there. Acknowledging that we did and thanking him for an incredible afternoon and evening, the father waved us off. I was wistful and didn't want the night to end. Being away from home and family, I felt for that brief time together, Suad and her family were my home.

On the road home, Nabil asked about my time with the women. I told him about the food, unrestrained chatter, off-color jokes, and free-wheeling music and dance. I told him it was both wonderful and disconcerting. Nabil wasn't surprised. As a youngster in Jordan and Lebanon, he had seen his sisters unbridled at gatherings with friends and family filled with food and dance. Outside the Gulf region, in the Levant, women were not segregated nor required to wear the abaya and hijab. How was his experience in the men's tent? I asked. Much different. The men were somber; they spoke of politics and family life, but only on a superficial level. There was certainly no music, singing, or dancing. Many of the men, including Nabil, took naps on cushions after dinner. He mentioned he enjoyed the music and laughter coming from the women's tent and that I must be happy. Regardless, Nabil said the men lavished attention on him and treated him like a brother. The time in the desert with Suad and her family reminded me of the summers with my Native American clan and how they once welcomed a "foreigner" into their family – my dad. We, two American expatriates, were now part of an extended Qatari family.

CHAPTER 8

WORK LIFE

Before moving to the Middle East, we were wary about adjusting to a new work culture. However, in Saudi Arabia, a nation considered "different" by most in the Western world, and despite a challenging start, weeks would go by when I felt I could have been in the U.S. at my government job as an economist. Deadlines, meetings, consultations with colleagues—all the familiar trappings of a typical American career. After months in the Kingdom, I had become accustomed to flowing robes, my modest dress, and chats with female colleagues over cardamom coffee. Nabil had accepted a job with the Engineering group at KFSH a couple of months after our arrival in Riyadh, and we both found ourselves dominated by work on the weekdays. I supervised a new automated budgeting process for the most comprehensive budget to date, which was both familiar and challenging. Although I had developed financial models and systems in the U.S., at KFSH, I felt some pressure to perform given my expat and gender status. Nabil headed up maintenance for nearly 200 small to medium-sized ongoing construction projects across the hospital—KFSH was in constant expansion. We drove to and from work together, our buildings adjacent to each other, in our prized Jeep Cherokee. We often went home for lunch and, on occasion, shared a meal at KFSH's cafeteria or dined at a formal restaurant on the premises where waiters placed cloth napkins on diner's laps. We had a feeling of contentment, or a kind of settling into a new life, which suited me, especially, more than the one in DC.

Our personal lives were filled with varied experiences and more social opportunities than we had time for. From pool time and feasts of fresh fish with expatriate friends on Fridays to square dancing and Taekwondo lessons, choral concerts featuring Beatles and Rolling Stones tunes on guitars, and meals at a favorite Turkish restaurant with our expat and Al-Omari friends, our social calendar was always full. In all my daydreams about Saudi Arabia, I never imagined myself in a floral green knee-high dress with full white petticoats doing the do-si-do.

It was customary in the Kingdom to have "help" in the form of people who cooked, cleaned, and took care of the laundry. I felt somewhat conflicted about this, grateful for the extra support, but, at times, embarrassed for this guilty pleasure. It did mean we had more free time for outings and events—all manner of Arab-themed and Western entertainment. Word of mouth was the most common and safest form of communication among expatriates. We plunged into Western-style activities more often in Saudi Arabia than in the U.S., aided by extra discretionary time and the push from fellow expatriates.

Despite the routine at work, there were those times that reminded me we weren't in the U.S. Although English was the official business language, Arabic was often heard between Saudis and other Arab coworkers. Over time, I didn't really notice, and even understood some of the accents from the Levant region, since Nabil was Lebanese. I was struck, particularly in my early days, though, by the predominance of the use of the phrase *Inshallah* or "if God wills" in daily speech at the office. I heard Nabil's mother, sister, and other relatives use this phrase from time to time when we visited Lebanon. In the Kingdom, however, it appeared to be threaded through much of people's speech, and it was rare not to hear it in between a few sentences at a time. Though they might not have known Arabic, expatriates were quick to learn this widely used phrase within days of arriving in the Kingdom. "Inshallah" followed many expressed thoughts, wishes, queries, and responses. The phrase was so common it often became entrenched in the vernacular of the ordinary expatriate.

"Can we meet today at 1:00?" "Inshallah," came the response. Or "Do you think we can have that report finished by the end of the day?" Without hesitation, the reply was "Inshallah." One day, when Nabil and I were rushing back to work after a medical appointment, we found ourselves in the middle of a crowded elevator.

The elevator stopped on the second floor, and a gentleman outside asked if the elevator was going up; several inside responded automatically, "Inshallah." It wasn't long before I found myself saying "Inshallah" in meetings, during workplace and personal conversations, and I still use it today.

Other, less transparent customs left me slightly bewildered. I quickly learned, for instance, of the male Saudi habit of letting doors close behind them, regardless of who trailed, as they stepped briskly through the halls of the hospital complex. In time, I realized that women did not hold doors open for each other either. I found this disheartening; however, Nabil explained that Saudis presumably wanted to avoid any gestures possibly construed as flirtatious or inappropriate. Ironically, in the States, I regularly asked men to step through a doorway before me in an effort to reinforce the notion of gender equality.

I had to adapt to different kinds of working relationships in the Kingdom. Early on in my Saudi career, I sensed an unspoken rule on appropriate interactions between the sexes. When I first arrived on the scene at the hospital, the relationships with my Saudi male colleagues were cordial but less familiar. While Saudi women greeted me with sweet, shy smiles and offerings of cardamom coffee, on my first day, Saudi men rendered polite handshakes, steely reserves, and no "small talk." It became apparent that my male colleagues were not hostile, just observing their Gulf customs. In the weeks that followed, I was pleasantly surprised when this seemingly restrained working relationship gave way to an almost familial association; I was referred to as "sister," which afforded me a certain level of respect. I valued the straightforward affiliations with my male colleagues; they felt both safe and reassuring. I sensed they looked out for me and "had my back."

Working "shoulder to shoulder" with my female Saudi counterparts, I came to learn they had an acute appreciation for their career opportunities, were extremely hard-working, and remained intensely disciplined, particularly those without young children. I especially admired the work ethic of Laila—in her 20s, single, and reserved—often early to work, head buried in financial reports, willing to work on weekends without complaint, and somehow finding the time to train me on financial systems. I don't believe Laila ever invited me to her office for cardamom coffee, unlike my other female Saudi workmates.

I often felt like a surrogate mother or big sister to some of the younger female Saudi women, one of whom even stopped by my office regularly to discuss some of her more private marital challenges. "My husband isn't spending enough time with me," she fretted on one occasion. "Sometimes he goes out with other men and doesn't tell me where he's going or what he's doing," adding, "I feel that maybe he doesn't love me anymore and is not interested in me."

I admit that at times, I felt off-balance during these encounters, appreciative yet daunted by this level of trust from a workmate; I couldn't recall ever having these kinds of intimate discussions in the American workplace. "Marriage is complex and challenging," I began tentatively, trying to give my best Oprah advice. "It has its 'ups and downs,' and there are some points during a marriage when the husband and wife feel distant. You just have to nourish the marriage like you have to water a flower to make sure it grows and stays healthy."

I sometimes felt unworthy of the level of respect and trust I received from these young women, believing it could be due to my nationality. Still, I remained captivated by the unexpected authenticity of both my male and female colleagues.

At other times, I treaded lightly around cultural and traditional roles for women and men and the appropriate interactions between the two. More formal meetings required gender segregation, while regularly scheduled departmental meetings were mixed. It was at the larger, more formal gatherings of work colleagues, such as the time we welcomed a new Director of the Finance Group or celebrated the retirement of a fellow workmate, that I made an intentional effort to respect the customs of the host country. It was second nature to want to walk across the room to my male Saudi co-workers, but I had to remind myself not to. I knew it would be unseemly, at the very least, to approach my Saudi male co-workers clustered on the far side of the room to say "hi" or anything else. These instances left me feeling stifled and unsettled, wondering how this custom could promote a healthy workplace. Perhaps because KFSH and other hospitals in the Kingdom were the rare workplaces where men and women could mingle, society dictated that some vestige of tradition remain at the hospital.

My male Saudi teammate, Saad, was smart, exceedingly polite and respectful. Soft-spoken with an elegant bearing, Saad could have been from a prominent family; however, I didn't know for sure. Our working association was easy from the beginning; surprisingly, he seemed to have no issues with a female American boss. He listened attentively, asked relevant questions during our work meetings, and produced solid work. Ours was a more traditional supervisor/subordinate relationship, making it less familial than the one I shared with Saudi male peers outside my group. I also contended with the matter of my Lebanese American subordinate, Mazen, who had worked for a couple of prestigious American companies in the U.S. Cordial and self-assured, Mazen gave off an air that he knew better than others, particularly me. Mazen regularly solicited Abdullah for my job. Fortunately, I had encountered a similar situation several years earlier with an ambitious colleague when I was a finance manager with a U.S. government agency.

Thankful for the straightforward working relationship I had with Saad, I felt somewhat discouraged, at times, with Mazen. Bright, highly technical, and analytical, Mazen was an asset to our group. I needed to squelch the competitiveness and encourage more of a team effort.

I decided to speak to Abdullah about Mazen.

"Abdullah, I wanted to talk to you about my group. Things are going well, but I'm concerned a bit, about Mazen."

Abdullah looked at me quizzically; "How so?"

"Mazen does a great job and is technically skilled at what he does. But he seems to have issues with authority. He's not always receptive to me being his boss."

Abdullah leaned across his desk. "Mary, maybe you and Mazen could share managerial responsibilities. You could be a supervisor for several months, and Mazen could take over supervisor duties for a few months. You two could continue rotating responsibilities between you."

It was apparent Abdullah wanted Mazen off his back and had been thinking about this as a solution.

Maybe the trace of a frown or glare in my eyes told him this wasn't going to happen, and the matter seemed to drop from further discussion. Moving forward, I found myself focusing on promoting a balance between the team effort concept and maintaining clear lines of authority.

Through those first months and beyond, friends and family regularly corresponded with us. They wondered how work and our private lives were going in this distant land, particularly since Saudi lifestyle and culture were largely a mystery in the early 2000s. For our friends and others outside the Kingdom, there was little formal reporting on what it was like on the inside, leaving much to the imagination, unfortunately. Our e-mail missives to family and friends provided glimpses into our own lives, at least, in this remote Gulf country. I think folks were surprised to hear of my rather "normal" work experience, our sometimes unusual and frequent social activities, and our general level of contentment. I checked in with myself, from time to time, about my feelings on our new life as I wrote e-mails to close ones back home. Other than that first dreadful night in our apartment at Olaya 8, I was continually startled at my lack of sentimentality over my old life in the U.S. Even American holidays like Christmas failed to evoke strong feelings of homesickness, although I was grateful for not having to storm malls and buy presents that were often superfluous.

I was mostly comfortable and valued in my job with a slew of expatriate and Saudi friends, and often had too many social events to fit into a weekend. Of course, I was privileged as a straight, married white woman with a white-collar job in the Kingdom. And I was heartened by feeling that I could not only learn from and enjoy this culture but could feel good about telling people back home about all I was experiencing, giving them another perspective of what it was like to build a life in the Kingdom. And, very importantly for me, I looked at my watch less because I didn't feel as impatient, restless, and bored. I was increasingly "living in the moment" through the good, the challenging, and the strange.

Nabil and I often talked about work in the evenings over dinner or lunch on the hospital grounds. His workplace interactions were distinctly different than mine. He had two promising offers of work after we arrived in the Kingdom. One as a teacher of math and science at the American International School of Riyadh, and another as an engineer at a German company. Nabil preferred to continue his career as a civil engineer, and KFSH offered a job in the Engineering and Maintenance Department with a package superior to the other offers. Although our work buildings would be adjacent, allowing us to commute and have lunches together, the work environment was more challenging for Nabil. He complained during one of our lunches at the hospital cafeteria that most of his Saudi co-workers, all of whom were male, would disappear for hours without any notice. Sometimes, his staff informed Nabil they would be gone 15 minutes for prayer time, only to show up to work an hour later. The Saudis were a powerful force protected by the government and hospital and viewed Nabil as an outsider. With an unemployment rate close to 25 percent, Nabil was another expatriate taking a job from a local. Many times, in meetings with outside contractors, Nabil's co-workers excused themselves to drive their wives to an appointment or social event, and Nabil was left alone to run the meeting. Nabil had no recourse for reporting or disciplining his colleagues or staff. This was challenging for Nabil, but he mostly took it in stride, knowing this would likely not be his last career opportunity.

One evening, we grabbed falafel sandwiches on our way home from work. I asked Nabil what he thought about the differing treatment we received from our male Saudi colleagues. Nabil believed Saudi men wouldn't dare treat a woman outside their tribe unfairly, especially a Western woman. Women in the Arab world were regarded differently than men, and more so in the Gulf. There is debate over why this is so. Some say they are the weaker sex and need to be protected. Others say they are treated with utmost respect and put on a pedestal. Although more progressive, my young friend from Qatar told me the conventional thinking in the Arab Gulf (among the older generation) held that men take care of women with the woman's focus on the home and children, much like 1950s America. This friend, Suad, a young 20-something and newly minted lawyer, thought times were changing in the Arab Peninsula and women were viewed differently. Suad let it be known to me and others that she planned to be the first female judge in Qatar and help support her family. The changing times were definitely evident in my workplace. However, there was a noted difference in behavior among the men in my office.

I looked over at Nabil as we gobbled up our sandwiches at the kitchen table.

"Why does Mazen repeatedly go to our boss asking to take my position? I asked."

"It's obvious, Mary. He isn't Saudi." Nabil was always matter of fact like that.

Nabil's frequent feedback helped me understand the subtle cultural differences between countries in the Arab world.

Although feeling more comfortable in the Kingdom over time, there were always new insights to absorb, new insights to decipher. For example, most expatriates we met at work and socially were unusual in some way or another, at the tail end of a normal curve. We, ourselves, were among those who were different. I often felt out of place and detached, at least socially, in a country, the U.S., known for its freedoms and possibilities, and Nabil was certainly "out of the box." I left a perfectly fine life, in many respects, for a place with harsh and stringent cultural mores just to avoid unsettling boredom. In our several years in the Kingdom, we found certain categories that expatriates typically fell into. Those who were escaping something: a staid existence in my case, or family issues, the past, a breakup, and such. And then, some relocated to the Kingdom for financial opportunities. This was the case for those highly credentialed with PhDs and eminently trained medical researchers.

I marveled at Saudi Arabia's diverse mix of expatriates from all over the world with the largest proportion comprising manual laborers hailing from southeast Asian countries like Nepal, Sri Lanka, and India. These workers, typically construction workers and sometimes retail clerks or "tea boys," were typically younger and from countries with high poverty rates and few opportunities. They were essential, in high demand, and the foundation of the country, performing the menial jobs that Saudis would never consider. Young male Saudis, just out of college, were more interested in securing managerial jobs; however, they lacked the expertise to do so. There was one office in my department with the name of a Saudi gentleman and the title of "Finance Manager" on the door, however, that individual never showed up to the office. I never met him, but his name was on the payroll. Although a rare circumstance, it unnerved me that this occurred at all. I couldn't believe someone, probably influential, could get away with being paid for staying away from the office.

The plight of the manual laborer tore at my heartstrings while in the Kingdom and later in Qatar. They were paid poorly, although often higher than in their home countries, and were sometimes left unpaid for several months in the Arab Gulf. They were treated shabbily and provided overcrowded and dirty accommodations. The construction workers were the low men on the totem pole in the Kingdom, below even the "tea boys" and retail workers. Although there were restrictions on working outside in the summer heat, these mandates were often overlooked. It was common to see these men on cement pads of high-rise buildings under construction in the midday heat that could top 100 degrees Fahrenheit.

Nabil and I felt helpless seeing these men in dire circumstances, however, they and we had little recourse in this unfortunate circumstance. If the workers were to complain, they would likely be deported, not paid, or punished in some other way. I felt embarrassed and ashamed that we could do little more than provide bottles of water for those on the roadside after completing their shift. On a few occasions when on the way home from work or on an errand with me, Nabil stopped his car at a construction site along the road. He got out and gave each man near our car a bottle of water. It would have been inappropriate for me to do so as a woman. Nabil always had a big box of bottled water in our car trunk in case we encountered laborers. Most often, the men were surprised and suspicious of Nabil, eyes downcast, as Nabil approached them. However, once he handed the water to them, they often gave him a thankful smile. One time, when at the Dairy Queen drive-thru in Doha, Qatar, we saw a Southeast Asian laborer doing landscaping work around the building. We noticed him looking at us as we gave our ice cream order. Nabil ordered a third ice cream cone. When we received our order, Nabil handed the extra ice cream cone to the worker. The middle-aged man couldn't contain his happiness; he bowed in our direction and waved us off as we left the premises. Nabil often gave laborers at his own worksite crackers and bread. We knew these were paltry efforts in the end, but we hoped against hope these workers would ultimately return to their countries and families with financial resources to better their lives.

While my own work life had become mostly regimented and clear-cut, this was not always the case outside the office, even on the hospital grounds. Most days, the many hospital buildings, combined with the overall make-up of the staff, made it easy to mistake the KFSH premises for a small town or planned community. Browsing the magazine racks in the hospital grocery store always brought me back to reality. Black magic marker blotted out the bare arms, legs, and cleavage of the female models on the magazine covers.

My limbs stiffened when I first opened one of the women's magazines to find each of the pictures of young models with similar blackened arms and cleavage; each magazine I flipped through was the same. Later, I discovered that one of the informal duties of the Mutawa, or religious police, involved shielding the community from even the slightest hints of sexuality.

This sort of seemingly nonsensical "Mutawa activity" provided fodder for uneasy chuckles and long discussions about our mutual unconventional experiences within the Kingdom— at weekend expatriate gatherings or evening fetes. Many of my single female expatriate friends who remained in Saudi Arabia for an extended period eventually concluded that the financial rewards and unique professional and personal experiences gleaned from life in the Kingdom outweighed concerns over eccentric and baffling pursuits by the Mutawa.

The places Nabil and I encountered Mutawa were in malls, places of large gatherings, and Western-oriented shops. Hanaa and Samer coached us on how to spot the religious police; they wore a ghutra over their head without the round black agal, and their thobe was mid-calf length rather than to the ankle. And they had long beards. In the malls, they appeared in pairs with an armed policeman. The first time Nabil and I visited a mall solo, we were holding hands and encountered such a trio. As a novice, I did not have a scarf over my head. One of the Mutawa growled, *"ghatee, ghatee"* (cover, cover) and I promptly put my scarf, which was around my shoulders, over my head. The other Mutawa screeched, *Sheel, sheel* (remove your hand). I could feel Nabil's hand twitch in mine as he pulled it away, and I knew we were in trouble. Nabil responded with "She's my wife" in Arabic. "She's your wife in your house, only," was the clipped response. My mind darted and blurred with thoughts of the distressing "Mutawa article" from my Washington, DC neighbor as I waited for further interrogation. Would Nabil be taken away in handcuffs? And what would I do then? I was thoroughly relieved when, suddenly, the threesome purposefully strode away. As we walked further down the corridor, Nabil said, "That was so stupid; they're just trying to show power." Although rattled at the thought we could be hauled off at any time, whether true or not, I settled myself with the idea that the Mutawa wanted expatriates to respect their culture. They needed Saudi Arabia to remain conservative and not become another Dubai.

Otherwise, we regularly observed these religious individuals as private citizens, without their entourage, on and off hospital grounds where they blended in with the general public. I was surprised to see them speak openly with men and women (more with men, however) at the hospital, where they seemed reserved and polite, much like the larger Saudi population.

The official Mutawa was known for unpredictable behavior. One Valentine's Day Eve, Nabil went in search of red roses for me and was happy to find a flower shop on the hospital premises that was selling roses. He went back the following day to purchase the flowers only to find out the Mutawa had swept through the flower shops throughout Riyadh and disposed of all red roses. And then there were the seemingly random years the Mutawa forbade the sale of Christmas trees.

Several months into our stay in the Kingdom, we had another, scarier encounter with the Mutawa. We had many wonderful and uneventful restaurant meals in Riyadh; however, there was one exception. We were seated for dinner at Crystals, a posh restaurant in the center of Riyadh, with the wife of our tax accountant. Crystals, located in the striking Al Faisaliyah Tower, holds a magnificent hotel and extensive retail and office space. Our table was immaculately set with one of the arrangements of fresh flowers encased in a glass receptacle at each place setting. Imposing dragon figures embellished the plates atop the glass cases. I did a double-take over the extravagance and glanced over at Nabil, who was shaking his head in apparent agreement.

The restauranteurs knew our friend Edna and surprised us with complimentary hors d'oeuvres of sushi with fresh fruit, followed by luscious mushroom soup, appetizers with bits of lobster, calamari, and shrimp, which I mistook for the main entrée, and a huge platter with hearty-looking lobster, tuna, hamour, more shrimp, and other fish I couldn't place. Seven waiters skillfully and graciously served us, expertly balancing attentiveness with consideration of our privacy. I was filled to the brim, completely absorbed by the food, spices, impeccable service, and setting. We could not, however, forgo dessert, a variety of exquisite chocolates served on a multi-tiered silver tray. Midway through our meal, Nabil leaned over and whispered, "Look at those two tables." I surveyed the room and saw unusual activity at two nearby tables. One with three young women two tables away and the other with two men at an adjacent table. Nabil said, "They're exchanging phone numbers. Look, the woman is holding up two fingers and now four fingers. And now she's holding up eight." I tried not to stare but noticed one of the men tapping his cell phone as the woman signaled with her fingers in the direction of the man. Soon afterward, the twosome was on their phones, darting glances bouncing back and forth.

I was surprised at the bravery of these young people, as open flirtation is forbidden in the Kingdom. Taken by the unexpected diversion and satiated, I left the restaurant appreciative and content, with a smidgeon of guilt at overindulging. Nabil, Edna, and I chatted lightheartedly as we walked through the lobby of the building when out of my peripheral vision, I spotted three men in Saudi garb approaching. As they came closer, I saw two of them in the shorter thobe and ghutra without agal. "They're Mutawa," I thought. I immediately covered my head with the black scarf around my neck. And soon, they trailed us, getting ever closer. Nabil grabbed my hand. Why were they following us? What could we have possibly done? As we picked up the pace, Nabil scanned me and Edna head to toe.

"Edna, you're not wearing your scarf! Put it on!"

Edna's eyes widened, and she rifled through her purse. "Oh no, I forgot it!"

Under his breath, eyelids twitching, Nabil barked, "There's a women's restroom. Get in there."

My body heat rising and somehow sensing we shouldn't appear to be blatantly disappearing, I took Edna's arm, and we expeditiously strode into the bathroom. Every one of my nerves on edge, I looked over at Edna in the corner of the restroom. Her eyes red with tears welling, she frantically searched every corner of her purse for her scarf. I was scared and infuriated by the situation. I couldn't believe Edna forgot her scarf and we were being hounded by the Mutawa as a result. We were in an upscale establishment frequented by Westerners. Why would the Mutawa be harassing us? What would happen if we left the restroom too early? Would the Mutawa arrest Edna, or perhaps Nabil, since he was our escort and should have ensured that our dress was proper? I could just envision Nabil outside the restroom with the Mutawa being worried out of his mind for our safety and perhaps planning a course of action. His possibilities were extremely limited, though. If he made too much of a fuss, he could have been carted off to jail. Would we be in this restroom all night? At my wits end on how to not be dragged off by the religious police, it seemed like nearly half an hour before Nabil took the risk of opening the bathroom door, calling out, "Mary, Edna, come on out. The Mutawa are gone." Spent, I was certain that the evening would not end well. Dazed over what had just happened and the panic of what could have happened, we made our way to the car. We climbed into the Jeep, an eerie silence filling the car on the drive home.

CHAPTER 9

9/11

After living in the Kingdom for 10 months, we became more comfortable with Saudi customs and traditions while holding a healthy concern for the Mutawa. Despite the several run-ins with the religious police that could have led to jail time, particularly for Nabil as my escort, we learned how to balance full lives while remaining discreet. We had many friends, both Saudis and expatriates, who kept our lives centered and content. Having slipped into a comfortable new rhythm, I could imagine staying for an indefinite period.

September 11, 2001, started as an ordinary workday. Driving into work, Nabil and I talked about the wonderful weekend getaway we just had to Abha, a village in the mountains of southern Saudi Arabia near the Yemen border. We visited an unusual women-run basket souk, rode an aerial tramway from Jabal Al Sooda through the rugged Sarawat mountains, learned about the *flower men* of the Tihama, toured the multi-tiered clay houses of this highland region and a "hanging village," and encountered bands of wild baboons. The trip was beyond what I could have possibly imagined: exciting, scary, and rejuvenating all at once. I imagined visiting again.

Once I got back to work, my day was consumed with collecting data for a financial report that would be discussed the next day, as well as a usual conversation during a mint tea break with female colleagues. Later in the workday, a bit after 4:00 PM, I heard several people scrambling through the corridor speaking tangled Arabic. I couldn't understand what they were saying. The inflections were high-pitched and choppy, yet sober like someone had just witnessed a horrible accident and was telling his colleagues about it. I left my office and found my colleague, Joseph, an Indian national who had worked as a financial analyst at KFSH since the hospital's inception in the 1970s. He and others huddled in a tight scrum, their voices overlapping like cascading water. I couldn't discern what was going on. Something about planes and New York City. Had a plane hit a building in New York City? And maybe more than one?

I called Nabil in the adjacent office building.

I spurted, "Something's happening in the U.S. Something about planes hitting buildings in New York. Have you heard anything?"

"No, I haven't," replied Nabil, a trace of concern in his voice.

"Come on over to my building. Let's find a TV. We need to figure out what's going on."

Tensions rose in the few short minutes it took Nabil to get to my office. People were gathering in offices and hallways, looking upset. A colleague shouted from inside an office that a second plane hit a building in New York city. My head spun.

"Have you seen what's going on in the U.S.?" hollered a colleague from another financial department as he repeatedly pulled on his beard.

"No, we haven't," we yelled in unison.

"There's a TV in one of the manager's offices. It's over there!" the man shouted.

Nabil and I scurried into the office. Others had squeezed together, watching the unbelievable events unfold in New York City. CNN was reporting that there were two planes. I couldn't believe what I was seeing. An image of a plane flying through an entire building. Plumes of smoke spilled from the upper floors. And a video of a second plane blasting through another skyscraper. More billowing smoke and fire. People were jumping out of windows. They suspected commercial planes. One hit the North Tower of the World Trade Center in Lower Manhattan, and the other the South Tower. I felt detached, unable to absorb it all. What about family and friends at home? Would there be more attacks? Silence permeated the office, eyes glued to the TV. Now and then, scattered Arabic and an air of foreboding filled the room over the agitated tones of the TV newscasters.

"We have to get home!" I muttered in a daze.

I had hardly finished my sentence before Nabil led me through what had become a throng of spectators. No one seemed to notice our departure.

We rushed through the building, people in motion and nervously chattering along the way. All I wanted was to be with my husband and two poodles in the safety and privacy of our living room. I needed to block out the noise and decipher for myself what was going on in America. Arriving at our Jeep in the hospital parking lot, we clumsily climbed in, and Nabil sped away at a fast clip toward the Diplomatic Quarter. We hardly said a word; the only thing I heard was the roaring of our Jeep's engine.

As Nabil parked the car adjacent to our building, I felt numb. I barely recall my feet finding their way, but Nabil's arm in mine steered us out of the car and toward our building. As we approached our apartment, we saw several people at the end of the street. We were drawn to them. They were American hospital staff; one of them, face ashen, confirmed the first and second Twin Towers had fallen to the ground. Also, something about the Pentagon. I asked the man instantly, what about the Pentagon? He said initial reports said that it also had been struck.

"Oh, no," I cried out, tears pooling in my eyes. I reached out and grabbed this total stranger and held him close. I wanted to feel better; I wanted us all to get through this insanity. Somewhere in my being, I felt he probably needed a hug, too. Nabil shakily reached out to the man; they shared a deep embrace. Nabil and I hugged; I never wanted to let go.

We had to get to our apartment to see and hear first-hand what was going on in New York and Washington, DC. We stumbled up the stairs and dashed to the TV. I gasped. One tower was slowly collapsing like vertical dominoes; dark smoke and soot spilled out of the crumpling upper floors. And it wouldn't stop until the whole structure was a pile of steamy rubble on the ground. It was a replay of the South Tower falling multiple times.

I turned to Nabil; there were no words.

Glancing back at the TV, I saw another replay of the building toppling to the ground. Something was different, though. Through my haze, I concentrated on the disjointed words coming through the TV. The second tower, the North Tower, buckled floor by floor to the ground on a continuous loop. Hordes of people, men with ties and suits and women with work dresses, their faces and clothes covered in gray ash, floundered away from the buildings through clouds of heavy soot. The ghastliness contrasted with the supreme bravery of the New York Fire Department rushing into the smoldering buildings shortly after the planes struck.

Soon, we heard news confirming that a third plane struck the Pentagon and a fourth crashed in Pennsylvania.

I was in a jumble of thoughts, but I knew I had to be in touch with my family. They were in Georgia, but was there a possibility that they could be in danger? They lived near Atlanta, the capital of the southeast; could they be a target? It was impossible to get through on the phone. Dad wrote the first e-mail on the morning (EST) of 9/11/2001, shortly after the attack. The last e-mail from me to my parents had related the incredible visit we had to Abha just days before 9/11.

Dad wrote: *Hi Mary and Nabil—As you are probably aware there has been a rather significant terrorist attack on NYC and the Pentagon. We have been following the events since early this morning and I must say at times it was like watching a Hollywood movie. It is at times like this that, naturally, we become increasingly concerned about your safety. It is the randomness of these types of attacks that give us concern. We remember the marine barracks in Beirut, the Cole recently, the various airline incidents (most notably Lockerbie). I sincerely trust that our confidence in the security mindedness of the Saudi government is warranted and takes all the necessary measures to protect its expats, especially the two that are most precious to us. Keep us posted. Love, Mom and Dad*

Dad was composed in his e-mail, which was his way. It was comforting to hear his steady, level voice come through at this moment.

I wrote back several days later that the attacks seemed unreal; the enormity of it all would take some time to completely fathom. There was greater military security at the entrance to the Diplomatic Quarter, where we lived. At both the Diplomatic Quarter and KFSH, military personnel were positioned with automatic machine guns. Anti-aircraft weapons fitted on military jeeps were placed around the city and pointed toward the sky. The whole world seemed on edge. As advised, Nabil checked under our car before we left for anywhere, a completely nerve-wracking practice. I remembered my distress in early 2000 when traveling with the US-Saudi Business Council from one meeting to another; I watched guards search under our official car with long rods attached to oversized mirrors before entering Saudi government and business locations. Even then, Saudi Arabia was on alert.

For the time being, we would "sit tight" and watch CNN. Not having encountered anything resembling preparations for battle or war, the thought of the U.S. or the Kingdom having to fend off potential terrorist activity was deeply unnerving. To survive, I became philosophical about it all, creating emotional armor. If it happened, it happened. Nabil had been through war; many countries around the world were on a war footing.

An immediate concern surrounded the friends we knew at the Pentagon and federal buildings close to the Pentagon, including my own former DC agency. Had they made it through the assault? We sent hurried e-mails. One who was working at the Pentagon had escaped immediately after the attack and driven home with other friends from the office. We were relieved to hear the news.

Others we heard from said they were okay, and those who worked in the district indicated there was complete gridlock in the city as people attempted to flee the disaster. There was one person we hadn't heard from who worked at the Pentagon. Nabil wrote all the mutual friends we knew, and we waited anxiously each day to hear. Four days later, we found out he was okay; he had been on a business trip to Alabama.

Within a couple of hours of the attacks, a friend wrote: *Here in the Washington DC area, we're stunned as is the rest of the country. I was across the river at my office about 2 miles from the Pentagon, and the smoke was clearly visible. The federal government shut down. As I write this, the DC National Guard is patrolling the city in Humvees... they have been federalized, as have the Maryland Natl Guard. DC, VA and MD have declared states of emergency. One of the most dramatic aspects of this terrible day is the silence in the skies over the DC area, skies which normally carry the sound of planes landing and departing from nearby National Airport ... that silence is broken only by the sound of sirens and the occasional fighter jet (yes fighter jet) that is among those that are patrolling the airspace over DC. That's what it has come to... the Air Force and the DC Air National Guard is providing air cover over the Nation's capital. Today's attack was not just against buildings, planes and their occupants. It was an attack on a free society, on free speech, on free thought, the freedom to associate, the freedom to be different, the freedom to be a peace-loving American, whether born here or an immigrant. The temptation may be to blame the foreign-born who are now here in the U.S., even though the majority are likely to be hard-working immigrants to this great country, immigrants just like the millions who have previously arrived and helped make this country great. We cannot bring back those who have died. We cannot erase the damage and the pain. We can, however, vow that we will defend our freedoms and resist the temptation to isolate our Nation and restrict our freedoms. To do otherwise would be to grant the terrorists yet another victory. The Chinese symbol for crisis is a combination of the symbols for both danger and opportunity. The crisis we face today, as horrific as it is, represents an opportunity to demonstrate our resolve to attack those who have attacked us, while at the same time defending our precious freedoms. God bless the people on those hijacked planes, those in the Trade Center towers and at the Pentagon, those who died trying to rescue them and those who are still risking their lives to help. And God bless the United States. Washington, DC*

Our friend was exquisite in expressing what we and many Americans felt on that awful day.

Another friend wrote about support from the international community. The scenes of the playing of the 'Star Spangled Banner' at Buckingham Palace and the singing of 'Amazing Grace' in Germany brought *many people here in the States to tears. In closing, God Bless America and all of our friends. Even though it will never be quite the same, life will slowly resume. When we meet next, the hugs and handshakes will have much more meaning.*

Nabil and I were disheartened to watch news reports of a small group of Palestinians celebrating in Israel, but later learned that most Palestinians were very much against what they saw on TV. The cameraman filming the cheering Palestinians had threats against him by other Palestinians, who were distraught over the scene. We also heard that a certain number of patients on the KFSH hospital wards were pleased over the attack; big, powerful America was caught flat-footed and vulnerable. Nabil, the emotional one in our small family, was agitated by such rumors.

"Mary, I can't live in a country that wishes harm to our beautiful country, America," Nabil exclaimed over breakfast of Lebanese omelets.

I twinged. "I'm amazed, but not really surprised, Nabil, with your patriotism for the U.S."

After all, this was the same Nabil who grew up loathing America and Jews. Chanting in the streets of Mafraq, Jordan, when he was 11 years old, "Death to America, death to Israel, God bless our leader Yasser Arafat." And here he was, fully standing with and supporting America. Over the years, Nabil told me almost everything about his challenging and conflicted childhood and how, ultimately, he was grateful to become an American citizen.

I wrote Dad and Mom that we were keeping a close eye on anti-American sentiment. I thought it was a more limited viewpoint, but Nabil didn't necessarily agree with me. He was more inclined to leave the country and leave those sentiments behind. For my part, I drew a parallel with people in America who were against "all Arabs" in the U.S. and abroad. These sentiments were irrational and felt from a perspective of ignorance or heightened passions. I told my parents that we continued to feel safe but were aware and cautious. We were discussing various courses of action based on different scenarios and would definitely keep them informed of all that we felt, heard, or did. I added it was interesting to observe and "take in" events and reactions from a different perspective given the country we were in. Though horrific, we were in truly historic times.

Although I wanted to appease my parents' worries, Nabil and I were anxious and alert. Each day brought fears of what might happen in America or to us.

In time, we would find out from news reports that 15 of the 19 attackers were Saudi and were part of Al Qaeda. I was sick to my stomach, baffled. Saudis were my colleagues, friends, confidants . . . But this was Al Qaeda, a different animal. Personally, though, the rug had been pulled from under me. I had been "alive" in Saudi Arabia, reawakened by the generosity of the Arab culture and easy social mixing; I was more human and less dependent on my logical side. I was enmeshed in the expatriate lifestyle and all its perks: local plays and concerts, holiday choirs, and Tai Quan Do lessons. Living in KFSH housing, there were no bills to be paid (most service costs like rent, water, and electricity were covered by KFSH), and securing inexpensive housekeepers was the normal practice, all of which made a thriving personal life possible. But this Al-Qaeda threat was too serious and pervasive; we didn't want to become targets. Maybe Nabil was right in wanting to leave the Kingdom. And a question swirled, almost imperceptibly, through my mind during those first days. Was I betraying my own country by considering to stay in Saudi Arabia? We agreed to wait to receive instructions and direction from the U.S. Embassy in Riyadh.

In the next couple of weeks, I became more reflective, and wrote Dad and Mom: *When we first woke up this morning, I was glad we* weren't in the U.S., as Nabil is of Lebanese heritage, and American people are so outraged, as they should be. It is sometimes hard, though, for people to separate out individuals from groups of fanatics. We feel fortunate to be where we are. Nabil and I were at our Saudi friends, the Omari's, home last night. (The family with the seven daughters.) They were terribly distraught over what happened in the U.S. They were very warm and supportive of Nabil and my concerns. It was such a good break to be away from the constant media attention for a short period of time. It was obvious how much the family did not want to believe that an Arab group could be perpetrators of such acts. They kept repeating that Saudi Arabia was like a relative to the U.S.—that Saudis love Americans.

We were in constant touch with family. It was important for us to let them know, daily, we were okay, and for them to let us know they were okay with our decisions, although I knew they were very concerned.

Dad wrote in response to one of my early e-mails: *Americans are finally seeing violence and death on their very doorstep. As you know our wars have always been exported since the Civil War. Seeing such devastation on our very soil is certainly different from seeing it in the Middle East nightly on the TV. It is inescapable not to come back to the devastation wrought by these horrific acts. I personally think you are as secure where you are as anywhere. If you were still in DC, you would have been dangerously close to the attack on the Pentagon.*

I was relieved that Dad was keeping a balanced perspective.

We felt a bit more relieved when we received an e-mail message from KFSH Medical and Clinical Operations (MCO), headed up by a Saudi. "I continue to believe that the Kingdom is one of the safer places in the world to live and work. We have received assurances from the relevant governmental agencies that additional measures have been taken in Saudi Arabia to protect its citizens as well as the expatriates working within the Kingdom. However, if some of our expatriate staff would prefer to return to their homes, either on a short-term or long-term basis, special measures have been taken, in conjunction with Personnel, Finance, and the Passport Section, so that their departure would be facilitated." MCO even arranged for an Employee Counselor to moderate focus groups where employees could air their concerns with their co-workers.

Nabil and I continued to have many lengthy discussions about what we should do after the 9/11 attacks. When I returned to the office on September 13, I was surprised when Abdullah, my boss, made it a point to ask if my family and friends were safe in the U.S. He seemed relieved when I told him everyone was fine. Several days later, as I walked through the office area, I practically bumped into Abdulaziz, another Saudi finance manager, as I rounded the corner between our offices. "Oh, sorry," practically speaking over each other. I rarely interacted with Abdulaziz, as we were in different finance sections. He always seemed reserved; our interactions were more formal and tended to be limited to larger Finance meetings we both attended.

"How are you doing, Mary?" his voice warm and friendly.

"I'm okay," I responded, surprised at the informality. This would be the first time I had a real conversation with Abdulaziz.

"I mean about the attacks in America."

I considered saying I was all right, concealing my true horror over the attacks in my home country. However, I could sense he earnestly wanted to know my emotional state.

"We are both very concerned about staying in the Kingdom, and Nabil feels strongly that we should leave," I said.

"Mary, I want to tell you something," the manager declared.

My throat tightened, anxious about what might come next.

"If anyone came through those doors threatening you, I know

that I, or any of your co-workers, would stand between you and the attacker. We would never let anything happen to you."

I took a breath. My limbs relaxed.

"Thank you," was all I could muster.

Later in the day, on the way home, I told Nabil about the manager. Nabil didn't know the man, so he wasn't sure how to take what he said. It was a bit of a turning point for me, though. I felt cautiously optimistic.

In the days after 9/11, official news reported that the Saudi government was one among many other Arab governments that supported the U.S. against Al Qaeda. The news was a comfort. Since the U.S. relationship with Saudi Arabia would remain friendly, we determined it was safe to continue working and living in the Kingdom.

On October 7, 2001, the U.S. attacked Al Qaeda forces that were hiding in the mountains of Afghanistan.

Within some months, we adapted to a new normal. We knew the threat was out there but were distracted by the routine of work and a full social life. I continued to be ever-busy with refining the new budget process at work. And we resumed our Friday fish dinners with expatriate friends, and social events at the U.S. Embassy, even venturing out to camp in the desert.

CHAPTER 10

LOVE AND MARRIAGE

One afternoon, when Nabil and I lived in Qatar, we were out shopping at Souk Al-Waqif, a popular marketplace in Doha, and stopped for lunch at a favorite café. This particular souk was often teeming with Qataris and expatriates wandering the maze-like cobblestoned alleyways. The smells of spices mixed with bakhoor and lamb roasting on huge spits for shawarmas, permeated the air. Nabil and I ordered *manakeesh*, a spicy dish with za'atar -- a mixture of thyme, sumac, oregano, marjoram, and sesame seeds, on freshly baked pita bread. Our Indian waiter asked if we wanted the Jordanian or Lebanese za'atar. Nabil later told me he didn't know the difference. Sentimentally, he simply said, "The Lebanese kind."

Nabil leaned over to one of the two women eating at the table next to us. Both in abayas and headscarves, one middle-aged and the other younger were in deep conversation. Bursts of intense, muffled conversation between the women were interrupted only by careful sips of Turkish coffee.

Nabil boldly asked, "Excuse me, please, ladies, what is the difference between Jordanian and Lebanese za'atar?"

The older woman, who we later found out was named Mai, fell silent. She raised her eyebrows. Men typically don't address women in public in the Arab Gulf. She glanced at me, probably doing the mental math of geography: Westerner, definitely. Mai regained her composure, and was most kind to explain that Jordanian za'atar was often green and Lebanese often red (and somewhat spicy, as the sumac is stronger). Mai asked where we were from and was impressed that we both spoke Arabic. Nabil disclosed he was Lebanese, and he taught me some Arabic. We chatted about ourselves and how we came to Qatar. They were surprised it was my idea to come to the Middle East. After several minutes, Mai and her daughter, Fatima, excused themselves as they were very busy planning for Fatima's wedding.

"*Mabrouk*" (congratulations), I said enthusiastically.

"*Allah ybarek feekie*" (God bless you) came the reply.

As she collected her shopping bags, Mai asked me, "Have you ever been to a Qatari wedding? My daughter is marrying a Qatari man."

"Unfortunately, no, I haven't," I replied.

"We need to change that," Mai said with a thin smile.

Enthralled by the thought, I beamed inside, and we exchanged phone numbers. A couple of weeks later, Mai called me, inviting us to a barbecue dinner at her home. I happily accepted, and we savored barbecue lamb, chicken, and mezze and met Badia and Rami, friends of Mai and her husband, all Palestinian, the following weekend.

As we all left Mai's home, Rami half-grinned at Nabil and insisted, almost commanded, that Nabil and I come to a barbecue at their home the next weekend. Although a bit perplexed, as we had just met, we were delighted at the invitation. Like Mai and her family, Rami and his wife, Badia, had lived in Doha for many years. We became fast friends with Rami and Badia, spending nearly every weekend with them. They had four children, Randa, Ali, Rula, and Adel, ranging in age from late teens to early 30s, all born in Doha. Still, they were not allowed Qatari citizenship, per Qatar immigration policy. As is the tradition for unmarried adult children, they all lived at home. Badia was petite with expressive green eyes that revealed her sensitive soul. At the same time, Rami was tall, solid and the captain of the family who enjoyed frequent gatherings of family and friends. The eldest child, Randa, was quiet, well-read, and divorced. In the Arab Gulf, it is customary for a divorced woman to move back into her parents' home or her brother's if her parents are deceased. Randa was more subdued than the other three children and would often retire to her room before our evenings came to a close. A favorite of ours; Randa was down to earth and a good listener. She seemed to have a greater sense of the world, having been married and divorced. Randa was held in high regard within the family; she worked in the finance arena and was the primary breadwinner. This was rather startling, however, refreshing, as Arab Gulf women are not typically the main household providers.

Badia worked as a schoolteacher, and Rami was more retired than anything. Ali, in his mid-20s, and Rula, in her early 20s, were the outgoing ones in the family—Ali with his animated stories, and Rula directing the music, dance, and sing-alongs at our get-togethers. Rula had sparkling blue eyes; I was never sure if they were her natural color or contact lenses. Young Gulf women were prone to change their lovely brown eyes to blue or green one of the few ways to distinguish themselves, as the abaya was dictated by their culture. The youngest child, Adel, was sort of in-between in terms of personality. Being the young one, he was polite, friendly, and a first-year college student. The family introduced us to popular Arabic music, including the Lebanese singer, Fares Karam, famous for his *dabke* (Arab line dancing) tunes featuring the tabla and *mijwiz* (Arab flute). Rula joyfully taught us the Palestinian, Jordanian, and Lebanese intricate footwork of the dabke, which includes leaps and stamping. Our times with Rami, Badia, and family were always festive with day trips to the desert, sometimes with henna artists, or excursions to the beach where we'd all swim fully clothed. When our close American friend, Anna, visited us for several weeks in Doha, our Palestinian friends could not have been kinder, pampering her with fine jewelry, lavish homemade meals, and henna sessions.

One evening sitting outside in their courtyard sharing an elaborate meal of mezze with stuffed grape leaves and squash, baba ghanoush, hummus, and a full hamour, Badia rose ceremoniously from her seat, her face flushed.

Holding on to the back of her chair, with a soft, confident voice, she said, "I have something to announce."

The table became silent. I steadied myself for what I knew would be significant news.

"Our son, Ali, has met a beautiful lady. Her name is Zahra, and we all went to visit her family. They seemed to be very nice, and Zahra is not only pretty but also very kind."

Almost in unison, Nabil and I shouted out, "*Alf mabrouk*" (a thousand congratulations), a popular celebratory expression that I learned in Saudi Arabia when one of my work colleagues had a baby.

I even did my version of ululating: my right hand cupped over my mouth, and I hummed hard with my tongue brushing up and down against the back of my upper front teeth.

"We cannot wait for you, Mary, and Nabil to meet Zahra and her family."

Nabil and I beamed proudly, feeling grateful to be considered part of the family.

Nabil asked Ali how he met Zahra. He loved hearing peoples' stories.

With an impish smile, Ali disclosed that he met Zahra when driving to work. She was on the side of the road standing by her car, and Ali sensed she needed help. He pulled over, changed her flat tire and asked Zahra to follow him to the mechanic's shop to fix the tire. Ali and Zahra determined their families came from the same area of Palestine. Since the two families were Palestinian, Ali told Zahra it would be great if their families met. Because of their shared background, Zahra and Ali felt comfortable exchanging phone numbers. As Palestinians, it was not odd for them to meet this way. The remainder of the courtship and ultimate marriage would be mostly conventional for the young couple (except for the wedding reception).

As we sat for our dessert in the family's lush courtyard surrounded by colorful cut flowers and green foliage, Badia, her eyes glowing, revealed, "When we visited Zahra's family in the last few days, they told us their family rejected other proposals, but were happy to accept our family's proposal."

I had goosebumps, feeling the same sense of pride and joy that I knew our friends must be experiencing.

On another occasion at our home, Rami and family brought a large full hamour with rice from a fresh seafood shop. The silver tray, carrying the white meaty fish, was nearly two and a half feet long. The side eye of the fish stared at me, and I looked back guiltily as Nabil and I carried the tray to the back courtyard behind our villa. Earlier in the day, Nabil and I arranged the patio with a long table covered by a white tablecloth with decorative swirling designs embedded in the fabric. Sitting in the middle of our vegetable garden surrounded by a fully blossoming magnolia tree and colorful flowering bushes, our table held lit candles, along with Nabil's tabouli and fattoush. When Badia, her husband, Rami, and four adult children arrived, along with Ali's fiancé, Zahra, we warmly welcomed them and led them to our back patio.

As we sat in the calm night air enjoying our meal, I was very curious to know what dating was like in the Arab Peninsula. I had stereotypical images of veils and arranged marriages. Was that even accurate at all? Although they were Palestinian, Rami and Badia said their marital customs were similar to those of the Arab Gulf. Rami leaning forward, explained that the *Jahaa*, the engagement ritual, and the *Aqed Zawaaj*, the marriage agreement, were integral parts of the marital process, both solemn rites taking place in the presence of a religious sheik. Eyes intent on ours, Rami continued. The marriage agreement, or Aqed Zawaaj, was signed by the bride and groom, the bride's father, the groom's father, and two male Muslim witnesses.

Although Nabil had lived in Jordan and Lebanon through his early 20s, he had no occasion or reason to attend Muslim wedding preparations. He grew up in a Christian household and community. He had only witnessed his oldest sister, Aida's wedding when he was four years old and his other sister, Sonia's, wedding as an older teenager. These ceremonies were traditional Christian events. We were both surprised at how solemn, holy, and structured the pre-marital practices were in the Arab Peninsula.

After our guests left and we were getting ready for bed, Nabil and I agreed it would be a unique privilege to attend any of the functions of the traditional Arab Gulf marital proceedings. So, Nabil was more than delighted when several months later, in Spring 2008, Rami invited Nabil to attend the Arab Jahaa for Ali, (men only), the holy event in which close family members, friends of the bride and groom, and a religious sheik, assemble at the home of the bride's father to formalize the engagement of the bridal couple. While Nabil was with the men, I was at our housing compound clubhouse with Ali and Zahra's female family members and friends, preparing for a celebratory reception.

Later, Nabil told me he was asked to drive Rami and Mazen, Rami's best friend, to Zahra's parents in the lead car to the Jahaa; he was honored to do so. It was an exhilarating scene; the procession of cars became longer and longer the closer they were to the bride's home, as more vehicles followed behind Nabil's car, honking in revelry. The tone soon became somber, though, as Nabil said he and the two men were seated next to Zahra's father in the garden in front of the house. There were maybe 100 rented wooden chairs in a huge circle. Rami sat to the left side of the bride's father, Mazen next to Rami, and Nabil next to Mazen, a place of privilege. Ali sat to the right of the bride's father. Soon after, more men arrived at the Jahaa and filled every single chair in the garden with knees touching. The Muslim Sheikh arrived several minutes after all the men gathered, and sat between Ali and the father of Zahra.

The Sheikh solemnly spoke in Ali's direction: "May Allah shower his blessings upon you and join you together in goodness. And may you have many children." The Sheikh continued with recommendations to the groom on how to have a good marriage and be kind and fair to his future wife and their children. A few minutes later, the Sheikh rose from his chair. The congregants stood up, and the groom and fathers of the bride and groom and Nabil shook the Sheikh's hand and thanked him. Rami paid a fee to the Sheikh, and the Sheikh quietly slipped into the night. Soon after, Rami and Ali exchanged hugs and planted kisses on the cheeks of Zahra's father. Nabil felt somewhat awkward, as he didn't know what to expect at the Jahaa and wanted to be respectful of the special occasion. Although he was the only non-Muslim man at the ceremony, and despite some initial jitters, he ultimately felt as if he was one of them and was grateful for the experience.

While Nabil and the other men attended the Jahaa, the women and I decorated the clubhouse with streamers, balloons, and banners. Rula became our makeshift DJ. The music, contemporary Arabic, was loud and the dance free-flowing. Some sipped aromatic cardamom coffee along the perimeter of the room. Most women wore colorful and stylish dresses, and others wore simple abayas. Perfume and bakhoor filled the air. The occasion culminated with the shrill, undulating intonations from several of the women erupting into the night air, signaling the arrival of the bride, groom, and male relatives and friends, Nabil among them. Zahra was in an exquisite blue gown with alluring makeup. The gathering expanded with the arrival of men and the bride and became a spirited celebration, the guests feasting on an assortment of catered food, mounds of lamb and rice, and Lebanese mezze. Before leaving, Badia presented Zahra with a gold watch, necklace, earrings, and a bracelet in a pink velvet gift box. Zahra remained restrained (it would have been bad-mannered to behave otherwise); however, the slight glint in her eyes revealed her delight. Similar gifts would be conferred on Zahra by Badia with a certain ceremonial flourish before and at the time of the wedding; a customary marital gesture along the Arabian Peninsula.

One Friday evening, we gathered at Badia and Rami's home with Badia's relatives for dinner. As we enjoyed cardamom coffee and *knafeh* (a sweet dessert cheese pastry saturated with syrup), Um Essam (mother of Essam), Badia's second cousin, abruptly interrupted the group's conversation. She asked Badia how much money she and Rami were paying for the *mahr* (dowry) for Ali and Zahra's wedding.

While I bristled at this audacious question, Badia didn't flinch when responding about the wedding cost.

"Oh, you all are paying more than we did for Essam's wedding," Um Essam replied.

The two ladies competed on who would ultimately pay more for the extravagant wedding gown, wedding hall, food, wedding music, decorations, and flowers.

Badia boasted that she paid more for the *jahez* (jewelry, dresses, and accessories) for Zahra, the bride.

It felt odd to think about the solemnity of much of the marital ritual contrasted against the extravagance of the final wedding celebration. I was not only surprised to learn that the groom's family paid for all wedding expenses in the Arabian Peninsula but at how freely money matters were discussed. Nabil explained later that evening that it is not uncommon in the Gulf and the larger Arab world to openly discuss money concerns. It didn't matter the setting or who asked the question. It was natural to hear relatives, neighbors, or friends ask how much your house or car cost or inquire about your salary. Several Saudis and Qataris asked us how much it would cost to buy Maci and Coco, and Badia and Rami felt no qualms about asking about Nabil's and my income. I would never get used to this.

We were all so connected that Badia and Rami invited Nabil and me to attend the Aqed Zawaaj (marriage contract) ceremony, which would take place before the wedding celebration for Ali and Zahra. This ritual, segregated by gender, would be held in early summer 2008. I was astonished by this great honor normally bestowed only on family members. When Nabil and I arrived at Badia and Rami's home, the designated location for the special ritual, Nabil was immediately ushered into the salon along with the other men, including the fathers of the bride and groom, male family members and close friends, and the Sheikh. I was directed into the adjoining living room with Badia gingerly holding my hand as she guided me to a chair next to hers.

Nabil and the men sat along the walls of the salon, with the Sheikh seated between Ali and Zahra's father. The Sheikh solemnly prayed verses from the Quran while the men bowed their heads. After the prayers, Zahra's father called out to Zahra in the living room to come into the salon. Zahra slowly and with intention, like a soldier, entered the salon. As the ritual progressed, Badia diplomatically asked the women in the living room to be quiet during the ceremony so she and the rest of us could hear the proceedings in the next room. It seemed they wanted to be ready the moment all relevant parties signed the Aqed Zawaaj.

In the salon, Zahra stood alongside Ali, and the Sheikh gestured where the bridal couple needed to sign. Ali signed the marriage agreement first. Ali then passed the pen to Zahra, and she soberly signed the agreement next to Ali's name. The witnesses were next. The agreement was passed along to Zahra's father for his signature, then to Rami, and finally to the Sheikh. Zahra's father quietly said "mabrouk" (congratulations) to his daughter, and she gracefully exited the room.

When the marriage was official, female relatives and guests cupped their hands to their mouths, producing the familiar high-pitched tones as the mother and sisters of the groom chanted good wishes for the bride and groom. The experience enthralled me; my skin tingled, excited yet somewhat overcome with the honor of being at such a sacred event.

It was several months between the time the Aqed Zawaaj was signed and the wedding reception for Ali and Zahra where the participants served as witnesses to the marriage. This period, common in Muslim communities, allows the couple to get to know one another, or court, before the big wedding reception. Unlike Western dating, a chaperone, typically from the woman's family, remains present on any outing. We had several trips to the beach or shared homemade meals with Ali's family following the signing of the Aqed Zawaaj and before the wedding reception. During these occasions, we often saw

Ali and Zahra in the distance, however, always in the family's view, chatting quietly and sometimes holding hands. To be seen together in public without a chaperone or to live together was forbidden before the ceremonial wedding reception.

Citizens of the more traditional Arabian Peninsula hold separate wedding receptions for the bride and the groom. I had heard some amazing stories about these surprisingly vibrant women-only weddings. Ali and Zahra and their families, however, were Palestinian and held a magnificent, boisterous, and gender-mixed wedding reception celebration. It seemed like no time at all had passed since the day we struck up a conversation with Mai in the cafe and now, the day I was attending her daughter's wedding.

Nabil already had the good fortune to attend a conventional male-only Gulf Arab wedding when we lived in Saudi Arabia. We would have entirely different experiences. Although politely greeted at the door of the male-only wedding of a work colleague, Faisal, in Saudi Arabia, Nabil found the sober nature of the event rather bewildering. The wedding ritual itself was held in a large hall designated exclusively for these occasions. Nabil found his way to the groom, seated in a plush red cushioned chair with a gold frame in the front of the hall. The groom, positioned between two older men (presumably the colleague's father and father of the bride), extended his hand to Nabil, firmly shook it, and said: *"Alsalam alaikum"* (Peace be upon you); his countenance restrained. Nabil shook hands with the two older men and introduced himself; however, neither Faisal nor the men introduced themselves to Nabil. Although Nabil felt uncomfortable, it seemed to be the tone set for the occasion; formal and somber. Nabil, at one point, tried to take a photo of the groom but was quickly intercepted and sternly told, "No pictures allowed." Unlike informal gatherings of Arab males at cafes and restaurants where collectives of men seem intimate and jovial, traditional functions for men are typically marked by more subdued pursuits. Music and flowers were absent from the wedding ceremony in Riyadh; controlled whispering penetrated the room. The entire ritual was understated, marked by muted conversation during which servers offered cardamom coffee and dates. After an hour and a half, a feast was served, followed by knafeh, and shortly thereafter, the men departed the wedding hall.

In contrast to formal gatherings of men, women-only events give Arab women the opportunity to cultivate a certain freedom to simply be themselves and appreciate their femininity. I was awkward and self-conscious at my first few women-only get-togethers, not knowing exactly how to act or what was expected of me. Adding to my discomfort was my concern at being viewed as an oddity, someone out of place. I wondered if these women regarded me with suspicion: the American girl seeing this type of celebration as simply a novel or quaint experience. I was initially surprised to find these women, who in public were often silent and covered in coal-black abayas, to be surprisingly open and joyous at women-only functions, transformed by their colorful clothing, ornate jewelry, and perfectly coiffed hair.

I attended the women-only wedding of Mai's daughter, Fatima, in Qatar in 2008. The wedding invitation itself, hand-delivered to our villa, foretold a memorable event. Lavender velvet encased the invitation with gold Arabic script laced over in elegant calligraphy, which seemed to shimmy in the filtered sunlight of our villa courtyard. Tiny mirrored gems sprinkled along the folds of the invitation. I visualized myself, an expatriate Cinderella, finally asked to the ball.

Only the most traditional of Arab families continue with the practice of women-only weddings – primarily natives of the conservative Gulf countries of Saudi Arabia, Kuwait, Qatar, United Arab Emirates, Bahrain, and Oman. These six nations, with ties going back to the ancient Najd Arab tribes of Saudi Arabia and Yemen, ascribe to Khaleeji culture: each country shares the same dialect, clothes, food, music, and the more traditional marriage customs, including arranged marriage.

The women-only wedding, a distinctly Arab ritual, unites women in unadulterated euphoria, celebrating and honoring the rite of marriage (a particularly pious experience in Arab culture). Despite being exposed to many novel cultural experiences during my nearly four years living in Saudi Arabia and over three years in Qatar, at the time, attending a traditional women-only wedding remained a particularly poignant desire of mine. Almost compulsively drawn to places, people, and experiences that swept me away from the conventions and comforts of my Western culture, I found this innate kinship with foreign locations and customs responsible for shaping much of my adult life, including my eventual decision to leave Washington, DC, my home of 17 years, and to relocate to Saudi Arabia with Nabil.

As the name suggests, these women-only weddings are reserved for females, allowing the bride and her family and friends to celebrate the cherished nuptials free of the restrictions that are faced in everyday life, such as wearing the traditional abaya and headscarf in public. Until then, I had lived vicariously through the experiences of my Arab and expatriate women friends who filled my visions of these celebrations with Arab women adorned in spectacular gowns, dancing with wholehearted abandon until dawn, and feasting upon the seemingly limitless banquet of fine cuisines served late into the night. I felt like a teenager who had just been invited to the prom, and I gently clutched the invitation close to me and hurried inside our villa. The laundry list of my daily errands and chores evaporated in the scorching noon sun as I mentally scanned my closet. What to wear?!

Female family members, mothers, sisters, and aunts are all responsible for selecting an appropriate mate for unmarried males from a pool of possibilities, including cousins, friends, neighbors, or strangers. Marriage to a cousin brings the greatest security and creates stronger ties within the family. At women-only wedding ceremonies, unmarried women are given the chance to catch the attention of female relatives of eligible bachelors by flaunting their figures in revealing gowns and proving their "moves on the dance floor."

The wedding reception was held at the Ritz Carlton on the outskirts of Doha. I was awestruck by both the opulence of the room, with its sparkling chandeliers and lush furnishings, and the assemblage of women. Women spilled out everywhere, some whispering discreetly in each other's ears or meandering through the room, reservedly and chastely kissing relatives or friends the requisite three times on the cheeks; others surveyed the room like critics ogling guests on the red carpet. Amidst these assorted guests a core group presided over all the guests, directing the sequence of events. I was enthralled, transfixed, and a bit unsteadied by the sheer spectacle.

After wading further into the room, I noticed a three-foot elevated platform with a runway that traversed virtually the entire length of the room. Alongside the runway, a female singer keened to the accompaniment of female musicians playing the tabla. Dotting each side of the extravagant catwalk were numerous round tables laid out with elaborate gold and burgundy place settings for dinner. A large golden rectangular pot with circular designs spread from the base to the rim and containing an abundance of colorful artificial flowers resided on each table. Ivory pillars rose from the elevated platform sporting gold inlaid designs with a sequence of curves that melted into each other; burgundy curtains dripped between the columns. Gold and ivory-colored stands with exquisitely crafted flowers bordered the stage. In the center, a red velvet loveseat awaited the bride and groom, who would make separate entrances later in the evening.

Mai, the mother of the bride, greeted me and my Jordanian friend, Wedad, when we entered the room. Though I had met her several months earlier at the sheesha cafe at Souk Al-Waqif, I abruptly passed right by her in the ballroom, mistaking her for just one of the many bejeweled and gowned guests. Gone were her long black abaya and head covering. What stood before me now was a vision that could easily pass for Hollywood royalty.

Mai gazed at me with impeccably made-up eyes – hues of blue covered her lids, and shimmering black outlined her exquisite ovals. A lavender dress clung to her curvaceous form that ended with a magnificent train; silver adornments glimmered in the artificial light of the luxurious chandeliers. Mai's hair was piled high atop her head; delicate ringlets framed her face and cascaded along the side and back of her head. Struck by Mai's splendor and extraordinary luminescence, I felt at once wistful that these Arab women were not permitted to let their natural beauty radiate in this way more often, and yet I understood and respected the desire to maintain and honor the deeply ingrained traditions and customs that dictated their reality. In a constant state of frenzied yet gracious motion, Mai played the roles of a skilled director, choreographer, and consummate hostess; she indefatigably welcomed her guests and ensured that not only was everyone comfortable but supremely happy—a staple of Arabic hospitality.

After many years in the Middle East, I had undoubtedly become acclimated to seeing traditional Arab women covered in black, seemingly deprived of identity and barely present – one ebony form identical to the next. I had to squelch any outward signs of sheer disbelief at the exceptional beauty of the women collected in the room as my friend, Wedad, a veteran of such gala events, coolly guided us to a table adjacent to the stage. We settled in amongst a throng of haute couture gowns with glittery and colorful embellishments (many with trains), plunging necklines, unconventionally stylish miniature top hats garnished with striking colors and glistening silver sequins rakishly tilted to one side atop flawlessly fashioned hair. I met the eyes of many women ringed with deep and rich shades of green and blue, their lids traced in thick, sultry black liner. Henna scrollwork artistically ran up and down hands, arms, feet, and legs. I reflected on my couture gown, ornate multi-tiered silver necklace with matching earrings, and painstakingly applied makeup and lost all hope of blending into this opulent jewel box.

Not long after we entered the hall, the room began to pulsate with music blaring from mammoth speakers mounted to the walls. Along the stage, frantic, rhythmic drumming by women resonated in the room while a singer belted out traditional Gulf melodies at a pitch that strained every nerve ending. Several young women in the audience sprang onto the stage, leaping and gyrating along the platform, simulating the traditional Gulf dance, a dance performed in countries along the Arabian Peninsula, in a zealous and ritualistic fever. I watched with a tinge of envy at the dancers' sheer lack of inhibition. I was brought back to an image of myself at that age, very shy, filled with uneasiness when first asked to dance to the comparably tame strains of Chicago by my future husband, Nabil, in the bar of the Hilton Hotel outside the University of Florida campus.

Wedad caught my intent gaze, her eyes playfully prodding me to take the dance floor. We both adored dancing, but neither of us knew how to dance the traditional Gulf dance. I bit my lip and shook my head, not wanting to risk exposing my two left feet. My love of dance, however, won over my trepidation of not measuring up to these graceful and bewitching creatures. I could sense legions of eyes, laser rays boring holes through me as Wedad and I made our way up the stairs to the stage. My gaze anxiously swept the platform taking in the hapless yet harmonious arm movements, inexhaustible and whirling hip action, pivoting shoulders and necks, and swirling fans of long, silky, coal-black hair slicing through the air. Seizing the fleeting sympathetic smiles from compassionate observers, I desperately tried to imitate the mystical moves, willing my body to sway and whip in the same mesmerizing fashion to no avail. I finally succumbed to the more familiar belly dance that I had learned from Nabil, his family, and other Arab friends, slipping comfortably into the oscillating circular movement of the hips and letting my arms billow out to the side, joyfully losing myself in the dance. Wedad persisted heroically with a blended version of Gulf motions and belly dance. Our inspired, yet futile, efforts were met with charitable applause from the audience. Emboldened and giddy over the audience response, Wedad and I made a second vain attempt at the nuanced movements of the Gulf dance. The most I could muster were inept leaps and helpless flailing arms. I felt challenging stares as my spirit deflated. Once at the security of our table, I caught a twinkle in Wedad's eye as she leaned over and whispered that she had overheard several of Mai's inner circle comment that the westerner and her friend might prefer belly dancing over the more traditional Gulf moves. To our delight the next song was a Lebanese melody, perfect for belly dancing. Wedad and I were back on the stage to the obvious appreciation of the audience.

Several enchanting young children, fixated on their older sisters and cousins' expert movements, gingerly climbed the stairs to the stage to imitate their revered relatives. From time to time, older women, completely covered in black from head to toe, save for their worn eyes, made their way onto the stage to throw paper bills over the dancers.

The scattered money would be collected at the end of the festivities to tip the singer and musicians. The bills twirled and fluttered across the stage in the same way the dancers cast their bodies about the platform. The women tossed out their money, cupping one hand over their mouths and crying out in shrill, undulating tones. I was intrigued and baffled by the incongruity of the scene. Only moments before, these nondescript women shrouded in black had appeared devoid of personality. Now, they shared the stage with such dazzling, spellbinding figures. Both sets of women, generations colliding, drew the eyes of enraptured onlookers. Perhaps these women cried out in sheer joy for their younger sister, given over in marriage; perhaps theirs was also a wail daubed with mourning, recalling a time and place that was only a distant memory for them.

Finally, the time arrived for the bride, Fatima, to make her anticipated entrance. Muted sighs rippled through the room. A viselike grip throttled my senses as I caught sight of a vision in white satin floating past me on the carpet. Fatima sparkled in a resplendent white modern wedding gown and veil, her figure in full display. Her serene eyes gazed regally, deep pools of black framed by sumptuous multi-colored shadows and lids heavily laden with charcoal black eyeliner – an Arabian princess. With each step, an attendant smoothed out Fatima's intricately embroidered train while other ladies showered her in rose petals. Fatima stepped up onto the runway and proceeded to the red velvet loveseat, where she sat composed, reserved, and glorious, with barely a smile. Around her, the scene erupted as many well-wishers kissed, embraced, and congratulated her while professional photographers clamored to get their shots of this stunning beauty. (Guests are not allowed to have phones or take photos at women-only weddings.) The sight of the lone alluring figure surrounded by rapturous family and friends tugged at my heart; it was a most joyous moment, and yet behind the beguiling eyes, I sensed a young girl unsettled over entering a distinctly new chapter in her life, removed from the security of her family into the role of wife and mother. As I gazed upon this lovely bride, I silently shared her excitement and trepidation, willing a kind of mute solidarity with her and wishing her a life of happiness amidst inevitable challenges and change.

The audience commingled as fierce drumming accompanied by piercing intonations reverberated along the foundations of the hall. Fatima received her guests for nearly half an hour when a low murmuring filled the room. The mood shifted, and a curious tension began to swell. The fluid and graceful movements of the dancers were exchanged for fitful and spasmodic gesticulations. Disquieted and fleeting glances ricocheted through the space, and an apprehension hung in the air. Flustered and unsettled, I furtively scanned the room, struggling to unearth the source of the unease. As if on cue, the aggregation of women stealthily and nimbly masked their exposed skin with abayas and black headscarves. Wedad tugged at my scarf and covered her visible kneecaps. The groom's arrival, along with his father and brothers and the bride's father and male siblings, was imminent. Their entrance transformed the activity and energy of the room, bringing a sense of order and male authority to what had previously been an orgiastic celebration of women, pleasure, and decadence. The groom majestically and purposefully strode to the platform, climbed the steps, and made his way to his bride with the male family members dutifully following behind, faces implacable. I caught my breath as a black curtain was draped around the bride. Sensing my bewilderment and consternation, Wedad dropped her head and, in a hushed tone, divulged that custom dictated only the groom, his father, and the bride's father and brothers were permitted to see and congratulate Fatima; she must remain out of sight of the other male members of the groom's family. Camera flashes popped around the room like little sizzling bolts of lightning. The once divine and radiant bride became indiscernible to much of the audience, disappearing even further beneath the throng of family and friends who engulfed her in congratulations.

By nearly midnight, the male population had whittled down to its one distinguished member—the groom. Elsewhere, the illustrious gathering became briefly preoccupied with luscious culinary delights: a buffet laden with what looked like an infinite array of Lebanese mezze – hummus, tabouli, fattoush, baba ghanoush, *mutabal* (an eggplant dip). Fish and chicken skewered or braised in rich sauces and garlic swam in copious measures of parsley and mint with flat, oval leaven bread piled high in baskets. This was followed with indulgent and heavenly Arab sweets: baklava, knafeh, and *mabroumeh* (sweet circular pastries encasing pistachios). Trading snatches of conversation over the wonderments of the evening, Wedad and I put our heads together like excited school girls, feeding our bodies on the sumptuous cuisine and our minds and spirits on the remarkable celebration.

Wedad and I decided to forgo the dancing and celebration, sure to continue unabated through the wee hours of the morning. We would collect our tired but happy bodies and ruefully wonder what twinges or aches might greet us in the morning, the physical souvenirs of such a spirited evening. In the early hours of the morning, the bride and groom unobtrusively made their way to the door amongst a cluster of attendants. Before exiting, several women delicately cloaked Fatima with an abaya and black head covering. This alluring Arabian jewel, like so many others, would now be just another raven silhouette amongst the featureless masses. But not to me; I would know differently.

CHAPTER 11

LOSING NABIL'S MOM

It was Monday morning, February 24, 2003, a work day. I had just left my building and was walking down the sidewalk to meet Nabil. We agreed to take a quick break and grocery shop at the KFSH store, which was something we routinely did.

I met Nabil near my building. He seemed placid.

"I just heard some sad news about my mom," Nabil said.

"What is it?" I exclaimed, my heart accelerating, half expecting the worst.

And it was the worst.

Head down, Nabil sounded surprisingly normal. "I just got an e-mail message from my mom's neighbor that my mom passed away."

I gripped Nabil's hand. "No! I'm so sorry, Nabil."

Nabil's hold on my hand tightened.

As a child growing up in the Middle East, Nabil's mother, Fatina, was his closest friend, and that special connection remained throughout his life despite not seeing his mama for long stretches, sometimes years at a time. Nabil appreciated his mother's love, wisdom, and encouragement. As the youngest child, Nabil was often left behind with his mother when his siblings went off to play. During Nabil's first 17 years of life, his father was frequently outside of Jordan on contract as a physician's assistant in Saudi Arabia. The few times he was home, there was often discord in the family; animated arguments between Nabil's father and mother. And Nabil's father clearly favored his two older sons. Nabil's dad perceived Nabil as being too close to his mother. He was even known to say Nabil should have been a girl.

During his parents' spats, Nabil was openly allied with his sisters on his mother's side and the two brothers with their father. Nabil's father seemed to not understand his sensitive son. As a youngster, Nabil spent hours with his mama in the backyard garden of their Mafraq, Jordan home sharing oranges, apples, and grapes from the vine. The other siblings were outside with playmates, and Nabil and his mother had alone time. Nabil's mama routinely confided in her young son about troubles with her husband or missing her homeland, Lebanon, and her relatives. Nabil always had a listening ear for his mother. He never minded being at her side, patient and quiet, letting her talk even if he couldn't understand some of it at his young age.

When Nabil left Lebanon in 1978 for the U.S., it was often impossible to stay in touch with his mother by phone due to Lebanon's civil war. The lines were often cut due to shelling and bombings, so it was sometimes months between their phone calls. It was a great joy when Nabil reached his mama back in the early 1980s when I first knew him, but upsetting when the lines went dead in the middle of their conversation. Lebanon was often cut off from the world during its civil war that raged from 1975 to 1990. Given the instability of Lebanon, we were shaken with uncertainty by these terrible routine phone lapses. We never knew if Nabil's mom was okay. Nabil's nightmare pictured his mother being shot, hit with shrapnel, or worse, having little chance of survival due to her diabetes. And hospitals prioritized the military or militia fighters. There were long periods of anxiety before Nabil and his mom talked again, with Nabil glued to the TV between classes, monitoring Lebanon's breaking news in the interim.

Jehan, Nabil's sister, became Fatina's main caregiver in the mid-1980s when their mother's health began deteriorating due to her diabetes, a heart condition, and a broken hip. Nabil was closer to Jehan than his brothers, and as the years went by, Jehan gained more respect and admiration in Nabil's eyes. With the onset of Fatina's first major medical issues, Jehan and Nabil were in regular touch regarding their mother's health. A couple of weeks before his mother's passing, Jehan phoned us.

Voice shaking, Jehan disclosed in Arabic, "I have something to tell you. The doctor told me that Mama's lungs were filling with water. I'm scared. Do you know what this means, Nabil?"

Nabil looked worried. "I don't know, Jehan. Turning to me, "Do you know, Mary?"

"No, I don't, but we can check with our nursing friends at KFSH and let you know, Jehan." I was at a loss and frightened.

During a lunch break, Nabil and I visited Melanie, a KFSH nursing friend, and she explained water in the lungs was not a good sign. Nabil's face blanched. Sadly, Nabil's mom's body was breaking down. As we walked back to our offices, Nabil's hand was limp in mine. I didn't really know what to say; neither of us did. A tear formed in the corner of my eye. How would Nabil be in this world without his mother? He had reconnected with her in the couple of years since we moved to Saudi Arabia. We were fortunate to have visited Nabil's mother and sister, Jehan, in Beirut, Lebanon, every few months. It was always an event.

I'll never forget our first visit to Lebanon in 1996, before we moved to Saudi Arabia. A few years earlier at our wedding in the Washington, DC area in September 1993, we promised Nabil's mother a visit to Lebanon before too long. Determined not to miss our nuptials, Fatina had bravely flown from Beirut to Washington, DC, via Heathrow Airport on TWA. It was a challenging process to get Nabil's mama from the Middle East to the U.S. She was mostly blind in one eye due to her diabetes, did not speak a word of English, and recently had hip surgery. But she had always been a resolute woman with a great spirit. Nabil arranged for a wheelchair and attendant in London for his mother's connecting flight, as well as at Dulles Airport just outside DC. Since the U.S. Embassy in Beirut was closed at the time due to an earlier bombing related to the years-long civil war in Lebanon, Fatina traveled by bus accompanied by a neighbor to the U.S. Embassy in Damascus, Syria. It is not an easy journey for a 72-year-old woman in poor health.

Nabil and I were overjoyed to see his mother, the last passenger, at the end of the jetway in a wheelchair, assisted by airport staff on that late summer day. I didn't anticipate crumpling into a ball of tears when I first embraced Nabil's mother. It could have been because I had never met either of Nabil's parents, although I had spoken with Fatina and Nabil's sister, Jehan, on the phone many times. Jehan spoke in brusque Arabic and only slowed down when attempting her few words in English.

"Hi Micha, how are you? ... Are you *mneeha* (fine)?"

Prompted by Nabil, I would reply, "*Ana mneeha, wa entee?*" (I am fine, and you?)

Jehan had only traveled once outside Lebanon's borders when she and Fatina visited Nabil's oldest brother, Basem, in Italy. Jehan had no interest in leaving her native Lebanon. She lived with and cared for her mother, had many relatives inside and outside Beirut, and enjoyed a multitude of friends who were like family. Nabil and I often asked Jehan if she would like to visit us in the US and, of course, extended an invitation to our wedding. But her answer was always the same. She didn't want to leave Lebanon. So, it always made me happy when she did her best to converse in English when we spoke on the phone. And I did my best to improve my Arab vocabulary for the next time.

Although Nabil's mother spoke no English, the warm lilt of her voice and Nabil's translation conveyed the love and devotion she held for her son and soon-to-be daughter-in-law, even on our first phone call.

"*Habeebtie, ana smehet annek ashyaa helweh kteer.*" (Sweetheart, I heard a lot of nice things about you.)

"*Shukran, ya Mama.*" (Thank you, Mama.)

"*Mesh adra astana lashoofek.*" (I can't wait to meet you.)

"*Ana kaman, ya Mama.*" (Me, too, Mama.)

"*Deree balek ala halek wala Nabil.*" (Take care of yourself and Nabil.)

"*Shukran, ya Mama. Tabban, ya habeebtie.*" (Thank you, Mama. Of course, my sweetheart.)

In the Arab world, a daughter-in-law is a daughter. Nabil's mama was like a mother to me before we even married.

Early on in our relationship, Nabil told me the story of how he first came to the U.S. in 1978 through a seemingly strange mix of coincidences and the reaction of his mother and family. Nabil would attend the University of Florida as an engineering student. On the night before flying to the U.S. to attend college, a farewell party was thrown for Nabil in the family's Beirut apartment. Nabil was anxious about the unknown yet hopeful he would complete his studies and graduate as a civil engineer. As the party wore down and before bed, each female member of his family came up to Nabil with long faces, holding back tears, and offered positive words.

Jehan told him never to fall in love with an American woman. They were ruthless. Nabil grinned when he told me Sonia, his second oldest sister, said she was concerned about an American woman staking him out and Nabil never returning home again. Nabil didn't think much of either of these warnings; he was mainly concerned with how he was going to learn English and how he would become an engineer. Nabil's mama's take was different. She trusted Nabil's decisions and wanted Nabil to keep in mind that we were all children of God. If he fell in love with a woman who was not Lebanese, as long as he was happy with her, then his mama gave him her blessing. I was amazed at the story and how advanced and wise Nabil's mother was in matters of love. Selfless, in fact.

On that cold December evening in 1996, before we left Washington, DC, for Beirut via Amman, I told Nabil I was eager to visit his mama, Jehan, and other relatives and friends. Nabil was excited, too. However, he didn't know what to expect, having been away from that culture for so long.

Although we had only a several-hour stop-over in Amman, Jordan, some of Nabil's relatives, the children of his oldest sister, Aida, who was in Chicago at the time, came to the airport to greet us. Nabil had not seen them in years. There was Kasim, his oldest nephew who was like a brother to Nabil growing up in Mafraq, Jordan. Only five years younger than Nabil, they spent time in Mafraq playing chase and hide and seek, and Nabil taught Kasim soccer. And then there was his niece, Linda, only a baby when Nabil last saw her 19 years earlier. Nabil's eyes glistened.

Color rising in his cheeks, Nabil bear-hugged each niece and nephew in turn. I had not seen Nabil this emotional since seeing his mother at Dulles Airport in 1993. Minutes of unrecognizable happy babble, and they all turned to me. My eyes lit up as Nabil introduced me.

"*Khaleenie aarefkum ala martie, Mary!*" (Let me introduce you to my wife, Mary!) Nabil yelled out excitedly.

"*Marhaba, Mary. Ahlan wa sahlan feekie fe Ordon!*" (Hello, Mary. Welcome to Jordan!)

Unrestrained loving hugs followed. Warmth flowed through my body; my face flushed. I immediately felt part of Nabil's tribe.

They insisted we stay with them for a couple of days.

It was an offer we really couldn't refuse. I knew this was a big deal for Nabil, but I couldn't help being concerned about some of the practicalities. Jordan was a developing country, after all.

"What about our luggage, Nabil? Will the airlines allow us to send it on to Beirut without us on the flight?" We had our carry-ons with our essentials that we would keep with us.

"Don't worry, Mary, it will work out."

And it did.

What didn't work out so well was getting in touch with Jehan to alert her we would be late to Beirut by several days. We attempted to call Jehan in Lebanon (less than an hour's flight from Jordan) several times and were met with, "You cannot complete this call as dialed." I was astonished we couldn't reach Jehan and worried she would be concerned about us. Even though it had already been six years since the end of Lebanon's civil war, there were still lingering effects. Nabil had the creative yet outrageous idea to call my dad in America and have him call Jehan in Lebanon. My Dad was bewildered but understood once Nabil explained it was easier to call from America to Lebanon than from Jordan to Lebanon. I still had concerns, as Dad spoke no Arabic, and Jehan's English was minimal. When Nabil called Dad back, Dad said Jehan was relieved to hear we were alright, as she had gone to the airport, and we never showed up. I was reassured.

Constant noise and movement – cars honking, people on the roadsides gesturing wildly, and nearby lamb meat rotating on a rotisserie outside a tiny cafe. I tried to catch all the details through the car window as Kasim's vehicle passed through Amman, the capital of Jordan, on our way from the airport to Kasim's home. Much of it blurred like a collage.

Our days in Amman were filled with high emotions, joy, reflection for us both, and great excitement for me at experiencing my first Middle Eastern city. That first night in bed, Nabil told me he had to learn how to reconnect with these people, his family, who he had not seen for two decades. Nabil was overwhelmed and confused but certainly happy to be in Jordan, his birthplace. I, myself, was blissful about being in a new culture, Nabil's culture. Food was a central theme, along with cardamom coffee (*gahwa*) and perpetual chatter. We enjoyed *molokhia* (thick green leafy vegetable) with rice and chicken, stuffed squash and grape leaves, and more in the evenings. It was all a first for me; I couldn't get enough!

I was enthralled with my newfound Jordanian family, and I believe they were with me. The conversation was primarily in Arabic, but they tried their best to accommodate me. And I did my best to keep them laughing with my "baby Arabic." Mostly, though, my mindset changed abruptly. This was a different lifestyle, focused heavily on family, time with friends, and communal eating. In the Middle East, outside the Arab Gulf in countries like Lebanon, relationships between relatives and friends are more tactile and effusive. In contrast, people of the Arab Gulf tend to be reserved in their daily lives, however, revel heartily at parties with family and friends. As Lebanese Christians, Nabil's family, men and women, made it a point to embrace and kiss my cheeks when we first met. This would never happen in the Arab Gulf; outside the nuclear family kissing is limited to the same sex. Dynamic chitchat was a part of every day with Nabil's relatives, with topics ranging from family to politics to what we would eat for dinner. The most protracted conversations were about food and eating. I appreciated and was intrigued by this peek into another world, another way of life.

Kasim, Nabil's nephew, was kind enough to drive us to Mafraq, around 40 miles from Amman, where Nabil was born and spent his childhood and where Nabil's father, Kareem, was buried. Nabil later told me he imagined Israeli warplanes overhead. He showed me the location of the Arab Liberation Front (ALF) headquarters; he joined this militia group as a young boy. The ALF building was now a simple residence; the ALF and other militia groups that were so prevalent during Nabil's childhood no longer existed. Jordan became a peaceful country in the 1970s after Black September. One block away stood the arches of the Latin Church, where Nabil hid from Israeli bombs.

The church was just as Nabil remembered, with wooden pews, the Virgin Mary to the left of the altar, Jesus just behind the altar, and Saint Joseph to the right. When Nabil attended church as a youngster, females sat on the left-side pews and males on the right. Our hearts uplifted with these remembrances, Nabil asked the young priest if he would bless our marriage, and he graciously did so. On that beautiful, peaceful day in early winter, all the raw, traumatic memories seemed like a dark dream.

Nabil's childhood home was only two blocks away. The home, its exterior made of uneven stone, had two bedrooms, one toilet room, one shower room, and a backyard filled with trees and vines -- blackberries, grape vines, and an olive tree. I could just imagine Nabil in this backyard with his beloved monkey, dog, deer, rabbits, and chickens.

Although they were pets for Nabil, the family consumed all but the monkey and dog.

Looking for Nabil's father's gravesite in Mafraq was painful for Nabil. Nabil's dad had passed a year earlier, and Nabil was unable to attend the funeral. They had not spoken for years, and there were unresolved issues. Nabil's shoulders slumped as he drifted through row after row of gravesites, quietly scanning the names on the headstones. He read them to me as I followed over the coarse ground with wild desert bushes and spots of muddy earth. Nabil's brow crumpled; I knew he was frustrated. I felt helpless not being able to read the names. Kasim was on the other side of the cemetery, nervously probing, also turning up nothing. There was a man in the distance with children rambling through the grounds. Nabil approached the stranger, hoping against hope that he might know something. After all, Nabil's father was highly revered in Mafraq in the 1950s and 1960s as the only reported medical professional, a skilled physician's assistant, in the area.

A flicker of recognition, "Ah, Kareem Khouri, he's buried over there." The man pointed his index finger toward a gravesite the next row over, behind some brambles. Nabil thanked the man and said he was sorry for the man's loss. The man and his children continued somberly through the graveyard.

Nabil, Kasim, and I, heads bowed, ambled over to Kareem's final resting place. The tears hit Nabil and then me. They were uncontrollable. Nabil rubbed his hands over the grave, what was left of his father, memories flooding back. Faces tearstained, eyes swollen, we walked back to Kasim's car.

On the car ride back to Kasim's home in Amman, Nabil quietly wiped his tears and put his arm around my shoulder. He tentatively leaned over to speak; Nabil said he was glad to have the chance to visit his father's gravesite and talk with his spirit. I think the experience provided some resolution for him.

We were on our flight from Amman to Beirut, Lebanon, the next morning.

Shouts of "Nabil" and "Mary" ricocheted off the walls as we arrived at Beirut International Airport. We had just deplaned, gone through immigration, picked up our luggage, and were walking through the end of the corridor to the arrival hall. We peered through the throngs of people at the far end of the room, and Nabil spotted Jehan clustered with others, all screaming our names. Nabil seemed numb and foggy; his eyes were unfocused. "Hold my hand," he whispered. His legs were about to give out.

Jehan fell into Nabil's arms, sobbing when we reached the visitor's area. Hardly getting the words out, Jehan stuttered, "Nabil, Mary," as she let go of Nabil and grabbed me. I was overwhelmed by Jehan's passion, somewhat unnerved by the entirety of it all. As she trembled against my chest,

"Hi, Jehan! Finally, I get to meet you."

"Ana bahebek, Mary. Enti okhtee." (I love you, Mary. You're my sister.)

"Ana bahebek kaman, ya Jehan," (I love you, too, Jehan) caught up in the moment, my basic Arabic tumbled out.

Engulfed by tight hugs and kisses from people I didn't know or barely heard of left me breathless; I had never been greeted like this. I caught sight of Nabil buried in hugs and spirited conversation.

"Marhaba, habeeptie, keef halek." (Hello, sweetheart, how are you?) he told a neighbor and friend from his past.

"Eshtatelek kteer." (I missed you a lot.)

Faces aglow, arms entwined around us, we walked from the airport terminal to a neighbor's car, an old Mercedes Benz, parked just outside. It was not unusual to see second-hand Mercedes in Lebanon; however, it was very unusual to see American cars, as they were too pricey. Jehan motioned for us to get in. Kamal, a neighbor and friend who Nabil knew during the Civil War in the 1970s, was jovial and enthusiastic about being our chauffeur. Hayat, Kamal's wife, sat up front with Kamal, and Nabil and I squeezed in the back with Jehan. I noticed small tears, scratches, and discoloring on the backseat upholstery as I climbed into the car. Remaining friends and neighbors piled into other vehicles, and we started our procession to Nabil's mother's apartment. Not a silent moment as we drove from the airport to the family home; constant talking -- catching up for lost time -- wild driving, and continuous honking. The Mediterranean, rolling hills, distant mountains, and grand Cedar trees formed the backdrop of our highway drive. It was reminiscent of my childhood days in the San Francisco Bay Area, where the Pacific Ocean meets the Santa Cruz mountains.

My perspective changed, though, as we approached the city of Beirut, where gaping holes in high-rise apartment buildings became commonplace. The result of artillery warfare during the 15- yearlong Lebanese Civil War and the intercession of the Syrian military in 1976. Syrian tanks and jeeps sat at the side of the roads, especially just outside the airport. I was nervous; what were we getting ourselves into? Lebanon's Civil War ended in 1990. I thought any remnants of the War would be long gone, particularly the Syrian presence. (Syria withdrew from Lebanon in 2005.) Nabil later told me he was afraid of being stopped by Syrian soldiers; he had flashbacks of being flagged down several times as a teenager by Syrian soldiers or militia members as he traveled in or out of Beirut in the 1970s. Lebanon's Civil War was raging during that period. Each time, Nabil had to state his religion with a gun leveled at his head. And each time, he was lucky.

As we exited the main road from the airport and entered the outskirts of Beirut, the driving became more chaotic. Traffic lights were mostly non-functioning, and those that worked were not followed. Roundabouts were useless, with some drivers simply going the wrong way. Dismayed at the seemingly complete lack of driving etiquette, I wondered if we would make it home safely. This was very different from the U.S. or even Jordan. Jordan had a modest economy, though, with fewer cars per capita, and drivers followed the rules. Beirut was a cosmopolitan city with all the inherent city-driving issues and beyond. All the while, those around me chatted and laughed unperturbed, Nabil included. As I hung on tightly to Nabil's hand, he whispered, "Welcome to Beirut." Sloping roads became more prominent as we approached Jehan and Mama Khouri's apartment in Antoneieh, a neighborhood outside Beirut proper. Small restaurants, retail shops, and shoppers appeared out the window. We turned right on a steep downward tilt and took another right into a small parking area of the apartment building where Nabil lived in his late teens.

Parking was underneath the four-story simple cement building. We walked along pretty white marble tiles with light streaks of pink and gray to the back of the building. Nabil and Kamal pulled our luggage to the elevator door, and Nabil and I crowded into the small compartment with whatever luggage fit. The tiny lift reminded me of the cramped elevators in Europe; a nice memory. Kamal and Jehan followed with more luggage. Kamal went back for another trip for the rest of our bags.

Exhausted but enthusiastic about seeing Nabil's mama again, three years after our wedding, and meeting other relatives and friends, Nabil and I made our way down the small corridor. While it was exciting and somewhat unnerving to see everyone at the Beirut airport, especially after our astonishing unscheduled time in Jordan, it was even more emotional to see Nabil's mother at the door of her apartment. Dressed in her traditional dark dress, cinched at the waist and imprinted with small red and blue flowers, I plowed into her arms, shaking and trying to restrain my tears, Nabil's mama yelled out: *"Ya meet ahla wa sahla! Ya meet ahla wa sahla!"* (A hundred welcomes! A hundred welcomes!)

Nabil, tears in his eyes, was behind me shouting, *"Keefek ya Mama?"* (How are you, Mama?) as he fell into a tight embrace with his mother.

A flood of people rushed to the doorway from the next room. *"Ahlan Mary, ahlan Nabil!"* (Welcome Mary, welcome Nabil!)

Loving hugs overtook us, with three kisses planted on each of our cheeks. Nabil's eyes twinkled.

"Are these your relatives, Nabil?"

"No, these are my neighbors who I knew in the mid-70s."

The rush of people, family, and neighbor friends coming and going through the small apartment became routine during our two-week visit. The love and heartfelt interest in us was almost unfathomable. However, the two-bedroom, one-bathroom unit held the care, tenderness, and celebratory spirit well.

Soon after we entered the apartment, we were made to smell and taste pots and plates of savory food before even emptying our bladders. Stuffed intestines, tabouli, fattoush, fresh fish, hummus, manakeesh, and more. Mama Khouri's refrigerator was crammed with flavorful dishes. Someone grabbed my hand, and before I knew it, I was led out of the apartment and up the stairs. Where are we going? I thought as I looked at the young woman's encouraging eyes. Looking behind, I saw Nabil, smiling with his arm around Jehan, following us. We turned a corner, and my new friend opened the door of another apartment. She ushered me into the dining room and opened the refrigerator; the kitchens were too small to hold refrigerators. "More food from Mama

Khouri!" The lady pulled my face for a closer view and smell. Jehan, just behind us, wriggled through and, with her finger, gave me a taste of raw meat: *kibbeh*. Whew! With the same finger, she dug in and gave Nabil a taste.

Overwhelmed yet gratified over the welcoming hugs, incredible cuisine, and overall aura of joy, I was swept along by the merry celebration and enthusiasm of the family. Feeling less self-conscious and more at ease after some days, I still knew we were in the middle of a meaningful time. Many conversations centered around cuisine, not my forte, however, the heightened excitement over the correct way to make hummus caught my interest. And what would we have to eat later tonight, for breakfast tomorrow, for lunch tomorrow? Where did the ingredients come from? What was the mix of spices? Discussions and sometimes disagreements erupted over appropriate herbs. And so much time spent on meal preparation. Lebanese meals were plant-based, influenced by the Mediterranean region, unlike Khaleeji countries where meals were more meat-based.

Turkish coffee with cardamom flowed all day over the next couple of weeks, with relatives squeezed on the couches in the living room. I played word games with myself to remember names and faces. A cousin from Nabil's mother's side was named Jehan, like Nabil's sister. Cousin Jehan's mother was named Laila, which I knew meant "night" in English. Another cousin was Noor "light." These cousins were often together, so they were "night light" for me.

Drumming and dancing filled most of our nights. Arab women in tight jeans with long dark hair rolled and whirled to the rhythmic beat of Lebanese and Egyptian music. Nabil told me ahead of time that Lebanese women dressed more fashionably than those in Jordan and elsewhere in the Middle East. Lebanon saw European visitors in the summer and had historic ties to France after World War I. I did my best to replicate the refined movements of these Lebanese beauties. And I was cheered on, although I knew I was trying too hard and was mechanical. I didn't really care, as I knew of the Arab custom that ensured all guests felt welcomed and well cared for. Night after night, I watched these lovely creatures moving like they had not a bone in their body, effortlessly catching the soul of the music.

Jehan and Fatina made sure I had hot water showers. Evidently, Nabil told them as an American I was used to daily bathing. I would only find out later that something similar to shredded tree bark was specially stored for my showers and was placed in a compartment near the toilet with a match used to start the fire that heated the shower water. The heat only lasted for an hour. Fatina warned me to keep the window open slightly during my shower so as not to get asphyxiated. Nabil knocked on the door every few minutes to make sure I was still conscious.

Jumping out of the shower, I closed the window and quickly dressed. There was no central heat to combat the December cold that seeped through the window during my shower time. Jehan and Reham, a neighbor and friend who lived upstairs, were waiting outside.

"I'm going to do your *seshwar*," Reham half shouted.

"What do you mean?" I asked.

"I'm going to dry and do your hair," came the reply.

"Okay, sounds great. Thank you." Although it was slightly odd, I was going to fully appreciate this kind gesture; a cultural experience. And, besides, it wasn't appropriate to decline such generous offers in the Arab world.

Reham pulled and fluffed making gentle curls in my hair as Jehan stood nearby satisfied with Reham's creative turn. Jehan brought out a carrier with makeup, and lined my lids with Arabian eyes, my lips with cherry lipstick some of which she used to color my cheeks. And we found a little black dress in my suitcase that they insisted I wear for that evening at Jennah ("heaven") restaurant with live belly dancing shows. All the pampering was difficult to get used to, but clearly generous and heartwarming. Every day was like my wedding day. Feeling guilty, at times, with all the attention, I wondered how I could repay all their kindnesses. According to Nabil, it was their honor to spoil me; I was the wife of the cherished brother.

That night, at the hilltop restaurant, a belly dancer focused on our table with arms flowing and hips gyrating as we dined on Lebanese mezze, and more than 20 different dishes: za'atar, olives, *labneh* (yogurt dip), goat cheese, mutabal, baba ghanoush, fattoush, tabouli, kibbeh, gyros, shish kabob, kafta, to name a few. Cave-like beige interiors, beautiful colored lights and lanterns, diners dressed in their finest, and light conversation made me feel like I was in an Arab fairyland; transported to a different realm. Quenched with food and emotion at close to 3:00 AM we made our way to the car. The hired driver cautiously made his way down the mountain and on back roads to Antonieh and Nabil's mother's home. Fatina was up waiting for us, sipping a mix of *babounaj* (chamomile) and *maramiyah* (sage) herbal tea. She could not sleep as her diabetes was acting up.

We had many more trips like this to Lebanon in the early 2000s when we lived in nearby Saudi Arabia. One included a wonderful drive with Mama Khouri, Jehan, and neighbor friends to Mount Lebanon bordering the western rim of the country and the Mediterranean Sea. Lush greenery, windy roads, and snow-peaked mountains greeted us as we climbed the range. A woman on the side of the road in a tiny village baked saj bread over a large metal dome outside her small cafe. We had to stop. We told the lady the aroma was lovely. She kindly gave us a sample of fresh Arabic flatbread hot off the dome. Adding a dollop of labneh from goat, made this traditional mountain delectable complete.

I took bite by bite, slowly savoring the fresh unleavened bread and soft cream as the woman looked on with a triumphant smile.

Rich in Biblical history, Mount Lebanon carries the Jesus Christ statue in the town of Zouk; Christ is displayed on a mountaintop, arms outspread to the Mediterranean. Nabil took me there and to several caves high in the mountains with scenes of Mother Mary holding Jesus in her arms. I knew these sites deeply stirred Nabil, and therefore me. He went to his knees and prayed intensely at each. Nabil was a Maronite Catholic, and the Virgin Mary was considered the Mother of God. Watching Nabil's mama light a candle in her bedroom most evenings worshipping the Virgin Mary, carrying a rosary in her hands, and wearing a black lace veil over her head for church strengthened my notion that sincere faith is supreme, no matter what kind.

As we traveled further north, we fell upon the Cedars Ski Resort, where skiers from Lebanon and Europe plowed the slopes. One could not help but feel a spiritual connection to this place. It is reported that in the Bible, the "Cedars of Lebanon" are mentioned at least 70 times. The historical influence is pronounced, as well. The Phoenicians, the first traders in the world to sail the seas, used wood from the Cedars to craft their boats. Many Christian Maronites, Nabil among them, take great pride in saying they are Phoenician, not Arab.

In 2002, Nabil's mother's diabetes took a terrible turn. Mama Khouri would need to have her right leg amputated below the knee to stave off gangrene that had started in her big toe after an injury. Nabil and I were heartbroken, and made arrangements to take the next flight out from Riyadh to Beirut. We filled out the necessary paperwork at the passport counter of the KFSH administrative building downstairs from where I worked on the second floor. We had our exit visa and were ready to leave early the next morning, Friday, the second day of the weekend. My boss, Abdullah, had been kind to let me go using family emergency leave.

Nabil and I hardly slept that night, worried about Fatina, however relieved that we were in the region and could be with her. We arrived early in the morning at Riyadh International Airport and started making our way through immigration, only to find out we did not have a re-entry visa to come back to Riyadh. I was crushed, and Nabil looked like he wanted to cry.

"Are you kidding me? What is going on, Nabil?"

"Didn't we sign everything?" I was completely exasperated.

Nabil looked at me angrily: "You know, one of the main reasons we came to this region was to be close to my mom to support her in a situation like she's in now. And here we are so close to Lebanon, but we cannot leave."

I rarely saw Nabil this defeated. Without the appropriate documents, it was impossible to change the immigration officer's mind.

Feet and spirits dragging, we drove home and waited anxiously for the next day, Saturday, the first day of the workweek, to resolve our issue. The next morning, we spoke with the passport staff.

"What are you two doing here? We thought you were in Lebanon."

"There was a problem with immigration, we couldn't fly yesterday. We didn't have our re-entry visas."

Faces pallid, the passport staff sincerely apologized for their dreadful mistake.

We were on the next flight to Beirut. We rushed to Nabil's mother's hospital room after arriving at the airport. Fatina had her surgery the previous afternoon.

Nabil's Mom yelled in Arabic, "They cut my leg, Nabil! They cut my leg!"

Nabil wept and hugged his mom. Fatina and Nabil's tears fell together.

The room was filled with people; Jehan, friends, and neighbors. Salwa, a neighbor and friend, broke out into song. I was surprised. Nabil leaned over and said Salwa was singing a Lebanese *tarteeleh* chant about the Virgin Mary.

"Our loving Mother of God, take care of us, our Mother, Virgin Mary."

Eyes moistened; everyone was transfixed. Although I didn't understand the Arabic, I had goosebumps as Salwa lifted her head and closed her eyes, velvety notes spilling out.

Nabil's mother was in the hospital for a couple of weeks and used a wheelchair when at home. She despaired at not being ambulatory. In time, she didn't want to move from her bed to watch TV in the living room. We would visit Mama Khouri in the coming months. Nabil and I sat with his mom in her bedroom, holding her hands. Her statue of the Virgin Mary ensconced in rosary beads sat on a nearby end table, the candle lit at its base. Nabil cut fruits, apples, and oranges, feeding his mama by hand, as he did as a child, keeping her engaged by talk of politics, a favorite subject.

Fatina passed away at home on February 24, 2003. Although expected, we weren't ready. Nabil and I traveled back from Saudi Arabia to Beirut to attend his mother's funeral. On the plane ride, Nabil was in his own world. I had my memories of Fatima's hugs, cheery smile, laughter, and loving soul. Her spirit and memory will always be with me and her treasured son, Nabil. Although he appeared calm, just before we landed, Nabil, eyes downcast, told me he felt heartsick over losing his mother and dear friend and guilty at not holding her hand when she passed away. He also worried about what would happen to his sister, Jehan, who sacrificed her own life to care for their mother over many years. We had to remind each other that we had the privilege of visiting Nabil's mom numerous times while living in Saudi Arabia and to be with Jehan and other family members and friends in Beirut mourning his mother's loss.

CHAPTER 12

ILLNESS & TERROR ATTACKS

"I don't like this," Dr. Jalal deadpanned to Nabil as he lay supine on the exam table that morning of March 19, 2003. The sterile white walls closed abruptly around me as I sat in the corner of the room, doing my best to process the doctor's words. Nabil's face turned ashen. In the following weeks, Nabil was diagnosed with colorectal cancer; only one month after his mother's passing.

Nabil visited a KFSH general practitioner several times between 2002 and 2003 for bleeding from the rectum. The doctor initially thought Nabil had hemorrhoids. He was put on a daily course of Metamucil. However, the bleeding continued but was not severe. Nabil never complained to me about pain. He grew up in an environment where men were brave and never showed weakness. The only hint that something was different, or possibly wrong, was in the months before his diagnosis; Nabil was only able to carry one five-gallon container of water rather than two up the apartment stairs to our dispenser.

One afternoon at work, Nabil felt moisture on his office chair as he stood up to go to the restroom. He reached down to find the source and saw blood covering his work chair. He tugged on his trousers and found more blood saturating the back of his pants. Nabil told me later he knew he had cancer.

Nabil called me at my office.

My voice trembling at the news, "Nabil, we have two options. Either we see a specialist immediately, or we go back to the U.S."

We saw a KFSH specialist the next day. I was inside the exam room as Dr. Ala Jalal supervised Nabil's exam. The intern didn't find anything. Dr. Jalal examined Nabil and felt a growth in the rectal area that greatly concerned him.

As soon as we exited the exam room, I made the excuse to Nabil that I needed to use the ladies' room.

I dashed into a nearby restroom, tears falling.

"Please let Nabil be okay! Please let Nabil be okay," I cried out to the universe.

This was one of only two times I wept during Nabil's medical ordeal. Like Nabil, I suspected cancer.

Dr. Jalal ordered a lung x-ray. Other scans were ordered, as well, and all came out clear. If it was cancer, it had not spread. We were hopeful.

However, when we met with a KFSH oncologist, he told us most likely Nabil had cancer. Nabil would have none of it, but just in case, he briefly thought about fleeing to Europe so as not to expose me to the ravages of cancer. He later revealed that he wanted to escape from reality. A colonoscopy confirmed Nabil had colorectal cancer. Nabil asked the doctor if he had ever been wrong before. "Never," came the response. We were in for a fight.

Nabil would need major surgery, maybe an ileostomy, and be hospitalized for an extended time. We were ravaged. What to do next? We would have to tell our family, our bosses. Should we stay in Riyadh or go back to the U.S.?

My parents were startled. They suggested we return to the U.S.

"What if the hospital where you work doesn't know how to deal with Nabil's case?" my dad asked.

Dad continued, "If you guys are concerned about the expense, I would be happy to help."

Mom chimed in, "The most important thing is for Nabil to receive the best medical care."

My heartbeat accelerated and different thoughts from just a few minutes ago poured in. A bit of light. A bit of hope. We had a definitive plan B.

However, Nabil's initial thoughts were to stay in Riyadh, especially since all of Nabil's medical treatment—surgeries, hospital room, and meds— would be free.

I needed to talk to my Saudi boss, Abdullah, the manager who expressed initial concerns about my skill set and ability to lead the financial unit that had been opened for me. Thankfully, Abdullah had since come to see me as a team player and a valued member of his department. But I was still concerned about trading on his good graces as I entered his office to tell him I might miss substantial amounts of work due to Nabil's medical challenge. The words barely left my mouth before Abdullah told me, "Mary, while Nabil is in the hospital, I am not your boss. Nabil is. When he tells you to take off, take off, and I'm not going to charge you any leave time." My entire body relaxed, encouraged by Abdullah's graciousness and relieved that work would not be a real distraction. Nabil's boss was also understanding. Nabil's health came first and he should not worry about work while he was sick.

Despite the reassurances, Nabil and I were still panicked over having a critical operation so far from home. Prolonged talks filled our work breaks, dinners at home, and bedtime. Dad's concerns rang through us. Could we entrust these doctors with this radical surgery and to make reasoned and crucial medical judgments?

I made a call to my brother-in-law, Sam, a physician at a prestigious hospital in the U.S.

"Should we have the surgery at KFSH or in the U.S.?"

"Don't do anything yet. Send a tissue sample to our lab in the U.S., and we'll test it," Sam said.

"And don't agree to surgery until we look at the sample and I speak with Nabil's doctor!"

We arranged for Nabil's KFSH doctors to FedEx a sample to Sam's lab. The report came back very similar to the KFSH findings.

After speaking to Nabil's doctors, Sam told us the course of action and techniques followed by the KFSH surgeons, all Saudi, would be the same as those followed at Sam's renowned hospital in the States. So, Nabil and I agreed he would have colorectal surgery on May 26 at KFSH.

There had been travel warnings from the U.S. State Department going back to February 2003 that Westerners could be targets of terrorism. Out with the dogs on the morning of May 12, 2003, just two weeks before Nabil's surgery, I caught snippets of conversation in the neighborhood about potential violence in the city. It seemed Western compounds might be the targets of attacks. My blood pressure elevated, imagining our friends or colleagues hurt or worse. And what if the Diplomatic Quarter became a target?

"Nabil, what should we do? What do you think happened?"

"Let's see if we get a Warden message from the U.S. Embassy. And let's turn on CNN."

Later that day, news reports came through—three Western compounds scattered throughout Riyadh, including Al Hamra, Dorrat Al Jadawel, and Vinnell, had been struck by car bombs. My head pounded; I felt the blood vessels surge in my head. This was too close! 9/11 was always on the fringes of my mind. I knew terrorist forces could hit us—this was a politically turbulent region, after all. Still, after two and a half years of relative safety, I never truly believed it would happen in Riyadh. Like those news reports where you hear about a tragic event, a weather catastrophe, or a kidnapping and say, "Oh, that would never happen to me."

On that fateful day of the attacks, our dear Japanese friends, Kamin and Kana, as well as colleagues of Nabil's, lived at Al Hamra, one of the terrorist group's targets. Foggy and deeply distressed, I asked Nabil how to find out about our friends. Nabil reached for his phone and dialed Kamin and Kana. There was no connection. My pulse quickened—I was inert; a certain hopelessness set in. Nabil was notably unflustered. I wasn't sure if he was strong for me or if it was because he had already experienced the atrocities of war and conflict as a child.

It would be a couple of days before we heard from our Japanese friends. They had felt the effects of the bombing at Al Hamra; broken window glass filled their bedroom, and Kana suffered a mild head injury from flying glass shards. Our friends sounded distracted, obviously in shock over the event.

Until May, we had only witnessed this kind of violence while in the Kingdom at a distance, through the news. On March 20, 2003, two months earlier, we were with Kamin and Kana at their villa in the Al Hamra compound, watching TV newscasts. News reporters announced that America had started a military campaign against Iraq to eradicate supposed weapons of mass destruction (WMDs). (It was ultimately determined that WMDs did not exist.) Awestruck as missile contrails sailed through Baghdad's night sky, followed by constant explosions and news reporters broadcasting the grim events, I turned to Nabil. The disturbing images completely consumed him and our Japanese friends. I couldn't fathom what was coming through the TV screen: massive destruction and Baghdad was only a little over four hours flying time from Riyadh.

We had received warning messages about real and potential terrorist attacks before even relocating to Saudi Arabia; one only a month before we left Washington for Riyadh to start our new life. There was an Al-Qaeda attack on American interests on October 12, 2000. The terrorist group had struck the USS Cole, an American naval destroyer, off the coast of Yemen. The event stopped us in our tracks; Yemen bordered southern Saudi Arabia. In a matter of weeks, we would board a plane to Riyadh. Our Washington, DC house had been sold, our furniture sold or given away, nearly a year was spent on a grueling process to complete endless contractual documents, and we had finally received hard-fought approval to bring our pooches into the Kingdom. My heart was too invested. With each new warning, I hid behind a cloak of denial.

While our friends escaped with minimal physical injuries during the May 12, 2003 assault on Al Hamra, the emotional trauma was formidable. I was American, after all, and had not personally experienced anything close to terrorism, especially not the detonation of a bomb 30 minutes away from my home. This just couldn't be happening to us and our friends; the craziness was palpable. Nabil found out several days later that an uncle of a colleague was picnicking with friends and family at the Al Hamra compound at the time of the bombing. The uncle lost his life. Nabil never conveyed his condolences; he didn't have the courage. The event brought back traumatic childhood memories for Nabil, as he experienced war and terrorism first-hand in Jordan and Lebanon. Sadly, 39 people were killed, and more than 160 were injured in the three bombings across Riyadh.

Escaping Saudi Arabia and moving back to the U.S. was out of the question since Nabil's surgery was only a couple of weeks away. Nabil and I agreed to keep a low profile while we were in the Kingdom until Nabil was done with his surgery.

"As soon as I feel well, you, Maci, Coco and I will leave," Nabil asserted.

"What if other compounds are bombed next week before your surgery"? I asked, my head spinning with the possibilities. None of them were good.

Nabil replied, "We will make a decision accordingly."

Luckily, there were no more bombings in Riyadh as the surgery date approached.

As the day of the surgery arrived, we could not disregard the fact that Nabil would receive life-saving medical care. I asked my Western religious friends to teach me how to pray, and I led a prayer as we all held hands.

"God, please let Nabil live. God, please let the surgeons' hands be steady, and the doctors be healthy during the surgery. God, please let Nabil and me get through this." And my prayers continued for the coming days, weeks, and months.

Expats, Saudi friends, and colleagues gathered with us in Nabil's hospital room the evening before his surgery. During a quiet moment, a Saudi friend prayed a verse from the Quran Kareem over my Nabil, a Maronite Christian, as there was no access to Bibles in Saudi Arabia. It was fine; we could use all the prayers we could get.

Early the next morning, Nabil and I were by ourselves. I kissed Nabil and told him I loved him; he told me the same and not to worry. I held myself together as they wheeled Nabil out of the room to the OR. As I stood alone in the hallway watching Nabil's stretcher moving slowly down the fluorescent-lit corridor, only the top of his head visible—a swath of dark curly hair—the transporters and stretcher turned a corner, and Nabil was gone.

I started thinking, *What if Nabil goes to Heaven while he is under anesthesia, or something goes wrong with the surgery? How can I continue without him?*

After all, he was not only my husband but my best friend.

I paused and frantically asked myself, *Why am I referring to him as 'was'?*

No, no, he is, he is, almost shouting at myself.

I was alone for several hours before a nursing friend, Melinda, came to visit. I had just found out Nabil's surgery would take a couple more hours than anticipated, as the tumor was growing diagonally and was difficult to reach. I shivered and imagined the unimaginable. What if Nabil didn't make it?

"Melinda, I can't stay in the room!" I exclaimed.

"Let's go see Tina and Diane," Melinda said as she put her arm around me and led me out of the room. Tina and Diane were also nursing friends.

I asked if we could all pray together and led another prayer. This time, I could not contain my tears. My friends embraced me and held me as I went to the recovery room to see Nabil a few hours later.

"Does anybody want pepperoni pizza?" I heard at the far end of the room.

Could that be Nabil? No, it couldn't be! All I could see around me were people, inert and gray, lying on stretchers. As we made our way to the back of the recovery room, I spotted Nabil, eyes and mouth open, covered from neck to toes in a hospital sheet, a couple of doctors and nurses at his side.

"Hello, ladies! Nabil said. "Are you ready for pizza?"

I could barely speak. "How are you, Nabil?"

"The question is, how are you doing, sweetie?" Nabil replied.

Dr. Jalal took me to the side. "We had to do an ileostomy." My heart skipped a beat. Nabil didn't know yet. He wouldn't have had the surgery had he known.

Dr. Jalal told me Nabil yelled out "hummus" during the operation. He was surprised Nabil would be talking about food. I said, no, that's Nabil's nickname for me!

Nabil would be in the hospital for an entire month. He fought through a serious infection, many procedures, scans, and two additional surgeries. While in the battle together, we fought our own separate battles, too. Nabil was confined to his hospital room, often in pain, and I was fighting for a balance between office time and time with my precious Nabil. Both of us were weary and ready for it to be over.

Nabil came home with his ileostomy bag still connected in late June. We were gratified that he weathered the storm.

Our two pooches were thrilled to see Nabil back home, though they sensed he was too weak to play. Deliberately following Nabil from the couch to the toilet, the couch to the bed, and the bed to the toilet, our oldest, Maci, would sit outside the bathroom door whimpering until Nabil emerged. Nabil hated the idea of having a bag for waste. Still, I continually reminded him it was only temporary until the doctors performed the reverse surgery and removed the bag completely. This always brought a hopeful smile.

In early November 2003, Nabil, moving slowly with his ileostomy bag still attached, and I took a short stroll around the neighborhood. We were still disappointed over a fluoroscopy test two months earlier showing a persistent leak in Nabil's colon forestalling reversal surgery. We were determined, however, to remain patient yet determined through this ordeal.

However, a few days later, around midnight, November 8, 2003, I jolted from the bed as a loud explosion reverberated through my ears and body, shaking the bedroom walls, bedframe, and my soul. Blood coursing through my veins, nerves tingling, I turned to Nabil who roused next to me.

"What the hell just happened?" I yelled, hoping against hope it was thunderclaps I heard.

"That was a bomb," Nabil answered anxiously, wiping his eyes as he sat up on the edge of the bed. "Stay away from the doors and windows."

It flashed through my mind that Nabil had lived through bombings during the Arab-Israeli Six-Day War and Black September in Jordan, and the Civil War in Lebanon.

It might have been Al-Qaeda, I thought, which meant there could be more bombs.

"It must have been close since it was so loud. Did you feel the bed shake?"

Nabil nodded. It occurred to me that he turned surprisingly calm.

I needed to do something. But what? There was nothing I really could do, and I didn't want to wait around for another strike. My thoughts immediately went to my parents, who were probably hearing about this in real-time on CNN. I leaped from the bed, rushed into the living room, and turned on the computer and CNN International TV.

My fingers flew across the keys. "Dad & Mom, you may have heard about the blast in Riyadh. We are OK and keeping our eyes on the news. Love, Mary & Nabil"

After several grueling minutes that seemed like hours, CNN reported that a bomb had gone off near the Al-Mohaya housing compound.

"Nabil, it was a bomb," I shouted into the bedroom. "And it was at Al-Mohaya. That's close, right?"

"Yes, it sounded very close by."

Smells of smoke permeated under the crack of our front door and through our window sills. Soon, the sounds of helicopters and ambulances blared through our apartment.

Phone calls and e-mails started coming in from friends and family, near and far.

Dad and Mom wrote, "We were worried. Thank you for letting us know that you're okay. We trust that you will make good decisions on what to do next." It was Dad's way to be nonchalant. He kept his worry inside.

As I lifted a window blind to look outside, Nabil shouted, "Stay away from the door and windows."

"I smell smoke, Nabil!"

"I do, too, Mary, but it's safer not to open blinds or be outside."

I quivered inside. Squeezing next to Nabil on the living room couch, he held me tight. I felt safe in his arms. Nabil told me we could either leave and go back to the U.S. this week or go back after his next surgery. He left the decision up to me, but that was harder than hearing the bombs and smelling the smoke outside.

Further newscasts confirmed that the expatriate Al-Moyhaya residential compound, just minutes from us by car, had been bombed and that, tragically, 17 people had died and 122 people were injured.

My head stirred with endless thoughts and conversations with Nabil. He had his heart-wrenching memories of war in Jordan and Lebanon, and high on his priority list was keeping me and our pooches safe. My mom and dad, and friends in the U.S. all encouraged us to come home. Certainly, this seemed like a practical solution and the safer alternative. However, we had invested time and money and had established and nurtured close relationships with both Saudis and Westerners. I was emotionally divided. Still, all options were on the table, including leaving the Middle East for good. One of my highest concerns was Nabil's medical condition, as he had his major colorectal cancer surgery only a few months back and was still experiencing the effects of the cancer.

Having been thrown into many dangerous and life-threatening situations during childhood and perhaps becoming somewhat conditioned to these events, Nabil also felt inclined to stay in Riyadh, in part a testament to the medical staff at KFSH. And Nabil was still wearing an ileostomy bag. Many issues remained surrounding the care of Nabil and his ileostomy bag: regular cleanings, handling mishaps, dietary requirements, and regular appointments with the KFSH medical team all were making a departure from the Kingdom problematic. Nabil was fortunate not to need radiation or chemotherapy. However, a month-long stay in the hospital and waiting for the ileostomy reversal surgery took a toll on Nabil.

We heard through the news that Islamic extremists were responsible for the 2003 bombings, part of an offensive against Westernization and Westerners themselves, possibly provoked by American and other allied troops planted in Saudi Arabia during the Gulf War with Iraq in 1991 after their invasion of Kuwait.

CHAPTER 13

WHERE TO RELOCATE?

My knees nearly buckled. *No, it can't be true,* I thought, as we sat in another of those colorless aseptic rooms. It was early December 2003, a couple of days after Nabil's second fluoroscopy. His first fluoroscopy exam had been in mid-September 2003. The doctor had found a leak in Nabil's colon. We were heartsick.

Dr. Jalal was showing us one of those cloudy X-ray images again on that sunny December morning. "You see, it's just right there" the doctor said as he pointed his pen at a very small dark area within an extended and larger gray area that was Nabil's colon. "There it is. It's the leak. Do you see it? It still hasn't healed." Nabil and I moved in closer. I squinted; all I saw was a tiny dark circle. "That's it?" I asked anxiously, pointing my finger at the blotch, astonished that this innocuous spot could continue to be the culprit, the reason my dear Nabil's reversal surgery would be further delayed.

"Yes, that's it," Dr. Jalal answered in too calm a voice.
I can't believe this. Not a second time!
Nabil was still looking at the x-ray on the wall, impassive.

"Are you okay, Nabil?"

"Yeah, I just want to hear what the doctor has to say."

My head throbbed.

"Will the leak in Nabil's colon ever heal?" I tentatively asked the doctor, firmly gripping Nabil's hand in my lap, small pools in my eyes.

The doctor grinned and let out a laugh that unnerved me.

"Of course, it will heal. It just takes time."

I only half believed him.

Nabil was scheduled for an operation in the coming days, December 8, to close the hole.

I was both hopeful and skeptical. We were first supposed to have a reversal operation in September or October; however, the unhealed leak moved it back to December. Now, instead of the expected reversal surgery, there was this continuing complication!

At least the surgery was a potential way out of this current conundrum.

Dr. Sala, Dr. Jalal's colleague, performed the surgery. The next day, in Nabil's hospital room, the doctor stepped inside and said, "Most likely, this will do the job."

My heart lifted, but I remained leery. I reminded myself that anything could happen; my protective shield was up in case it all went sideways.

Nabil, always the optimist, told me he trusted the doctors.

In any case, we would have to be patient until the next scheduled fluoroscopy on January 10, 2004, to determine if the hole in Nabil's colon had closed.

Earlier, just four months after Nabil's May surgery, we decided to travel to Cyprus, a nearly four-hour plane ride away. We needed the getaway. The trip would fall in early September, our tenth wedding anniversary. Our workmates and friends thought we were crazy; Nabil still had his ileostomy bag. But Dr. Jalal had okayed the trip as long as Nabil took it easy. We were used to packing; however, this time, we needed to include ileostomy materials – pouches, baseplates, and gauze pads for cleaning.

Cyprus was a beautiful weeklong respite. Despite my admonishments, Nabil insisted on going in the sea and jacuzzi. To my consternation and Nabil's embarrassment, Nabil's ileostomy bag dislodged twice while in Cyprus -- in the Mediterranean, and the hotel jacuzzi. Each time, Nabil wrapped a towel around his abdomen, and we rushed back to our room. Although cleaning and reattachment had become routine, I felt bad that Nabil had these episodes reminding him that he was still mending. These mishaps were more than made up for, though, by the glorious time we had tooling around in a rented convertible alongside the Mediterranean and lush green mountains. We stayed in the town of Larnaca, near the airport, and enjoyed the balmy waters of the property's tourist beaches.

A drive north into the mountains reminded me of coastal California and Nabil of his roots in southern Lebanon. In Troodos, a mountain town, we sampled locally-made wine. Driving to the southwest of the island country, we attended the Limassol Wine Festival in the beautiful seaside town of Limassol. Feasting on Cypriot food, including lamb cooked in a clay oven, as well as wine, music, and dancing, we were enchanted by a young man among the revelers gyrating in the traditional Greek manner as he stomped on grapes in an enormous wooden bucket.

Our last night in Cyprus had us dining in a cozy outdoor courtyard of a small hotel across the street from our lodging. We sipped ouzo and relished classic Cypriot food—yogurt, garlic, and cucumber salad; kafta; grilled chicken; hummus; grilled pork; and *loukoumades* (Greek ball-shaped donuts) and baklava for dessert. Our evening ended with

Nabil and me joining hands with other partygoers, snaking our way around dinner tables and the pool while dancing Zorbas-style. As I was pulled up onto a chair, I couldn't help but break out into my belly dancing. Nabil beamed.

Arriving in Riyadh following our revitalizing trip, we fell into our revised work and life routines. Nabil with a reduced work hour schedule and all the attendant meal and cleaning requirements surrounding his ileostomy bag. The doctors instructed Nabil to eat a high carbohydrate diet, including rice, bread, crackers, peanut butter, and no beans nor high-fiber foods, all of which were meant to thicken the gastric juices and aid in the proper functioning of the ileostomy bag and Nabil's reconfigured colon.

After the disheartening results of Nabil's fluoroscopy in early December and his subsequent surgery to close the leak, we needed another escape. Christmas was coming up in a few weeks, and we didn't want to spend it alone in Riyadh. We had heard about Sharm El Sheikh, Egypt, a tourist destination on the Red Sea and the south Sinai Peninsula, from co-workers and friends. Nabil visited the KFSH travel office, a floor below my office and inquired about flights and accommodations. The trip would be relatively easy for us since it was only a two-and-a-half-hour flight to Cairo and then an hour flight to Sharm El Sheikh. Despite the short notice, the agent was able to book us a flight. My hope was for another uplifting adventure for Nabil in spite of his continuing medical ordeal.

Our Cairo hotel had a view of the Nile. Like many, I had a romanticized image of this grand waterway: a majestic, beautiful, and historic river. I imagined Egyptians from eons ago, clothed in long robes, sailing in wooden boats along its tree-lined expanse, and farming its fertile soil. But what I was seeing on this Christmas Eve night after a crowded commercial flight was a somewhat brackish-looking river framed by an industrial skyline. It didn't help that we arrived in Cairo on a gloomy, stormy evening. We were in Cairo-proper, though, which carried a population of around 15 million at the time along with city pollution and hordes of unruly cars. The "idyllic scenes" of the river winding through an alluring desert fringed with bucolic greenery and palm trees were elsewhere along its four-thousand-mile banks.

We had one day in Cairo, and had to see the Egyptian Museum and the mummy exhibit. The hotel staff discouraged us from ordering a cab from the hotel, as fares would be cheaper on the street. Stepping outside the hotel, we hailed a taxi from the street corner. Within seconds, a cab was alongside us. "How much?" Nabil asked. The grizzled driver mumbled an amount. Nabil disputed the amount and asserted that our hotel management said fares should be half that. The driver bellowed, "Get in!" and instructed Nabil to hold tight onto his door handle as the door didn't shut properly. Nabil had to grab onto his door handle the whole way, a half-hour city drive from our hotel to the museum through intense car and pedestrian traffic, to avoid his door swinging open. I held onto Nabil as he held onto his door, hoping he wouldn't fall out onto the street. More than relieved that we arrived without injury at our destination, I was still somewhat shaken, thinking, *What's next?*

We walked tentatively into the majestic coral-colored Egyptian Museum. A glorious display of time-worn relics of ancient Egypt met us as we strode through the entryway of the museum. My mouth agape, I took a deep breath as we entered the Tutankhamun floor devoted to the Egyptian boy pharaoh of the 1300 BC century. I didn't know what to expect, but I knew I was privileged with the resources to be afforded a view of this extraordinary exhibit. Garish amounts of gold and ivory found in Tutankhamun's tomb filled a display in the museum. Gold slippers on the mummy's feet, gold casings placed over Tutankhamun's fingers and toes, and the gold enclosure where the ancient king's internal organs were buried separately. A spectacle – beautiful, awe-inspiring, but I couldn't help feeling that the blatant opulence was excessive, misplaced. A bloodline afforded this young pharaoh the gifts of an entitled life and death.

The next morning, we flew the "puddle jumper" from Cairo to Sharm El Sheikh. Greeted by hotel staff in colorful traditional garb – dark red fezzes with tassels and white, green, and red tunics gathered at the waist—drumming on tablas. We were disarmed by the colorfully decorated Christmas trees displayed inside and outside the hotel. It had been three years since I last saw holiday trees and decorations brandished in public. The Mutawa in Saudi Arabia did not allow Christmas displays, only the occasional sale of undecorated Christmas trees. Another restriction that had become a "new normal" for us. While I was never one to buy into the commercialization of Christmas, I admit to sometimes missing the carols and bright lights of the Christmas season.

The next morning at breakfast, I was startled to spy a couple of camels roaming between the hotel pool and beach, maroon rugs with circular designs spread over their humps. Obviously strategically placed for the tourists and promoting the hotel.

Later in the day, an old Mercedes taxi drove us 125 miles north of our hotel in Sharm El Sheikh to St. Catherine's Monastery, the site of the "Burning Bush" on Mount Sinai of Moses fame in the Sinai Desert. Planning for this trip drew me back to the epic movie, *The Ten Commandments*, directed by Cecil B. DeMille and starring the larger-than-life Charlton Heston as Moses. I eagerly awaited the visit, remembering the chilling scenes when God revealed himself to Moses through the grand "Burning Bush" and later returned to Mount Sinai to receive the "Ten Commandments" from God.

The two-and-a-half-hour drive was magnificent, taking us through a vast desert, wadis, and stony mountains of the Sinai Peninsula; Bedouin villages, camels, and sheep at every turn. Awestruck by the stark beauty of the Peninsula, I was similarly moved by the historical and biblical importance of the place. Also attuned to the politically motivated events of the area in past decades and possible safety challenges for us, I remained somewhat attentive throughout our drive. I would find out later that, like me, Nabil had concerns about being alone with this taxi driver in a vast desert with no real signs of civilization. Realizing, though, that there were no recent threats, I determined to fully appreciate this corner of the world that few would ever see. Saint Catherine's Monastery is located in its namesake, the town of St. Catherine's. Framed by Mount Sinai, it is reportedly the oldest Christian Monastery known in the world, dating back to 300 AD. Excited to view the esteemed "Burning Bush," I was instead surprised and somewhat disappointed to find a rather unremarkable overhanging prickly and dense desert bush, located in a relatively nondescript corner of the monastery's courtyard. Definitely not movie-worthy.

Our last evening in Sharm El Sheikh found us dining at the renowned Alf Leila wa Leila (One Thousand and One Nights) souk, scented bakhoor wafting through the night air. A fantastical marketplace with arched gateways took me back to the famed medieval Arab tales of my childhood. Enjoying stuffed grape leaves and kebabs, we listened to live Egyptian music, including songs by Um Kulthum, a premier Egyptian singer of decades earlier. It caught me by surprise when Nabil borrowed the musician's tabla and began drumming; I got up to dance, happy to be moved by the music I had grown accustomed to since living in the Kingdom. We both seemed relieved to be fully living life again in those moments.

Although care of Nabil's ileostomy bag and special dietary

restrictions, along with Nabil feeling less than par, was a constant, our trip had been a welcome breather from hospital stays and medical tests.

Unfortunately, Nabil's next fluoroscopy on January 10, 2004, showed another leak possibly caused by a surgical staple at the December operation site. And on and on it went; the next fluoroscopy would be in early April, with reversal surgery in mid-April if all went well. Although frustrated and concerned, I had to make peace with this; Nabil's medical issues could continue indefinitely, and he might end up with a permanent ileostomy. As long as he was alive, though, I would take what I could get.

"What is really going on here?" I asked Dr. Jalal during Nabil's follow-up appointment on January 14, anxious about the possible answer.

Smiling and seeming to understand my worry, he said, "Mary, because the cancer was in the lower part of the colon, the rectum, the dirtiest part of the body, infections and related issues are not uncommon.

I flinched.

He added, "The good news is that the colon itself is healing well, and after Nabil's final surgery, his digestive tract will return to normal."

Between November 8, 2003, the date of the Riyadh terrorist attack a few miles from our residence, and mid-January 2004, we noticed a significant increase in Saudi security presence at the Diplomatic Quarter and around Riyadh, in general. It seemed the Saudi government was preparing for another major attack. Nabil and I watched Saudi military vehicles moving in and around the Diplomatic Quarter, day and night. Seeing Riyadh on high alert, its military operatives at most major intersections in the city, and in front of high profile commercial and government buildings, naturally made me and Nabil very nervous. There were a lot of rumors that Riyadh, and specifically the Diplomatic Quarter, the location of Western embassies, could be targeted by terrorists. This meant we were potentially in harm's way.

We kept our eyes and ears open to catch the slightest hints of trouble. Nabil still had serious debilitating cramps that stopped him in his tracks, even from driving, at times. His ileostomy bag attached to the colon in his upper right abdomen restricted complete digestion and nutritional benefits to his body. Although we spoke of leaving Saudi Arabia, the practical reality was that we should stay to complete Nabil's reversal surgery. Was there another way?

"Nabil, I'm worried about what's happening in Riyadh! Should we consider having the reversal surgery in America?"

"I'm concerned my bag might not be able to handle the plane's pressure for that very long flight," he replied.

Trying to reassure Nabil, "Maybe we could use extra tape to keep the bag in place." I knew I was grasping at straws.

Nabil suggested we talk with his doctor. Dr. Jalal was pretty emphatic about Nabil staying in Riyadh for his final surgery. While Nabil could go elsewhere, KFSH had complete records and a history of Nabil's case and was following their prescribed protocols. They knew the intricacies of Nabil's case.

We were flattened; there were no real alternative options. We risked Nabil's health if we took a different route. We weren't even sure when Nabil's colon would be healed for reversal surgery.

We knew we had control, though, over what was next in our lives after Nabil's final surgery. Where did we want to live and work?

As we cleared the dinner dishes one evening in March 2004, I turned to Nabil.

"Should we ultimately go back to the U.S. or stay in the Middle East"?

"Maybe we should stay in the Middle East," came Nabil's reply. "What about you, Mary?"

I was surprised at Nabil's response.

I replied, "I'm really inclined to stay in the Mid-East region, but

I am worried about safety. And where would we go if we stayed in the region?"

This provoked more discussion and soul-searching. Feeling I needed more time in the region to grow, I became more settled on the notion of staying. I wasn't quite ready yet to return to what I perceived to be an unyielding and sterile work-life balance. Still appreciating the culture and lifestyle of the region, I wanted to complete my career in the Middle East. I was content with the expatriate lifestyle -- happily busy with ongoing events like trips to the desert, Christmas choral concerts, square dancing, and sometimes multiple dinners in one evening. Having lived in the nation's capital, Washington, DC area, for 17 years, we never had such a busy social schedule as in the Middle East. Life in the U.S. was sometimes lonely. We often had to initiate social events; otherwise, we might not hear from friends for months at a time. And our work life in Saudi Arabia afforded us the resources of time with extended vacation days, and money to travel frequently to memorable parts of the Eastern world, usually eye-opening experiences.

We ultimately agreed to stay in the region, but the question remained. Where would we take up residence? Countries like Jordan, Lebanon, and Syria were not possibilities. Lacking resources, such as oil or natural gas, they did not have the breadth of jobs or salaries that would make it worth our while to stay. We should focus on the Arab Gulf where natural resources were more plentiful. Dubai was out of the picture; the cost of living was too high. And, for us, Dubai was not a huge cultural draw. Although it had become popular for its impressive skyscrapers and glitzy lifestyle, it had turned into a mini-New York City. Kuwait didn't offer competitive salaries; it was already an established country. No significant new projects.

We considered Oman a beautiful Gulf country with rugged rocky mountains bordering the Gulf of Oman and the Arabian Gulf, where we had Omani friends who were like family. Unfortunately, the pay scale did not meet our needs.

There was one more obvious country.

"What about Qatar, Nabil? It's just next door, and they have a booming economy. Good place for an economist and civil engineer. Qatar has natural gas that's being sold around the world. As a matter of fact, a lot of expatriates are moving to Qatar for that reason."

And at the time, Qatar had the highest per capital income in the world.

Before I could finish my next sentence, Nabil said, "I'm going to call the U.S. Embassy in Doha and have them send us a list of companies in Qatar that might have an interest in an economist and civil engineer." And he did, right then. An embassy representative was accommodating indicating an e-mail would be on its way with the list of companies.

Relieved we were designing a course of action, I still harbored grave concerns over the basics. Nabil's health and our safety. While we decided to stay in Riyadh for Nabil's final operation, we could only hope against hope that there would be no more dangerous attacks on the country during Nabil's surgery and recovery time.

Starting plans to travel to Doha to meet with a variety of American companies and a smattering of Qatari firms, we still had the issue of Nabil's bag, the on-the-road maintenance, and concealing his ileostomy from potential employers.

We knew we had to move forward, though. Within a week after contacting tens of companies in Doha to secure jobs, we were able to line up several interviews for mid-March. Companies were not willing to pay for our airline tickets or hotels in Qatar. Without any real hesitation, Nabil and I decided to go to Doha for our interviews despite the effects on our budget.

Concerned and kept up some nights, I worried whether it would all work out. Our trip would be fast-paced with back-to-back interviews. Would Nabil's bag hold up, and would Nabil garner the gumption to confidently spar with prospective employers?

I told my boss, Abdullah, I would be going on a short vacation to Doha; of course, Abdullah could have suspected the real reason for our trip. He knew the challenges we, and other Western expatriates, faced.

We left our pups, Maci and Coco, at our residence with a KFSH nursing friend. We boarded the plane uneasy, wondering what the future might hold. I held Nabil's hand as we taxied to the runway, trying to gauge his emotional state. Seeming to understand, Nabil half-whispered that he was insecure about his ileostomy. He wanted to make sure his bag was not noticeable under his clothes when he was interviewed. I was also apprehensive about Nabil's situation but tried to put on a good face.

"Nabil, everything is going to be alright, and if it is meant to be for us to move to Qatar, then it will happen."

Nabil replied, a smile on his face, "I feel the same."

When we deplaned, I made sure to have my abaya ready. I heard that Qatar was less conservative than Saudi Arabia, but I still had to ask airport staff whether I should wear my abaya. "It's not required here," came the curt response. I still couldn't help but gawk at women in tank tops and western slacks in the Doha airport. After four years of traveling in and out of Riyadh's King Khalid International Airport, my mindset had settled on the belief that women wear abayas at public airports in the Gulf region.

We spent five days in Doha. Our modest hotel room in downtown Doha served as a makeshift office. A calendar with Post-it notes scattered about filled the double bed. I was in my element, organizing and planning for upcoming interviews while Nabil made calls confirming our scheduled sessions and arranging for new ones. We were surprised at the relative ease of arranging for interviews, perhaps because the Arab Gulf highly valued goal-oriented, serious-minded American workers, especially those with international experience. On occasion, we simply walked into a company on the list and presented ourselves to Human Resources. It was odd for us, (and for the Human Resources offices), to stone-cold present ourselves; however, our time was limited, and we were determined to hit as many companies as possible while in Doha. There wasn't always time to go through the additional steps for organizing an official interview. Explaining we were American expatriates residing in Saudi Arabia, I held my breath as we handed over our resumes to the Human Resources manager that first day. Could we meet with the Finance Department or Engineering office today? Quizzical looks. It didn't work that day.

We met many company managers and owners. It was all a blur at times. I felt sorry for Nabil, who had to keep his suit jacket closed to hide his ileostomy bag. It was hot in Doha, close to 90 degrees, but there was no other good option other than to keep his suit jacket tightly buttoned. When at DynCorp (a major contractor for the U.S. Air Force in Doha), one of the interviewers remarked about the hot weather and told Nabil he should feel free to take off his jacket. I tensed; would Nabil be discovered? With a glance at me and without skipping a beat, Nabil said something about the powerful A/C, and the interview carried on. Our interviews were promising, and Nabil was offered a job as a civil engineer. I was considered overqualified; however, DynCorp was willing to work something out with me if I didn't find suitable employment elsewhere.

"Can you start next week, Nabil?" the manager of the Doha branch asked.

"No, I can't start before September. We need to travel to the

States over the summer to see family." We couldn't start jobs anytime soon, as Nabil needed to have his reverse surgery and healing time before starting a new position.

"We need someone in a week, a maximum of two weeks," the manager emphasized.

With a half smile, the engineer who Nabil would replace jumped in, "I can't handle the Doha drivers anymore. I need to get back to Maine and my family."

Nabil lobbed back, "Come see the driving in Riyadh, my friend."

We all chuckled.

Although disappointed that our time frames didn't match and that Nabil would be giving up a competitive salary and employment package, we were determined to continue our search.

One afternoon, when Nabil was at an interview, and I was in the hotel reviewing interview notes, Nabil called, excited.

"Mary, I'm coming to pick you up."

I thought, "What, you're supposed to be in the middle of an interview."

Nabil continued, "I'm at Parsons with Robert. He wants to meet and interview you, too."

"Really, for what kind of job?" Parsons International was a Defense contractor, so I wondered what sort of economist or financial position he might have open.

Robert wanted to consider me for a possible position in another "leg" of the company that did financial consultancy.

Parsons was looking at opening an office in Doha, and Robert was tasked with doing reconnaissance to determine the profitability of such a venture. If the project was assigned, Robert might offer Nabil a job. It could be days, weeks, or months.

Robert and Nabil had a connection beyond employment matters; fellow Western ex-pats in the same field, both with gumption and drive.

Concerned that I wasn't appropriately prepared, my "interview" turned out to be more of a gabfest. Robert asked about our time in Saudi Arabia and why we wanted to relocate to Doha. Was it that unsafe in Riyadh? If Parsons International opened a branch in Qatar, it would hire staff from Doha and bring staff from Dubai.

Robert worked for Parsons International in Dubai; his family and life were there. Robert told Nabil that expatriates in Dubai were notoriously bad about saving money, as many spent their monthly earnings on expensive entertainment and consumer luxury items. Dubai prices tended to be much higher than Qatar's. Despite the unique financial challenges in Dubai, Robert aimed to stay there, like so many other expatriates in Dubai, probably drawn to the glitz and glamour. We met with Robert several times; the meetings were always hopeful. Perhaps Robert wanted to keep a hold on us in the event there were good opportunities for us and him; we wanted to keep a hold on him, too. My heart lightened a bit; we might have a fallback position.

While in Doha, I arranged for interviews with the standard large multinational accounting companies like Price Waterhouse and Ernst & Young; however, I didn't get far. I'm not an accountant. I sent my resume to the Finance Department at Education City with Qatar Foundation, half hoping to become the Finance Director, an intense job. I was shortlisted but did not get the job. And we both interviewed with Carnegie Mellon at Education City. Nabil held out hope for a job with Carnegie Mellon, a celebrated American university, which had programs in business, IT, and computer science. Education City opened other U.S. satellite campuses in Doha, as well, including Northwestern, Georgetown, Virginia Commonwealth, Texas A&M, and Weill Cornell. After interviewing with Carnegie Mellon, Nabil wanted the job as a Maintenance Engineer; the pay scale and medical benefits were good. Nabil had a lingering concern about his health, and the workweek at Carnegie Mellon was only five days. The workweek tended to be six days at Qatari firms.

Turner Construction, a large American company with an international presence, was on our list. They didn't have a current position for Nabil, however, if a suitable contracting job came up, they would be interested in hiring Nabil. David, one of the engineers who interviewed Nabil, suggested that Nabil approach I.M. Pei's engineering and architecture company, which was building a magnificent Islamic cultural museum in Qatar, the Museum of Islamic Art. While it appeared as a standard diplomatic response, *we don't have job openings, but here's another company you might try*, Nabil seemed to befriend David. It was Parsons all over again. Nabil insisted I go with him to a second meeting with David at Turner.

"Why? Do they have an opening for me, Nabil?"

"They might, you never know. But I just have good vibes from David."

I had mixed feelings about going, as I wasn't sure if it was good for me or Nabil, for that matter. Our time in Doha was limited, and I wanted us to focus on companies that we knew had vacancies for an economist or a civil engineer. I didn't want to waste this crucial time.

Nabil cajoled me into going. David had been in Doha for some time, and Nabil had the sense that David had good connections. We brought our list from the Embassy, just in case. David was in a large room surrounded by computers and wires. He pulled up chairs for us. The conversation was light.

"Nabil tells me you're an economist in Riyadh. How is it as an American woman living and working in Saudi Arabia?"

"It's good. It started with some challenges, but now I've adapted, and it's fine."

As David and I chatted, Nabil pulled out the list.

"You know, David, we have this list of companies that the U.S. Embassy in Doha gave us. Do you know any of these companies?"

David took the list. He skimmed through the pages and then slowly traced his index finger over the company names, one by one.

"You all should really consider some of these Qatari companies." David pointed to several.

"And I've heard good things about CDC and UDC. They're solid Qatari firms with some interesting projects."

We found out later that CDC was Construction Development Company, and UDC was United Development Company; sister firms with one managing director.

David continued, "Not all Qatari companies pay on time, but CDC and UDC do."

Nabil and I exchanged skeptical looks. We weren't really interested in considering a Qatari company. There was greater security and comfort in going with a known quantity, an American company. Although we worked at KFSH, a government-sponsored Saudi hospital, its beginnings were American-influenced. Americans built the hospital, which was opened in the mid-70s, and managed it until 1985 when the Saudi government took it over. American and Western influences continued to permeate the operation of the hospital with a goal-oriented outlook and an eye toward luring American and Western talent.

David was forward and compelling in promoting Construction Development Company (CDC) and United Development Company (UDC) as promising career paths for a financial analyst and civil engineer. Although not entirely convinced, Nabil and I thought there was no harm in checking out these companies.

The next day, Nabil and I walked into the offices of CDC located in downtown Doha. The building, unremarkable, was a three-story low-rise, and CDC was on the third floor. Double-paned glass doors brought us into the office area, a corridor with artificial leafy plants hugging the back wall. To the left was a distinguished fine wood door with the words "Management" on a metal nameplate. On the right was a similar door with "Human Resources" imprinted on metal. We went right and entered the Human Resources office. A South Asian woman, a receptionist, looked our way. We were walking in "cold;" no appointment.

"Can I help you?"

"We're here to meet the HR manager," Nabil said confidently.

I steadied myself. How would this work?

"Just hold on one second."

The receptionist disappeared down the hallway; we heard hushed tones. We could make out, "Miss Lamia, there are two people who want to meet with you."

"Who are they?"

"I don't know, but they seem to be westerners."

"Bring them in."

The receptionist came back out and led us to a large corner office, the desk covered with papers and files.

"Hello, I'm Lamia."

Lamia firmly shook my hand and turned to shake Nabil's.

Her eyes pierced mine. Her tall stature, casual chic ensemble, and large sparkly jewelry on her neck, wrists, and ears made her a presence. She jingled with any small movement.

We handed Lamia our resumes and informed her that we were Americans working in Saudi Arabia looking for job opportunities in Qatar since Riyadh had become unsafe.

Lamia glanced at each page of our resumes.

She looked up, straightened her back, and enthusiastically said, "There are resumes, and then there are resumes. I want to send these to the Managing Director of CDC."

"That sounds great," Nabil said. I smiled and added, "We appreciate it."

Lamia jangled as she left the office with our resumes to be copied.

We gave each other the thumbs up.

Nabil leaned over, "I'm sure she's Lebanese. I recognize her accent, and look how she dresses."

I thought the same thing.

When Lamia returned, she asked, "How long will you be in town?"

"Three more days," we responded.

We were gratified with the effortless introduction and interest in us, although I was unsure about whether I was fully onboard with this particular company.

We were surprised when Lamia called that evening to let us know we were both scheduled for interviews the next night at 6:30 PM. I didn't feel the need to overly prepare.

"I feel like this is only a practice interview, Nabil."

"I'm more interested in Carnegie Mellon at Qatar Foundation," Nabil declared.

Half an hour before our interview, we walked outside our hotel and signaled to the first taxi that was lined up along the street. We told the driver we wanted to go to Construction Development Company. He drove us through the town alongside the small shops of the computer souk. Within 20 minutes, we were deposited outside the CDC building. We went up to the Human Resources office where we found the receptionist, but few others, as the offices had just closed.

She looked at us quizzically, "Why are you here? Aren't you supposed to be interviewing at UDC?"

"UDC, what are you talking about?" I asked.

"You're scheduled to be at UDC, not CDC!" She ran over to her counter and jotted down the address for us.

We scurried downstairs, hoping the taxi driver was still there. Of course, he wasn't. We ran around the corner to a busy street, where we hailed a cab.

We arrived at UDC an hour late for our interviews. I felt terribly bad to be late, though this was tempered by the feeling that there wasn't a real future with this company.

While the CDC building was plain and dated with enclosed hallways, UDC was new; its main floor was a large open space filled with light, glass-encased offices, high ceilings, and a large mock-up of UDC's premier project – The Pearl, an artificial island à la Dubai's projects in the middle of the floor. I wasn't expecting this kind of flourish with a Qatari company.

"Pretty nice, huh, Nabil?"

"I didn't expect this, Mary."

We fell silent as the receptionist approached us sitting at the far end of the floor.

"Who's first," she smiled.

"I am," as I jumped up. I wanted to get this over with, especially the bit about being an hour late.

Walking the length of the large space, I braced myself as the receptionist guided me to a spacious conference room. Putting on a professional smile, I walked around the table and shook hands with three men and one woman. The man at the far end of the table, Kameel, in his mid-40s, of medium stature, with penetrating eyes, bluntly said, "You're late."

I shrank slightly, "I'm so sorry, but I thought the interviews would be in the CDC building."

His face remained unchanged, just those penetrating eyes during the entire interview.

Two of the interviewers were married; Adam was British and his wife, Rhonda, was Palestinian-British, and both had been with the company since the early days. The older man in the room, Abdulrahman, soft-spoken and measured in his speech, was Iraqi and was a founder of the company.

Adam and Rhonda from the Finance Department led the questioning, beginning with the basics of The Pearl. This massive island project would erect over fifty residential towers, luxury retail stores, and business offices. The project was at its beginnings; land was being reclaimed, costs determined for workforce and equipment and prices for residential and business units. Profitability was of primary concern. What was my previous work experience? What could I bring to the project given my work experience? Clasping my hands under the table, my interest piqued. I replied that I understood The Pearl was a complex project with a lot of moving parts; however, I played a major role in developing and running an intricate and successful new budgeting process at KFSH, a highly reputable 800-bed hospital. And I ran multi-billion-dollar cost studies for a federal agency in Washington, DC.

While I bantered with Adam, Rhonda, and Abdulrahman, Kameel at the far end of the table seemed to hang on every word I spoke, his elbows on the table, fingers intertwined, head resting on his hands, his eyes intense. He never asked any questions. Who was this guy? I assumed he was a staff person; he seemed young and perhaps a bit shy. Toward the end of the interview, Kameel, focused and self-assured, spoke. Although I had a good resume and experience, he wasn't sure my background was the best fit for their company. I straightened my posture; I wasn't going to let this pass. "I feel confident I have the right experience for most of the job requirements, and for the rest, I'm a quick study," I replied with conviction. Kameel's face eased ever so slightly. He carried on saying he noticed from our resumes that Nabil and I worked at the same hospital in Riyadh. Would we want to continue working together? "No," I said. "We didn't work in the same departments at the hospital. We wouldn't mind working in separate divisions, buildings, or companies." I thought it was an odd question. However, in the Arab world, family is a priority. I presume Kameel thought we had a pre-condition about working together, since our jobs were both at KFSH. We would later find out that Kameel was the Managing Director of UDC and the President of CDC.

Despite the awkward start, I felt good about the interview, pleased that I didn't hold back. I had been confident as I didn't think I had anything to lose. I was still not entirely vested in this company. It was Nabil's turn next. He disappeared into another nearby conference room. As I sat waiting, I wondered how Nabil would weather Kameel and hoped he wasn't anxious about his bag. Making some mental notes about my interview, I was surprised when Nabil reemerged only half an hour later with Kameel and three other men who turned out to be Kameel's father, Tony, Abdulrahman, and a staff member who was Lebanese. Nabil looked relaxed with the men, chatting and chuckling, almost like they were friends. Startled, I watched as Nabil made a beeline for me. "What just happened?" I wondered.

The men waved goodbye to Nabil and nodded in my direction.

"How was it?" I mouthed to Nabil as the four men walked the other way.

"It was good," Nabil mouthed back.

"Were they upset with you about being late?"

"I told them we thought the interview was at the CDC building. Kameel kind of smiled and said his sister, Lamia, never gave good directions. Everyone in the room laughed."

"So, Lamia is Kameel's sister," I said.

Grabbing my hand to leave, Nabil said, "Mary, it's all about family in the Middle East."

The receptionist had called us a cab.

Nabil was roused after the interviews. After climbing into the cab, he insisted we go to the Sheraton, a triangular-shaped building on the Arabian Gulf, one of the first major luxury hotels in Doha. In the taxi, Nabil told me that one of his interviewers, a staff engineer, was pleased to hear Nabil was from southern Lebanon. There seemed to be fledgling interest on their side.

There was an issue, though; the same as with other companies interested in us. If offered jobs, Kameel wanted us to start in a month or so. We could only start by September 2004. If things went well, Kameel couldn't wait a day longer than August 15th. There was another, bigger, issue for me: CDC and UDC workweeks were six days with only Saturday off. This was a deal-breaker for me.

"Nabil, I can't see this happening. The human body needs a couple of days rest."

"The package is good, though. The salaries are high, and housing is free, Mary."

I persisted. "I know, but we came to the Middle East to have a balance between work and life."

"I'm not too thrilled about the 6-days a week either," Nabil said. "But I think we should consider the jobs if they are offered to us."

I shrugged, not willing to give in just yet.

Exhausted after five days of interviews, we collapsed into the overstuffed chairs of the Sheraton lobby. A waiter in a black suit and crisp white shirt hurried over to get our orders. We selected our go-to dinner snack, Lebanese mezze: baba ghanoush, hummus, tabouli, olives.

With mixed emotions on our last night, I wasn't completely ready to leave. I wished we were further along in securing jobs, at this point. We made it hard, though, for potential employers by insisting on a start date in September, six months from the time of our interviews. But we had a reason beyond the recent terrorist attacks for being concerned about securing jobs outside of Saudi Arabia.

Very heavy on our minds was a call we received a couple of days previously from our doggie sitter in Riyadh. I thought back on that evening of the call as we sat at our small café table in the Sheraton lobby, sharing our baba ghanoush and hummus and some quiet moments.

At the time of the call, we were in our Doha hotel room getting ready to go out for dinner.

I was apprehensive to hear our sitter's voice as I answered the phone, my mind darting around, guessing what could be wrong. Did something happen with the dogs?

"What's up?" I asked, trying to stay calm.

Nervously, the sitter divulged, "A man with an Arab accent called here at the apartment and asked if Americans lived here."

I gripped Nabil's arm and put the phone on speaker. "We're being monitored!"

Eyes fixed, Nabil put his index finger to his mouth, "Let's listen to what she has to say."

The doggie sitter was quick thinking and told the caller, "No, no Americans are living here."

"And then what happened?" my mind swirling.

"Nothing, he hung up."

My mouth dry, we thanked the sitter and emphasized calling us immediately if the person called again or if there were any issues, at all.

Flustered and frightened after hanging up, I looked at Nabil. Heat rising in my face, "Nabil, I'm really concerned about going back to Riyadh."

"Mary, we have no choice but to go back and do my damn surgery," frustration in Nabil's voice.

A persistent ringing cell phone and Nabil's voice brought me back to the Sheraton lobby. Nabil was asking if it was my cell phone or his. It seemed to be mine. I dug into my purse, rummaged around, and managed to answer the phone before it stopped ringing.

A man with a deep, soft-spoken voice was on the line.

Slowly and deliberately, "Is this Mary Khouri?"

"Yes, it is," I said haltingly.

"This is Abdulrahman. We have decided to offer you the job of Financial Planning Specialist with United Development Company if you're interested."

I gulped, pointing to the phone and waving at Nabil.

"Hi, Mr. Abdulrahman," I intoned, wanting Nabil to know who it was.

"Oh, thank you. I appreciate it." Hesitating, "But I'd like to think about it before making a decision. Would it be possible to let you know by the end of the summer?" We had already spoken at the interview about the general terms of an employment package, including salary and benefits. We would be provided a house, car, and airline tickets from the U.S. to Doha whenever we were ready for them.

"We definitely need to know within that time frame, or sooner, if possible, but we will wait to hear from you. And we'll send you the final employment package."

"What about Nabil?" I asked.

"Yes, if you accept the position, we will have an employment package for Nabil, as well."

"Okay, that sounds good. I will be getting back in touch with you."

I hung up the phone. "Nabil, they offered me the job! And it looks like you have a job, too."

"That's great news, sweetie!"

"But I don't really want it."

"Mary, you should consider it!"

I shook my head. I just needed to leave it there. There was time to think about it. Things would be clearer after Nabil's next fluoroscopy in May, two months away.

And we had this real "Catch-22" situation. We needed to get out of Saudi Arabia but had to wait for Nabil's reversal surgery and allow time for recovery. It seemed we didn't have any good options other than to wait.

CHAPTER 14

MOVE TO QATAR

The thought of working six days a week continued to gnaw at me. As it was, I put serious energy and effort into my five-day-a-week working schedule. How could I sustain an additional day? My work ethic in the U.S., largely tied to wanting to display my prowess at not only getting things done but doing so meticulously, was exceedingly important to me. Like so many American career women, I was on that treadmill of putting in long hours, taking work home with me, and attending meetings even if I was sick. But by my early 40s, I was ready to step off that treadmill and envisioned an improved work-life balance in the Middle East. Living with Nabil for nearly 20 years by that time, I figured that social networking, connecting with other humans, was crucial in the Arab culture. Prior to moving to the Middle East, Nabil had provided a mini-Arab world for us in the U.S. with belly dancing parties, Lebanese food, and Turkish coffee readings for me and our friends. I knew I wanted more of that, and definitely needed to learn the art of being with and appreciating my fellow human beings, which seemed so effortless in the Arab world based on Nabil's stories of growing up in Jordan and Lebanon.

My previous work at KFSH in Riyadh helped to open up this new sensibility toward an improved balance between work and life that I was not so keen on giving up. I had enjoyed working hard in the U.S., but this new life was teaching me about enjoying so much more than my professional accomplishments.

If I took the Doha job, I imagined being drained by the end of a workweek and having only one day to recover. And having to do groceries and laundry on that day off. On the other hand, it was a job and would allow us to continue our life in the Middle East. I knew I had to come to terms with this and likely comprise in some way. Never easy for me; I liked things clearly defined and settled.

And we had more pressing immediate concerns. Nabil and I had several uneasy conversations in Doha about the call from the doggie sitter who was staying at our place in the Kingdom. Thinking that our lives were being monitored like in a spy movie made my skin crawl. I was troubled about returning to Saudi Arabia from Qatar given that our safety, and even our lives, could be compromised. If we ever felt hesitant or sentimental about leaving Saudi Arabia, this cemented our decision that we could not stay in the Kingdom.

While our security in Riyadh and acquiring a job in Qatar were paramount in my mind, we still had the issue of Nabil's reversal surgery for his ileostomy. We were now hearing his operation would likely be in early May 2004.

And we had to determine how best to exit Saudi Arabia when the time was right. How to tell my boss who had become more than a colleague, but rather a friend? I didn't feel great about leaving him in the lurch. And what to do with our belongings? Our initial move from the U.S. to Riyadh found us inanely transporting 42 pieces of luggage, including trunks, suitcases, and boxes. Although we had already sent some clothes and sundry items back to the U.S., we couldn't possibly lug all the remaining baggage back to the U.S., nor could we store it in Riyadh until our job situations were resolved.

There was a lot to consider.

The initial misgivings our loved ones raised when we first decided to move to the Middle East came back with renewed zeal after 9/11, and were only bolstered following the two alarming terrorist attacks in Riyadh in 2003. Living in the Middle East was not something we would recommend for many. It was just something that worked for us and for other Americans and Westerners who spent significant time in the Kingdom. However, with the Riyadh bombings just a couple of weeks before Nabil's initial surgery in May 2003 and then another in November 2003 during Nabil's recovery time, we realized how truly vulnerable we were.

Following the May 12, 2003 Al-Qaeda bombings, the U.S. Embassy closed for several days, and many Western expats made plans to leave Saudi. Security became tight around the city, including at KFSH and its housing compounds, and the Diplomatic Quarter. Military guards and tanks with firearms and artillery encircled these locations, constantly at the ready. Stunned and shaken, this was a world that didn't make sense to me. Truly too much to absorb, survival instinct kicked in. Part of my brain must have deadened. I focused on what I could control, things like Nabil's upcoming surgery. Although scary at the time, it seemed like the lesser of two evils. The doctors had assured us that Nabil would survive and recover from the surgery.

Security at the Diplomatic Quarter was on particularly high alert, with all its embassies and western occupants susceptible to attack. Concrete barriers stood at the two entrances, military guards performed several checks a day throughout the Quarter, and two tanks were permanently installed with firearms, artillery, and antiaircraft missiles at each entrance. Military guards with menacing eyes stood at the entrances to the Diplomatic Quarter, M-16 rifles slung over their shoulders, and police cars patrolled the Diplomatic Quarter throughout the day and night.

Although we lived in the Diplomatic Quarter, we were stopped each time we approached an entrance on the way back from work, an errand, or a friend's home. At these times, an intimidating guard looked through Nabil's open window and asked, threateningly, if we lived there. Nabil's answer was always, "Yes." The guard continued canvassing the interior of our Jeep Cherokee, his narrow eyes darting back to Nabil now and then. This ritual always set me on edge, reminding me that a terrorist assault could happen at any moment. And as hard as it was to imagine, we were among the targeted group. Otherwise, I tried keeping this terrifying thought insulated in my brain.

In late 2003 and early 2004 (before Nabil's final surgery), we gradually organized our place for a possible exit from the Kingdom, sorting through everything to find what we really needed – everyday clothes, toiletry items, important documents, including medical records and financial information. We gave away clothes and shoes to our housekeeper, as well as various household items we no longer needed – extra pots and pans, as KFSH supplied us with kitchenware. We packed trunks for the rest – heavy jackets and clothes, winter blankets, photo albums—to be sent to the States. By late January 2004, we sent the trunks from our Riyadh residence back to the Washington, DC area, where friends held it for us until our return. We had already sent five trunks home a year earlier after hearing talk of the U.S. attacking Iraq.

Amid these preparations and grave concerns over our safety, our routine included weekly visits to the stoma nurse to check Nabil's ileostomy and picking up medical supplies for changing Nabil's bag, as well as unceasing care of Nabil's ileostomy pouch at home. Parts of it were like a bizarre dream; there was normalcy in the midst of incredible strangeness. We were going about our everyday lives in what felt like a movie. It was just all so surreal.

During this time, I gladly became a part-time nurse, changing Nabil's dressing every day just after his hospital stay as one surface infection along the incision line lingered. We decided to avoid daily visits to the hospital to have the dressing changed by a "real" nurse. Later on, Nabil participated in the testing of new stoma equipment and materials. Nabil joked about being a guinea pig; always trying to be cheerful in so much anxiety.

I eventually continued long hours with the usually expected cardamom coffee breaks at KFSH as Nabil fell into teaching math and science at private schools in Riyadh; at first, part-time, and eventually full-time.

My family was particularly concerned about us getting stuck in Saudi Arabia.

Mom sent me an e-mail reminding me of the stories my aunt Catherine had told our family about living in England during WWII. *Before WWII, people living in Germany, who were at risk if a war were to erupt, trusted too much that there would be no war. They kept thinking that it couldn't/wouldn't happen. And when war finally did break out, it was too late for them to leave, and the natural consequences occurred.*

Mom continued, *Catherine remembers well the great sadness of that war. She was a young child then, and there was talk in her family of sending her and her brothers to a safer haven than where they lived in England. But something happened, and she and her siblings had to stay where they were . . . England was 'in the thick of it' during WWII. So, Catherine knows the perils of 'getting caught' somewhere and thus is greatly sensitive to your present situation. It should go without saying that you both are more than welcome, at any time, at our home to re-group or reconnoiter or just to rest.*

Appreciative of my family's worry and love, I felt, perhaps naively, that we had things covered.

I replied to Mom: *With regard to being 'stuck in Saudi Arabia,' we have several options in place to help us, which is not the case for all Western expats. First, we have multiple exit/reentry visas. Those without these special visas who want to leave the Kingdom have to visit the hospital's passport office, which is only open during normal working hours, and apply for a single exit and reentry visa. It takes at least a day to process these requests. Nabil and I, on the other hand, can leave the country at any time of the day or night, seven days a week. Secondly, most Western expats do not consider an escape by car to be feasible, while it is for us. We have several destinations in the region where we can drive or fly and stay for an extended period – Abu Dhabi, Jordan, and Lebanon, where Nabil has sisters, or Oman, where we have friends who offer a home free of charge for as long as we want. And we have an open airline ticket in this regard. We will continue to assess the circumstances and decide if we stay in the Kingdom, live and work in another Arab country, or return to the U.S. Also, Nabil is Arab, speaks fluent Arabic and is quite savvy in the 'Arab ways,' which allows us a more expeditious escape by car. Nabil can read the road signs in the region, as many are in Arabic. Now, of course, we understand that anything can happen, but we are planning with 'an eye' towards minimizing harm to ourselves. As you know, we have 'a few wrinkles' we need to try to work on, including Nabil's surgery and the administrative aspects of leaving our employment at the hospital. . . . We do know, at some point, we may need to leave immediately.*

After the November 8th bombing, 2003's second attack, I let my family know the Diplomatic Quarter had become even more heavily fortified with additional military personnel, tanks, and heavy artillery. I was sensitive to my family's worries. I decided to be as honest as possible about what I was seeing and experiencing in terms of the beefed-up military presence. I hedged, though, from time to time, trying to rationalize our predicament for our emotional health, as well as that of our families.

Nabil and I had many thoughtful discussions on what to do if we needed to leave at a moment's notice. It was bizarre to have to think like this, however, it had become an inherent part of our lives. My mind was becoming rewired in a sense. I was beginning to understand what Nabil felt like living between the two cultures. Nabil spoke, now and then, about having to balance and compartmentalize his younger life as an Arab militant in the Middle East with his recent life as a freedom-loving American citizen. The two barely intersected. Like Nabil, I was stuck between two worlds, the one ready to explode at any moment.

Around February 2003, when "weapons of war" in Iraq were first discussed in American news reports, Nabil and I agreed he would emphasize his Arab origins by speaking Arabic regularly to our Saudi workmates, friends, and government officials, and inform people he was a Lebanese native. The Saudis admired the Lebanese; they appreciated their perseverance and enjoyed holidaying in their beautiful country. In this regard, I was fortunate with dark hair and eyes, and that I spoke some Arabic. Colleagues regularly thought I was Lebanese, which I took as a compliment.

Within less than a week after the May 12, 2003 bombings and within a week of Nabil's first surgery, we received an e-mail from the U.S. Embassy in Riyadh. It was frightening to receive word that the American Embassy and Consulates in Saudi were developing possible evacuation plans for Americans. The message revealed that *"The Embassy continues to receive credible information that further terrorist attacks are being planned and could be imminent against unspecified targets in Saudi Arabia."* In my haze of mixed emotions, it was clear extreme precautions were being made to meet the threat; I was reminded, again, how truly perilous our current circumstances were. It all seemed like an alternate universe! This only happened in other far-flung countries.

Although understanding the real risks in the Kingdom, I had grown to love this area of the world and realized its impacts on me had been deep and lasting. There was a sense of belonging and rootedness; I was not ready to abandon this country and region, knowing I had more to learn and discover.

The Embassy e-mail read, in part:

EMERGENCY SITUATIONS: WHEN AN EVACUATION IS A POSSIBILITY

- Discuss possible contingency plans with family members. The United States is the designated safe haven. Families may go to any destination in the continental United States; employees are normally required to safe haven in Washington, D.C.

- Make a list of items to pack in each suitcase (normally each evacuee is allowed one suitcase).

- Make a list of items for carry-on baggage.

- Update current household effects inventory of items at post.

- Consolidate all personal records, financial documents, school records, etc.

- Prepare your house for departure -- secure valuables, if possible.

- Plan for pets. In almost all evacuations, your pets will not be allowed to go out on evacuation with you. Make advance arrangements for their care, food, etc. Keep the pets' records updated.

- Decide how money will be handled. Who will pay bills? Will you continue to use the joint checking account?

Was I dreaming?

Of course, Nabil and I wanted to be included in any contingency plans for Americans to be evacuated, although this possibility, at the time, seemed remote. If you were a U.S. passport holder, and wished to participate in the evacuation plans, you were to consult the Embassy or your Warden. It all seemed so sterilized and unnatural. No hand holding or *"Don't worry, it's going to be okay."*

I was in touch with Dana, the KFSH nursing head, responsible for thousands of nurses from all parts of the globe and for disseminating Warden messages to American KFSH employees. In response to my question about evacuation procedures for dogs, an issue of grave concern to us, Dana queried me through a preliminary e-mail:

Where do you live? Are your dogs small enough to carry on an evacuation plane? Are their vaccinations and papers up to date? I'm really not sure about the rules for dogs, but I will try to find out.

After receiving the Embassy's and Dana's e-mails, I was disturbed and confused about the potential issues with dogs. *There's a possibility we'd have to leave our pups behind? That is not going to happen!*

It was beginning to feel like a nightmare.

After the call with Abdulrahman on behalf of UDC on that balmy March evening at the Sheraton in 2004, I had to still my mind. There were too many unknowable variables. It was hard to know where to start.

At breakfast in our Doha hotel on our last day in Qatar, I asked Nabil, "When we go back to the States over the summer, what should we do with all our luggage and trunks? Especially given that I don't feel comfortable working 6 days a week at UDC, and we don't have any other offers."

Nabil replied, matter-of-factly, "I've been thinking about that. Let's ask Rachel, the rental lady if we can leave all our stuff with her."

I stared blankly at Nabil. "What do you mean?"

While in Doha looking for jobs, we spent time with Rachel, a realtor from South Africa, who showed us rental properties. We wanted to cover ourselves in case we accepted positions without free housing or a housing allowance. Although Rachel had been obliging in showing us rental properties, I thought it very inappropriate to ask if she would accept holding on to our luggage (everything we owned) while we were in the U.S. over the summer. We didn't even know if we would get jobs in Doha. This wasn't very sensible.

Nabil ignored my last question and continued, "And I could start calling cargo companies to make arrangements if Rachel agrees."

"I don't know, Nabil. It sounds so off-the-wall."

It wasn't long before we were meeting with Rachel. I was surprised that she wasn't really dazed at our query.

"My son has a garage; I can ask him."

"Wow, that would be great," I said. We would pay a nominal fee—the cost of transporting the baggage from the port to the son's garage. Perhaps Rachel was sympathetic to us, as the news of the Riyadh bombings was being reported all over the world.

At any rate, the stars seemed to be aligning.

I knew we had to go back to Riyadh and resign our positions. So much was up in the air, though. We still didn't know for certain when Nabil's reversal would be and if we would get jobs in Qatar that would interest us.

It still didn't make sense, though, that we make plans to move to Qatar when there was so much ambiguity. How could Nabil be so sure we should proceed with securing a cargo company?

And there was still the concern of our immediate safety in Riyadh when we returned to Saudi Arabia tomorrow.

"Nabil, I'm thinking you should dress like a Saudi when we fly into Riyadh tomorrow?"

"Why?" came the response.

"Because I'm concerned that we could be profiled at the airport if we come across as Westerners, Nabil. Everything is in such a state of flux, and you don't know who is with who."

In Saudi Arabia one never knew what sort of security official you might encounter at the airport. If they didn't like the looks of you or if they were in a foul mood, they could make life difficult for you, especially during those unstable times.

The next day, we were on the afternoon flight from Doha to Riyadh, Nabil in a white thobe and ghutra and me in a more traditional, fully black abaya. While pleased that Nabil's ileostomy bag did not present any challenges during our interviews in Qatar, I was worried about what might await us in Riyadh. I fidgeted with my abaya and put my book away as the flight attendant asked passengers to make sure our seat belts were securely fastened; we would land shortly.

Nabil collected our luggage from the overhead bins and adjusted his ghutra to fit just right atop his head. With a slight smile, he motioned for me to move from my seat into the aisle ahead of him.

Bothered by all the "what ifs," I clutched my purse, repositioned my abaya, and strode off the plane with forced confidence.

Approaching the immigration area there were segregated lines; one for single males only, and the other reserved for families. We joined the family queue. I was glad the line was moving fairly quickly but nervous about everything going on in Saudi Arabia. Stepping up to the immigration officer's booth, Nabil handed the man our passports. He grabbed them, and his fingers skimmed over the computer keys. He looked at Nabil. "Just wait here."

Oh gosh, what now? I thought, suddenly feeling very confined in my abaya.

Our passports firmly in his hand, the immigration officer went behind his booth to an office a few yards away. He was gone for only a few minutes. The officer didn't have our passports when he returned to his booth. I could barely breathe.

"Where are our passports?" Nabil asked, his mouth twitching ever so slightly.

"Follow me," he responded without an ounce of emotion.

He led us to a small room with a desk and chair and two uniformed men. The officer from the booth left.

The two gentlemen, grim-faced, stood like stone when we walked into the room. One with two stars on a holding bar over his chest was sitting at the desk, and the other with one-star insignia stood beside the desk.

Nabil asked, "What's going on?"

"We just want to check you two. You came from Qatar, and you're wearing a Saudi thobe."

The officer continued, "Your passport says you're American, but you have an Arab name."

Nabil responded, "We've been here for three and a half years and have legal visas since we're working at KFSH. So, why are you arresting us?"

The officer said, "I'm not arresting you. I'm only detaining you for interrogation. But your wife can enter the country."

Nabil said, "The U.S. passport belongs to the U.S. government, and you cannot hold them."

Nabil continued, "Well, then, can we call the U.S. Embassy?"

The officer said, "No need since I'm not arresting you."

"Then what do you call this if you're not arresting me?"

"I just told you. I'm detaining you, not your wife."

The officer told his colleague to search Nabil. When they found Nabil's ileostomy bag, they asked, "What is this?"

Nabil responded, "I have an ileostomy bag because I had cancer."

"What is that—the bag?" the officer asked.

Nabil provided a brief description.

The officer said under his breath, *"Maskeen"* (poor guy).

I jumped in, "Can I call my boss at KFSH?"

The officer immediately replied, "Yes."

I found my cell phone and called Abdullah. Thankfully, he answered.

"What's happening, Mary?"

"Nabil and I just arrived in Saudi Arabia from Doha, Qatar, and we're being detained at the Riyadh airport."

"I'm on my way! Can I talk with the officer, Mary?"

I gave the officer my phone, telling him my boss wanted to speak with him.

The officer stepped outside the office to talk with Abdullah in private.

When the officer returned, he had a friendly smile and handed me my phone.

"Can I get you both tea?"

Nabil said, "No, thank you, but can we get our passports back?"

"I'll return them to your boss when he arrives."

Nabil and I sat in that small office for nearly 45 minutes. I half-looked at the officer as he shouted on the phone. As he turned to us, he coerced a smile. I couldn't relax completely until Abdullah arrived.

I engaged the officer. "You know, we love Saudi Arabia. After all, it saved my husband's life."

The officer replied, "Welcome to Saudi Arabia," just as Abdullah came through the door.

Nabil and I let out a collective sigh.

"I'm going to get you all tea," declared the officer.

It would have been an insult to decline.

The officer picked up a business card and gave it to Abdullah. "If these people are ever in trouble again, please give me a call, and I'll help them."

Abdullah led us to his car.

On the drive to our apartment, I wasn't sure it was the right time, but I knew I had to broach the subject.

"You know, Abdullah, things are really unsettled and uncertain in Saudi Arabia. I know you don't want to hear this, but I think Nabil and I need to leave for good."

Composed, Abdullah replied. "You are like a sister to me, Mary, and Nabil like a brother. Whatever you feel is best, I support you."

Taken aback, all I could say was, "Thank you."

As soon as we arrived at our apartment, Nabil was in full gear, planning for a cargo company to inspect our belongings and provide a cost estimate for shipment to Rachel in Doha. Nabil let the cargo people know the final shipment of our household goods would not be before May 2004, as the doctors believed Nabil's reversal surgery would occur by then.

It was the latter part of April when we began shipping some of our belongings to Rachel in Doha to store in her son's garage. Friends in Saudi thought we were crazy to send all our belongings to Rachel, a real estate agent in Qatar whom we just met. I must say I felt pretty much the same.

In early May, Nabil had his long-awaited last surgery, the reversal of his ileostomy. The surgery went very well, and by mid-June, we found ourselves and our two pups inside a Saudia airliner flying from Riyadh to Washington, DC. We had spent weeks meeting with Saudia management about allowing our two pups on the plane. Saudia had rigid rules about prohibiting dogs in the plane's cabin. We explained that a small dog's health would be compromised in the cargo hold with the pressure and colder temperatures without us being there to comfort them. Surprisingly, management finally relented and we were provided formal paperwork allowing our dogs to fly in the cabin with us. We were astonished when checking in. The attendant at the airline counter declared we could not enter the plane with Maci and Coco. They could go by cargo.

"Look," I implored, "we have paperwork allowing the dogs inside the plane."

"It doesn't matter, no dogs in the plane's cabin."

Just as I turned to Nabil, a supervisor came to the counter and asked what the problem was.

"This man is not letting us bring our two dogs on the plane, even though we have special permission. See?!?" as I handed the supervisor the documents.

"It's okay, let them through," the supervisor ordered.

A sigh of relief.

And, of course, Coco could not stop whining and yapping despite having been given a doggie sedative.

We were let on board despite the initial obstacles; however, I couldn't completely relax until we left Saudi airspace. As soon as we settled into our seats onboard, a couple of Southeast Asian stewardesses came over and fawned over our two pups.

"Can we hold them? They're so cute!"

"Of course, they love everybody," I replied.

Once in flight, two stewardesses grabbed one pup each, cuddled them in their arms, and proudly marched through the plane.

This trip was different in another way. It was a final exit visa flight, which meant we could not return to Saudi Arabia without acquiring another working visa from a Saudi agency. It was bittersweet saying goodbye to our Saudi and expat friends. My finance group had a small farewell get-together for me in my boss, Abdullah's, office; nothing too fancy, as it was all on short notice, but emotional nonetheless. I hugged each female colleague and shook hands with my male cohorts. I asked Nabil if it was okay to hug Abdullah goodbye. He said it was fine. It was hard to let go.

Even though Nabil was a bit weak after his reversal surgery with gas cramps and constipation, we managed to have a good flight and rented a car in the Washington, DC, area. We drove along the east coast from Washington, DC to Georgia and the panhandle of Florida, and back all the way to the coast of Maine. We visited relatives and friends, and it was pleasant and heartwarming. However, it wasn't easy to relax and fully appreciate it all when neither Nabil nor I had jobs to go back to in the Middle East.

During our two-and-a-half months in the States, we did not communicate with CDC/UDC. I just wasn't enthusiastic about the expanded work schedule. A job with Carnegie Mellon that Nabil had held out for didn't materialize, and there were no other suitable jobs for me. So, with our hearts beating double-time, we signed our job contracts with CDC/UDC in early August 2004, and faxed them to their office in Doha. It seemed there was no way around the 6-day workweek for us. I knew I wanted to hold onto the experiences I had in the Kingdom and the general region, which had been crucial for my personal growth, so I would have to make the best of things.

CHAPTER 15

CAUGHT BETWEEN TWO CULTURES

Our flight back to Doha was scheduled for early September 2004. The company took good care of us. A CDC driver, sign in hand, "The Khouris," picked us up from the airport arrival terminal, expertly loaded our luggage into an awaiting car, and drove us to our new residence, provided by the company, in an expat housing compound. The company later provided us with our own vehicle and free gas. Nervous and excited, the view out the car window looked familiar as we travelled these same streets before in spring of 2004 during our job search in Doha. Our villa, located in the center of the city, was waiting for us: three bedrooms, and two and a half baths. A whitewashed cement wall encircled the compound. My boss managed to send us a few men with pickup trucks to move our household items from Rachel's son's garage to our new villa. Surprisingly, neither Rachel or her son charged us anything for storing our belongings, however, we did pay for the expense of transporting our goods from the Doha port to the son's garage.

Our villa was lovely, although older by Doha housing compound standards having been built in the 1970s. While the villa was spacious and certainly met our needs, Nabil and I were somewhat disappointed over the backyard enclosure, also bounded by a concrete white wall. The courtyard was half concrete pad and half dried up grass and wilted brown shrubbery, creating a limited area for our pups to "do their business." We would certainly need to work on that! Nabil appreciated gardening when we lived in the Washington DC area, and he spoke with the CDC maintenance men about breaking up the concrete pad and landscaping our courtyard with grass, bushes, and flowering plants. In time, Nabil relished planting and tending to a vegetable garden in our backyard that included tomatoes, cucumber, green peppers, and hot peppers.

Nabil's first day on the job was the first week of September, and mine was the week after.

Work at UDC was fast-paced and challenging. A different rhythm from the government-sponsored KFSH in Riyadh. UDC was developing the island project, The Pearl. Even before my first workday, I met twice with the contractor who built an intricate cost model representing all expenses for The Pearl, from dredging portions of the Arabian Gulf to building materials and equipment, finishings, and labor. Clearly, expectations were high for this luxury mixed-use island comprising residential, hotels, retail, schools, and entertainment venues. I needed a jump-start on managing this model. Once officially onboard, schedules and final deadlines were strict and always looming, work hours long. I worked closely with the Project Manager on the financial end, developing and producing profit and loss documents, income statements, as well as the cost model—all tools to support time-sensitive progress on this highly anticipated project. There were regular meetings in-house and with contractors and government officials. Meetings still included mint tea, cardamom coffee, and dates served by "tea boys," young Southeast Asian men. However, in Saudi Arabia, "tea boys" were more prevalent at higher-end meetings.

Though I had been seriously concerned with the 6-day workweek at UDC, I found my way to a reasonable pace and rhythm with the workload and the hours. The project fascinated me—it was enormously complex and flexed my analytical abilities to the maximum. I was responsible for gathering data points to create pricing for a variety of residential and retail spaces, and costs for building materials, labor, and overhead expenses. I fed the inputs through an intricate cost model, and presented results at management meetings. I was often at work until 10:00 PM or later before such meetings. My days were focused, and workdays passed quickly. However, as months passed and the latter part of the week neared, it was harder to maintain higher energy levels. By the seventh day, my day off, I crashed. I slept most of the day and struggled to do everyday chores like grocery shopping and laundry. I felt I had lost the balance I appreciated in Saudi Arabia. I hoped I could sustain the 6-day workweek, although I didn't think I could indefinitely. Thankfully, I didn't have to. After a year, the company went to a 5-day workweek. Possibly for expats like me who might be driven to find work elsewhere. Nabil's sister company, CDC, however, retained the 6-day workweek. Nabil somehow became used to it.

After some time in Doha, we appreciated exploring the city, its lifestyle, and its history. Originally a relatively poor pearling nation, Qatar became one of the richest countries per capita in the early 1970s after Qatar's development and production of natural gas reserves – drawing expatriates like us to probe career opportunities. By mid-2015, Qatar's population had expanded to approximately 300,000 Qataris and 2.1 million non-Qataris (expatriates). In talking with Qatari friends, we learned this wealth allowed Qatar citizens to receive ample assistance from the Qatar government: free land offers, and financial support for health and education-related costs.

Qatar and Saudi Arabia share an abundance of conventional souks – gold souks, livestock souks, fish markets, computer souks, as well as general souks like Souk Al-Waqif, a refurbished market with a patchwork of alleyways, in Doha, and traditional and colorful Battah Souk in Riyadh. Nabil and I always preferred the chaos, colorfulness, and aromas of the cobblestoned souks over the more hygienic and sober malls.

While Qatar is more progressive than Saudi Arabia, the two countries are among the six oil-rich Arab Gulf nations (the remaining four including Kuwait, Bahrain, United Arab Emirates, and Oman), and both find young locals frequenting upscale malls and couture shops over traditional Arab souks. However, none of the Gulf countries approach the glitz of Dubai in the United Arab Emirates.

I always had a particular interest in documenting the perspectives of women in the Arab Gulf; views on their culture, westernization, and their hopes and dreams. It was here that I discovered the opportunity to do freelance writing for a Qatari magazine. I interviewed several young female Qatari university students on their views of life in the more traditional Arab Gulf and the creep of Westernization in their small nation-state. These young women were grateful for the sitcom, *Friends*, fashion trends, the internet, and smartphones, much like young people in the West.

The young Qatari women formed other ties to the West in the form of the establishment of American branch universities in Doha. In 1995, Sheikha Moza, wife of then Emir Hamad bin Khalifa Al Thani, had the foresight to realize that education was the future of Qatar. She established Education City (within Qatar Foundation) and brought five American university branches to Qatar – Carnegie Mellon, Georgetown, Texas A&M, Virginia Commonwealth, and Northwestern. A couple of the young women I interviewed attended Northwestern University and another Virginia Commonwealth in Doha.

I felt privileged to be in a country that promoted diverse educational opportunities for young women. However, I knew the conservative traditions of the Arab Gulf circumscribed the aspirations of these young people.

Although similar in many ways, I was struck by the cultural differences between Qatar and Saudi Arabia, both Arab Gulf countries. Although Riyadh is a modern city, in many ways, Saudi Arabia always felt like the "real" Arab world, how I had envisioned it before we arrived, with its old souks sporting ancient daggers and sheaths; and as the land of Hejaz, it housed the two most holy sites in Islam. Qatar, on the other hand, felt more like a wannabe Dubai with glossy skyscrapers and non-stop development and construction.

Homelife in Qatar and Saudi, however, was practically indistinguishable. While in the Arab Gulf, I was intrigued by the massive homes behind seemingly impenetrable walls. Qataris and Saudis tend to have enormous homes to accommodate large numbers of immediate and extended family who are often in compound settings or, at least, in close proximity to each other. Ensuite bathrooms are the norm in the Arabian Peninsula, as are majlises—generally, one majlis area for men and one for women. As American expatriates, it was always a special treat to be invited to a Qatari or Saudi home.

Although Saudi Arabia and Qatar share Khaleeji (Gulf) traditions, including conservative dress (abayas and thobes), communal housing arrangements, cuisine, dialect, music, and dance, there are some definite lifestyle differences. In Saudi Arabia, women couldn't drive when we resided there. (Women were allowed to drive in the Kingdom in 2018.)

Not true in Qatar. When out for an errand soon after arriving in Doha, I was stunned to see a Qatari woman completely hidden in black, only her eyes uncovered, speed past us in her Mercedes as we drove to our villa. How could she see with her face mostly covered?? A Saudi woman driving the streets of the Kingdom would have been arrested during our time there, whether she was speeding or not!

When we first relocated to Qatar in September 2004, it was more open than Saudi Arabia. In Qatar, abayas were not required for non-native women residing in the Arab Gulf. Toward the end of our time in Qatar, though, it became more conservative; security men at malls chastised Western women for wearing capri pants or tank tops. Forever wary in our last couple of years in Qatar, I made sure to wear longer pants and less revealing tops in public so as not to attract attention. It was all a bit disturbing, and detracted somewhat from the latter part of my Qatar experience.

Curiously, it was more difficult to make friends with locals and expatriates in Qatar than in Saudi Arabia. Perhaps because Westerners were a novelty in the Kingdom; the proportion of Western expats in Saudi Arabia was significantly less than in Qatar. The Saudis wanted to know us, while the Qataris weren't as interested. While it took time to develop friendships in Qatar, within a few short weeks of moving to Saudi Arabia, we met the Omari family at the Kindi Square in the Diplomatic Quarter. The Omaris, a large Saudi tribe, became fast friends and remained so for our entire stay in the Kingdom. It was pre-9/11 and they were intrigued with us as Americans, and we were with them. We shared many elaborate meals at the Omari family home, time in the desert, music, and dance. I felt privileged to visit the family in their palatial home hidden behind blanched walls. I imagine we were the only Americans who visited the Omari family in their private home.

Not only was it harder to make friends in Doha, but social events were sparser in Qatar than in the Kingdom. Societal restrictions in Riyadh and a need for community lent themselves to "trailing wives," spouses who accompany their husbands to expatriate appointments, creating ways to stay active through developing popular expat events—plays, music concerts, desert trips. These events were advertised primarily through the grapevine. Nabil and I were never at a loss for something to do on our days off in Saudi Arabia. We were sometimes invited to two to three functions in one evening. While it was lovely to be invited, we had to watch our energy levels and sometimes had to pick and choose activities.

Life in Qatar was definitely more staid. Rather than hearing of expat and other events informally through friends, in Doha, we were mostly left to our own devices in finding entertainment and worked hard on nurturing and sustaining relationships.

After finding our "sea legs," we settled into a different rhythm of life in Qatar. Persistent, we sought out friendships through our compound community, and through work. Stray cats ran rampant through our compound, as they did throughout much of Doha, so we joined a "catch, neuter, and release" cat group with our neighbors providing a needed source of fellowship. But we obviously needed more friends.

As we walked back to our villa in Doha from a neighborhood cat group party, I told Nabil, "These expat parties are sometimes too quiet and 'cliquish.'"

"I agree, Mary. It's harder to get used to Western parties. I prefer Arab parties."

"Yeah, I know Nabil. Arab parties are much more alive with dancing, singing, laughing."

While much of our time in Qatar felt like life in the U.S.—working full days, and resting and doing chores on the weekends—our time became more balanced after a couple of years in Qatar when we connected with work colleagues, some of whom became close friends that continue to be a large part of our lives to this day. After forming a small pool of friendships, our free time in Doha ultimately included occasional wonderful meals at beautifully appointed restaurants like the Lebanese Layali's or the Egyptian Khan Farouk Café in Katara Cultural Village, a West Bay development featuring the Opera House and open- air Amphitheater melding Islamic architecture with Greek features. Less ritzy places like the well-known Turkey Centrale found Qataris blaring their car horns outside the restaurant for faster curbside service with throngs of expats inside. We savored Turkey Centrale's freshly baked ridged flatbread with sesame seeds paired with mezze—creamy and delectable hummus and baba ghanoush. The Pearl housed some of the most exclusive restaurants with elaborate crystal chandeliers and five-star meals. We appreciated the less elaborate al fresco dining and mostly preferred strolls with our pups along The Pearl's white-tiled plazas with sumptuous views of the azure-green Arabian Gulf—luxury yachts docked nearby. Although we favored the traditional Souk Al-Waqif for afternoon weekend jaunts, the opulent Villagio Mall sported high-end shops with a Venetian-style canal and gondoliers.

Weekends sometimes found us at the homes of American and British expat friends enjoying simple meals, BBQs, games, and laughter, or at Badia and Rami's, our Palestinian expatriate friends' house. We shared a wonderful year-long friendship with Badia and Rami, who could not have been more hospitable. Frequenting their home for joyous family parties, we were lavished with popular Arab music, dance, and huge platters of lamb and rice along with stuffed grape leaves, stuffed squash, *mjedderah* (lentil dish), shish kabobs, and so much more on white plastic tablecloths covering long tables in their front courtyard. Following our meals, I sat agape at the group engaging in the *zajal* (Arabic chanting that moved from one person to the next and told a story).

And then there were nominally priced WTA tennis matches at Doha's Khalifa International Tennis complex. It was exciting to see Rafael Nadal and Roger Federer play up close and personal. With extended leave time from work, we were also fortunate enough to take many trips to the near and far East from both Qatar and Saudi Arabia. We frequented gong concerts, prostrate with pillows, at expat friends' homes listening to the vibrations of the universe, and enjoyed walks along the gleaming Arabian Gulf waters with friends and our respective pups prancing and streaking along the beach.

Although it took time to form close friendships with Qatari natives, once we did, the connections ran deep. Our time with the Al Hamdan family ranged from intimate traditional Qatari meals in a red-hued majlis and a trip to the desert where we shared an elaborate Arab Gulf feast seated on the ground of gender-separated tents to a conventional Arab Gulf *azza* (funeral) for our dear Suad. Female family members from the Qatari Al Hamdan tribe shook with tears running down their faces as we embraced after a wonderful "final exit" farewell meal at their home before we departed for the U.S. for good.

What triggered our ultimate departure from the Middle East was a myriad of factors. It was 2017, and I had already turned 60, the age at which expatriates were required to depart the country. And Nabil would turn 60 in 2018. My parents were approaching their late 80s, and I wanted to spend more time with them. To top it all off, in 2017 there was an economic blockade spearheaded by the UAE, Saudi Arabia, Egypt, and Bahrain, prompted by perceptions that Qatar was acting independently of its Arab neighbors in foreign relations. Qatar supported the opposition to the GCC governments, like the Muslim

Brotherhood in Egypt, during the "Arab Spring" that started in 2011, all of which was covered favorably by Al Jazeera, the Qatar-sponsored news agency. In 2013, the Egyptian military overthrew President Morsi, who was backed by the Muslim Brotherhood and supported by Qatar, ultimately leading to Saudi Arabia, the UAE, Egypt, and Bahrain removing their ambassadors and thereby eliminating their diplomatic ties with Qatar in 2014. In time, GCC nations told their citizens to depart Qatar during the blockade.

Nabil and I were on edge. Qatar was becoming further isolated from the world. Many of our expatriate friends either discussed exiting the country or were making serious plans to do so. Although I had formed strong feelings for the Middle East and had largely assimilated to, and was grateful for, Arab culture, traditions, and all the friendships we had formed, I felt that perhaps I had reached the end of my learning curve. I knew it would be challenging, but I was ready to go home. Nabil, though, felt more like staying. It seemed that, for him, our time in the Middle East had reawakened a connection to this land.

Soon after the official blockade began in the early summer of 2017, Turkey and Iran were the only nations importing supplies and food to Qatar. The economic sanctions had severe implications for us. The UAE and Saudi Arabia blocked dairy items (eggs, chickens, milk), vegetables, and fruits and airspace; Saudi Arabia closed its border with Qatar.

"Nabil, I'm really worried about the food situation here in Qatar."

"Yes, I know, it's not great, but we can get by," Nabil responded, ever the optimist.

In the coming months, when we grocery shopped in Doha, some shelves were bare, and the eggs imported from Iran and Turkey often had blood in the yolk, and the milk sometimes soured in transit. To counteract these effects, Qatar brought in hundreds of cattle from

Australia and Holland. And we began to see live hens in grocery storefronts. Nabil slowly warmed to the idea that it was time to leave.

Even flying back to the U.S. had become somewhat problematic. When Nabil and I flew to the U.S. in the summer of 2017 for vacation, we had to fly around Saudi Arabia into Iranian and Iraqi airspace and over Turkey. The relationship between Iran and America had become increasingly antagonistic, so flying over Iranian airspace wasn't comfortable. I kept looking at my watch and calculating when we would enter Turkish airspace.

When we returned to Qatar from the U.S. in mid-August of 2017, many of our Western friends had already left and returned to their home countries. Nabil and I met with locals and some of the expats who decided to stay. Our friends who lingered in Qatar seemed to agree that the situation in Doha was not looking stable or safe. They warned us that the grocery shops were half empty due to the sanctions, which we found to be true after visiting Mega Mart, a Western-style store like Publix or Safeway, to buy significant groceries since we had been gone for much of the summer. We were shocked to see many shelves empty—very limited dairy products, and the vegetables and fruits looked as if they had been there for too many days. They were in bad shape; some would not have been on sale in normal times. In another store, a hapless-looking shopkeeper asked if we wanted to buy a hen or two; however, they were alive. We declined and went back to the car empty-handed.

The grocery stores were no longer the same in Doha.

"I just can't believe that we can't find even the most basic cereals," I thought to myself after leaving another smallish Doha grocery store.

Nabil interrupted my thoughts, "You know what? Seeing the shelves empty in the last couple of stores reminds me of Mafraq, Jordan during Black September in 1970 when the Jordanian army and the

Palestinian militias were in a deadly war or like Lebanon during the Civil War. At that time, my mom took care of food, always feeding us inexpensive and readily available za'atar mixed with olive oil. She made bread at home and always made sure to have a lot of flour on hand to bake the bread."

"But this is not wartime, Mary. We are not preparing for food shortages."

And then he said it, "I don't know about you, Mary, but I feel our time in this region is reaching its end." Nabil's voice shook and reflected a certain sadness.

I swallowed, "I fully agree, Nabil. We don't need to live in a world where the grocery shelves are barely stocked. We don't know how long this will last. I feel like it's time to go home, too."

With all the issues facing Qatar, we agreed to leave by late October 2017. We called cargo companies about moving our household items to the U.S. Although we knew in our minds, hearts, and souls that leaving Qatar was the right thing to do, every time we sold a piece of furniture, I asked myself, how could we do this? We were slowly giving up our lives in a region that had become so precious and consequential. I think we had a silent agreement to not talk about it so as not to change our minds. I kept reminding myself that we were ready to do this; we were going back to my home, where we would live peacefully without any shortages of food or other necessities.

I pondered my life in the Arab world. Besides learning more about Nabil's native roots and culture, one of our joint interests in moving to the Arab Gulf was to travel the world, which we did, to enjoy the expatriate experience, which we did. A distant second objective was to make money and build a better future for ourselves, which we also accomplished. However, I never imagined for a second that we would make friends with both locals and expats, who would become like family to us. It never entered my mind I was going to fall in love with the Arabian culture, food, music, and the simple lifestyle of the people. I had not accounted for this transformation; it was rather shocking when I thought about it. As the days went by, I tried not to look in Nabil's direction when expats arrived, one after the other, coming to our villa after seeing our Facebook ad about selling our furniture. I didn't want him to see the melancholy in my eyes.

I began thinking if I, as an American woman who was born and raised in America, was feeling sentimental and homesick for a region I lived in for 17 years, what about Nabil? He was born and raised for his first 19 years in the Arab world, and now add our 17 years in the region. How is Nabil feeling? When alone, especially, I questioned our decision to leave. I was going in circles.

On one of our days off in late September 2017, while having tabouli for lunch, Nabil must have been thinking the same thing about me.

Nabil asked bluntly, "Mary, are you feeling sad or having mixed feelings about leaving the region to go back to the U.S.?"

I hesitated, "I do have mixed feelings, Nabil."

I continued, "I didn't realize I was going to fall in love with the Arab culture that much. But we both know that we eventually have to go back to the U.S., And I feel sad because this is your region and part of your homeland."

Nabil interrupted me, "Don't be sad because of me. I love living in the U.S. as much as I love living in the Middle East."

I could tell Nabil was distraught about leaving his region, but he was trying very hard to hide it.

Once we finished our lunch, Nabil looked at me deeply, "We are not leaving the Middle East for good. We will be back to visit, for sure.

After all, we still have family and amazing friends in this part of the world. So, coming back to visit is a given."

I felt relieved.

By mid-October, we had sold most of our living room furniture: the couch, loveseat, and TV. The buyer of the TV was kind enough to let us keep it until our last day in Doha. We moved our lovely outdoor majlis benches with colorful red cushions into our living room. Only a year earlier we had bought the traditional furniture with cushions from a craftsman in Souk Al-Waqif. I just loved it and wanted to bring it with us to the U.S., but it just wasn't practical or cost-effective. I felt more of my soul chipped away as a family came by and said that the majlis benches were exactly what they were looking for.

Instead of having a "Ma salama party" (final goodbye), as there were so few friends remaining in the country, our Irish neighbors kindly invited us to a nearby Italian restaurant where singing waiters entertained the patrons. Our neighbor friend got up to dance to a 70s tune; all I could muster was a feeble attempt to rock back and forth in my chair.

The day before we left the Middle East, we spent a quiet morning with an American expat friend and her daughter. Nabil prepared us all tea, and we smiled, laughed, reminisced, and promised to visit each other in the States. It was a bit awkward; our friendship would never be the same. We would go back to our busy lives in the U.S. without time to nurture our friendship.

It was October 28, 2017, when Nabil, our Sally-girl pup (sadly, our dear Maci and Coco had passed in 2010 and 2013, respectively) and I sat at our gate at Hamad International Airport of Doha, waiting for our departure to the U.S. Nabil looked at me and asked if I could turn the time back what would I have changed in the 17 years of living in the Middle East. I confidently told him almost nothing. I knew part of my life's journey was to spend time in Nabil's region of the world and for Nabil to reconnect with it.

For me, it was priceless to learn the importance of investing in connections with other humans, to find that countries across the Arab world each offered their gifts of traditions and lifestyle, and to become a more fully-faceted empathetic being.

AFTERWORD

After spending some years in the Middle East—Saudi Arabia, Qatar, and other countries we traveled to—I formed a deep bond and fondness for the region. Both solaced and energized by Arab generosity, a trait rooted in both culture and religion, I felt more human, more patient, and aware of people's feelings, sentiments, sensitivities, and viewpoints. It was always gratifying, but still a surprise when Nabil and I were called brother and sister when visiting an Arab home. Once inside the home, our happiness—or that of any visitor—was paramount. It was an honor for an Arab family to accept guests. A Palestinian friend once told us that even if an enemy knocks on your door, you are well-advised to let them in and treat them royally. Now, whether this is always true is hard to know.

In our early years in the Arab region, although captivated by the Arab lifestyle and culture, I was anxious to get home for summer breaks, reassured to be enveloped by the love of family and friends and familiar surroundings. As the years went by, however, and by the time we moved to Qatar, I felt wistful about leaving the Arabian Peninsula for America; I would miss meandering along the alleyways of Souk Al-Waqif, walks along the Arabian Gulf, gatherings with Qatari and expatriate friends, and our two miniature poodle pups who would be staying behind with friends. I was a happy and content expatriate living a full and comfortable life in the Arab world.

As I connected my seatbelt and waited for passengers to take their seats on one of our Qatar Airways flights from the Middle East to the U.S., my mind wandered. I wondered if I were one of these Arab people and was born and grew up here, would I have been the same person? What if I had been like Nabil, growing up in poverty and war? Would I still be the same Mary I was now?

At the very least, I felt blessed to have experienced Arab culture and lifestyle first-hand. I admit that before going to the Middle East, during the initial years spent with Nabil in the U.S., I did not understand the Arab world or psyche. I knew that when we lived in the Washington, DC area Nabil sometimes yearned for his family, as well as his homeland of Lebanon and his adopted country of Jordan. When sitting quietly on our family room couch playing the dissonate ballads of Um Kulthum about unrequited love, I knew Nabil was homesick. However, I couldn't penetrate his mind or completely understand his struggle. And I certainly couldn't understand the doleful and inharmonious music of Um Kulthum. Nabil taught me to dance to traditional Arab music, the slow rhythmic movements of the hips and arms, but I couldn't really feel it. However, when we moved to the Arab region, and I watched Nabil's female family members and our Arab friends gyrating smoothly to the songs of Um Kulthum and more popular Arab tunes I began feeling attuned to the culture; in time, it would no longer seem foreign to me. It would just be my life.

It was only after some years of living, adjusting, balancing, and working in Saudi Arabia and Qatar that I began understanding life in the Middle East more broadly from my perspective. Although life was not perfect, and the region was rife with political turmoil, I began to feel a connection to the Middle East through a great appreciation of its traditions and rituals that focused on God (a higher power), family, and human relations. "People time" is important in the Arab region. I never could understand how, in the early years after I first met Nabil, he could talk easily for nearly an hour to his mother or sister in Lebanon or have lengthy chats with a stranger in Lowe's.

Of course, my experience was different as an American expatriate. Americans were treated better, paid better, and received better benefits than Southeast Asian workers who were the backbone of the Saudi and Qatar economies. The Indians, Bangladeshis, and Sri Lankans performed most of the manual labor required for building Riyadh and Doha's magnificent skyscrapers. My experience in the Arab world was advantaged; I was respected, I was appreciated, and I was treated well. Of course, I saw life in the Middle East through rose-colored glasses; my exposure to the Arab world was made better simply by being an American.

In any event, the Arab world forever changed me, both personally and professionally. I discovered there was an art to being with people. A sort of slow dance, a natural give and take, a conscious effort to learn about another person: their worldview, their life experiences, their sorrows, their triumphs. And for them to learn about me.

Although it was a deliberate and arduous process, professionally, I tapped into the significance of taking time to get to know my work colleagues. The sense of joy sharing cardamom coffee for no other reason than to talk about what we were having for dinner that night. Teamwork and collegiality were critical pathways to getting things done, even though it meant more "small talk" than I liked or was comfortable with.

In the end, like Nabil, I became somewhat lost between two cultures. It was difficult to leave the Arab region for the States and equally difficult to return to the Middle East after our U.S. holidays.

And while having returned to a plentiful life in America, I pine for the Middle East.

I don't have it all figured out. I think a lot about my years in the Arab region and still have complicated feelings about what it all meant. All I know is my time in the Middle East was invaluable; life-affirming. One of the more important lessons learned: we are all the same anywhere we go. The Saudis, Qataris, Lebanese, Jordanians, and others in the region and around the globe have the same emotions as me: joy, sadness, fear, boredom, anger, heartbreak, as well as similar life goals. We all want happiness, good health, and to feel safe with satisfying livelihoods.

I will miss the calls from the Omaris and the Al Hamdan family asking us, on the spur of the moment, to come over for mezze, cardamom coffee, or mint tea. The desert trips with boom box music and belly dancing with our expat friends and pups. The many lively and entertaining expatriate productions in Riyadh made our social life so full and connected us with home. And the world travel.

I have brought back several gifts from the Middle East – an appreciation for hospitality, the simple moments (stop and smell the roses and cardamom coffee), close familial and friendship ties, the delight of communal and cultural eating, the plights and joys of other cultures, respect for the elderly. I am eternally grateful for my time in the Arabian Peninsula.

ABOUT THE AUTHOR

Mary Khouri, originally from the west coast, has an advanced degree in economics. She worked for a Federal agency in Washington, DC for 17 years before moving with her husband, Nabil, a Lebanese American, and two miniature poodles to the Arabian Peninsula in 2000. In the Middle East she balanced her life between working as an economist/finance manager with her exploits as an American expatriate -- savoring local expat plays, desert trips, gong ceremonies, and communal feasts with Arab Gulf friends. Mary's 17 years in the Arab Gulf sparked an interest in writing about her enlightening experiences in this distant and often misunderstood land. She ultimately returned to the U.S. where she lives with her husband, Nabil, and their beloved poodle pup, Sally. Mary volunteers within her community focusing on cultural exchange and enjoys domestic and international travel with Nabil.

www.ingramcontent.com/pod-product-compliance
Lightning Source LLC
Chambersburg PA
CBHW020236170426
43202CB00008B/98